DANGEROUS
DEVOTIONS

JACKIE PERSEGHETTI

Chariot Victor Publishing
A Division of Cook Communications

Chariot Victor Publishing,
a division of Cook Communications, Colorado Springs, Colorado 80918
Cook Communications, Paris, Ontario
Kingsway Communications, Eastbourne, England

CAUTION: MORE DANGEROUS DEVOTIONS
© 1999 by Jackie Perseghetti.

Cover and book design by Image Studios, Colorado Springs, CO.
Illustrations by John Duckworth.

Scripture quotations used in this book are from the *Holy Bible, New International Version*
Copyright © 1973, 1978, 1984, International Bible Society.
Used by permission of Zondervan Bible Publishers.

First Printing, 1999
Printed in United States of America
01 00 99 03 02   5 4 3 2

Library of Congress Cataloging-in-Publication Data

Perseghetti, Jackie.
        Caution: more dangerous devotions / by Jackie Perseghetti.
             p. cm.
        Summary: Devotional on the Bible from Genesis through Psalms, including suggestions
for prayers and study questions.
             ISBN 0-7814-0250-6
             1. Bible stories, English—O.T. 2. Children—Prayer-books and devotions—English. [1.
Prayer books and devotions. 2. Bible stories—O.T.] I. Title.
BS551.2.P445 1999
242'.62—dc21
                                                                           98-51341
                                                                                CIP
                                                                                 AC

DEDICATION

Bill and Erika Griffin and
Emerson and Joyce Perseghetti,

who have modeled how to lovingly trust and follow the hand of God,
even when the valley of the shadow of death threatens.

ACKNOWLEDGMENTS

To my beloved husband Doug, who continually stands by my side encouraging, supporting, and being my best friend and partner. Thank you for helping me give "birth" to yet another book through all the late nights and tears. I love you. To Bethany and Ben, thank you for your faithful prayers, patience, and flexibility. Out of all the children in the world—if I could have my pick of anyone—I'd choose you two *every* time.

To my dear friends Marla Hartzell, Steve and Janis Wright, Pam Laughlin, Sharon Melhorn, and Evelyn Kuhn—a special thanks. Your constant prayers and words of encouragement backed by action meant more than you'll ever know. Thank you for being there.

To Steve Robinson, thanks for introducing us to caving—hence the theme! To the Kwiatek family, thank you. Inviting us into your home for the Passover feast was an experience we'll always treasure. To Sallie Simpson at UWM, Bob Plummer, Rick and Gloria Nulph, and friends at Faircreek and TEACH, thanks for your vital part in praying! Also, a special thanks to Donna (Marriott) Hines. You were a tremendous blessing as I tried to juggle both home schooling and writing this book. Thanks for being not only my home school coordinator, but my friend.

To my editor, Jeannie Harmon, thank you for your care, patience, and encouragement when the path before me loomed with uncertainties. Also, a special thanks to Chariot/Victor for such wonderful support in tough times, and to Elisabeth Hendricks for a great job line editing.

Finally and most importantly, the greatest thank you of all belongs to God who enabled me to write this sequel. Thank You, Lord. The glory and credit for this book belongs to You alone.

TABLE OF CONTENTS

TABLE OF CONTENTS

TABLE OF CONTENTS

TABLE OF CONTENTS

INTRODUCTION

CAUTION: MORE DANGEROUS DEVOTIONS?!!

Exactly! Here, the journey continues . . . OR, (if you haven't yet read the original Caution: Dangerous Devotions on the New Testament) it just begins! This book is considered "dangerous" because it might take you where you've never been before. It will probably challenge you to learn something you didn't know. It might make you stop and think—and will definitely cause you to grow! Whatever you do, don't read this devotional unless you are prepared for an adventure. Think you can stand the danger? Then read on!

Why the Old Testament? Just like exploring underground (caving), the Old Testament has lots of unknowns, twists and turns, and even tight spots and close shaves. For many, the Old Testament holds lots of unknowns and even more uncertainties! What does it have to do with us today? PLENTY!

But, don't take my word for it—come along and see for yourself. . . . The only equipment you'll need for this adventure is your own copy of the Bible. It'll be your map which charts the course as we explore. Here's a sneak peek at the various tunnels we'll be crawling through:

The first five books, Genesis through Deuteronomy, are rich with exciting events which lay the foundation for not only the Old Testament, but also the New Testament!

The books between Joshua and Esther are called "history books" (don't let that scare you off!) which are loaded with fantastic life lessons and examples.

Job and Psalms are books of poetry, but they're not for sissies! They deal with real issues of the heart.

Now that you know where we're headed, keep an eye out for these helpful symbols that will guide you along the passageways and through the twists and turns:

Getting Ready

tells you how to prepare for today's devotion.

The Journey

walks you through territory that will make you think.

exploring deeper

gives you verses to look up in your Bible.

  CROSSROADS presents you with a question and two possible options from which to choose. Which one is the right answer?

 THINKING ON YOUR FEET encourages you to think for yourself and apply what you've learned.

 DANGER AHEAD warns you of things in the real world that could prove to be a stumbling block to your faith.

SKILL TIME encourages you to put your faith into action—it tells you something specific to do to make your faith grow.

So, blow the dust off your Bible, grab your gear, and let's begin the journey together. Oh, along the way, we might see a small compass. Like any compass, we need to read it to get our bearings and make sure we are on the right track. Well, enough of that! Are you ready to journey? Follow me!

GETTING YOUR BEARINGS:
THE BOOK OF GENESIS

Where is the best place to start? Why, the beginning! Appropriately, the word "Genesis" means "origin," or "beginning." In this book we see the beginning of the world, humans, sin, languages, nations, and God's judgment. But let's not get ahead of ourselves! Genesis is the very foundation upon which the whole Bible stands. It is also a book under attack by those who don't want to acknowledge God. As you journey through Genesis, keep your eyes on the truth found here.

Genesis was written by Moses who wasn't born until about 300 years *after* the events in Genesis came to a close! Is this a problem? No. God allowed long life spans for the first man, Adam, and his descendants, so there would be firsthand accounts of information as truth passed from generation to generation. For instance, Shem (one of Noah's sons who lived through the Flood) could have passed along records to Abraham. Since libraries existed in Abraham's day, Moses would later have access to accurate information! Regardless of how God revealed His word to Moses, the message of Genesis is one God did not want us to miss!

As you journey through Genesis, keep your eyes open. Although the terrain may seem familiar at points, don't get distracted or discouraged. There are some important main tunnels you need to go down so you don't get lost later on. Stick with it, and be observant. This book has lots of twists and turns, ups and downs, and even a few bumps. When you exit Genesis, you'll be stronger for the journey!

11

SAID AND DONE!

TAKEN FROM GENESIS 1

GETTING READY

Just as you need to get yourself ready each morning before starting your day, so you need to ready your heart before you journey through God's Word. The best way to do this is to spend a few minutes in prayer. It doesn't need to be long—a simple sentence expressing a heartfelt desire will do. Each time you journey in God's Word, ask Him to open your eyes, and give Him permission to teach you.

THE JOURNEY

Have you ever wondered where you *really* came from? Did God *really* create everything, or did we evolve over a long period of time from simpler life-forms?

This lesson will be a little different from the others found in this devotional. Why? Because it is so important to our understanding of who we are, what we aren't, and who God is. In the very first verses of Genesis, we are told that God created the heavens and the earth. At this point, we can accept that as fact, or we can reject it. Was anyone (except God) around during that time to verify this? Can science either prove or disprove this? The answer to both of these is no.

In the beginning, God created. Darkness and void were all around until God spoke. Because of His power, it only took a spoken word on His part—and it was so. This is the God of the universe. This is the message He wanted to communicate to us. We need not worry about our worth or value—we weren't accidents or cells that happened to group together and form life. God specifically tells us that He created the heavens and the earth and the life found on the earth. God wants us to know that He is responsible for Creation. How did it happen?

Adam is the Hebrew word for "human being." It's related to another Hebrew word, *Adamah*, which is the word for ground. Interestingly, all the chemicals in our body are the same chemicals found in dirt!

First, Scripture says God created everything in six days and rested on the seventh day. He didn't rest because He was tired; God rested because He was finished and wanted to provide an example for us. That is the basis for our week to this day. (It is interesting to note that all known cultures throughout history revolve around a seven-day week!)

On day one, God created night and day by separating the light from the darkness. On day two, He created our atmosphere with just the right mix of elements to support life. On day three, God gathered the waters to form the seas and created dry land. He then made lush plants and fruit-bearing trees to cover the land. God saw that it was good. Day four brought the creation of the sun, moon, and stars, which would give light to the earth and mark days, years, and seasons.

The stage was set. On day five, God brought into existence the birds of the air and the creatures of the sea. He made them complete and perfect with everything they would need to produce more of their kind. He then created all the animals and insects and every living creature on day six—but He didn't stop there. God finally made the crowning achievement of Creation on that day. God made people.

God formed man from the dust of the ground and then breathed the breath of life into his nostrils. He made man in His image—not the way God looks, for we don't know what God looks like, but rather God made man with a soul. God wanted to enjoy a relationship with man, so He gave him a will to be able to choose, emotions so that he could feel, and a superior mind with the ability to communicate. This is where it all began.

What about evolution? Evolution is a philosophy with a lot of factual inconsistencies. Recent scientific discoveries have pointed out serious problems with the evolutionary theory that humans evolved from lower life-forms. Evolutionists still cannot point to adequate fossils showing the "in-between" stages of animals as they supposedly evolved over millions of years. As a result of these problems and new information, some scientists have been abandoning evolution as it was once taught in favor of a "creation" of some kind. In Genesis chapter 1, God told us this from the very beginning. He created it all.

exploring deeper

This is the exciting part, and where real growth and discovery happen! In this part, you will need to use a little energy. (Don't panic!) Your Bible is all the equipment needed for guaranteed success. Just look up the verse and answer the simple question. This exercise builds spiritual muscles and makes you strong in the Lord.

Open your Bible and look up Genesis 1:1. What does it say? (Go ahead, look it up and read it!) "In the beginning" mentions the creation of something—the creation of time! This verse also mentions the creation of space and the creation of matter—our universe and all that is in it. It's interesting to note that most other cultures, histories, religions, and sciences begin with time, space, and matter already existing. They don't know how it got there. Also, notice what the verse does not say. It doesn't try to prove the fact that God exists. That's because it was written in the beginning when no one doubted God.

DANGER AHEAD

As you read science textbooks, you will read about facts and "theories." Theory is different from fact. Don't be fooled into thinking that evolution is scientific fact. It's not. All scientists know that a theory must be tested to be scientifically accurate. That is, it must be repeatable in a laboratory under exact conditions. The theory of evolution is not based entirely on scientific results—but rather on a belief which rules God out. Evolution is not pure science; it's more of a religion. So, whose word would you rather believe? The ideas of those who weren't around when things began and can't even explain how matter came into being, or the word of the Creator Himself who was there? Think about it.

DON'T LOOK AT ME!

TAKEN FROM GENESIS 2-3

Getting Ready

Stop and pray. Ask God to open your eyes and help you understand what He wants to show you in His Word. Thank Him that He is a just, yet loving, God.

THE Journey

Have you ever done something you later regretted? You're not alone!

What happened? It was all so perfect just moments ago! Adam and Eve were ashamed and even wanted to hide from God—the very One who created them. The peace they once had in their hearts had now vanished. Something was dreadfully wrong. Adam's thoughts raced back, as he tried to remember everything that had happened in his life up to this point.

He recalled being given the task of caring for the Garden, studying what God created, and naming all the animals. The more he observed, the more he noticed how each animal had a mate, but Adam had no one suitable for him. A smile came to Adam's face as he remembered how God met that need. He placed Adam into a deep sleep, took one of his ribs, and fashioned a companion especially for him. When Adam awakened, there stood Eve! They were perfect for each other! Adam's smile quickly faded. He knew he was created to walk in the cool of the Garden with a loving God, but now all he wanted to do was hide!

Eve was having thoughts of her own. She felt guilty about what she had done. It was a horrible feeling she had never experienced before. Why had she listened to that serpent? Why hadn't she obeyed the one simple rule she had to follow? The serpent had tried to convince her that the fruit was really the most desirable thing in the Garden. He even promised her it would make her like God! All that power and knowledge seemed irresistible. The fruit—it looked so delicious! She wanted it. What harm could it do? Besides, the serpent said, "You will not die." Could he be right? The fruit looked so tempting! Besides, if God didn't want them to eat from that tree, He wouldn't have put it in the Garden in the first place! Before Eve knew it, she had grabbed the fruit and taken a bite. She turned around, noticed Adam, and offered it to him as well. After they had eaten, something inside of them seemed to change. Instead of wanting to be with God, they were afraid of Him.

"Adam, where are you?" God called out, knowing exactly where they were and what they had done. He had created man with a free will to choose, and the forbidden tree was a test of their obedience. Would they choose God's way or their own way? God knew Adam and Eve had been tempted and had chosen their own way.

> **"Sin" literally means "to miss the mark." It is living independently of God and centering on yourself as your own authority.**

"Have you eaten from the tree I commanded you not to eat from?" God questioned.

Adam panicked. "Don't look at *me*!" he said, pointing a blaming finger. "Eve gave me the fruit to eat."

Eve quickly added, "Don't look at *me*! The serpent said it would be all right!"

Because of their disobedience, sin had entered their lives. As a result, Adam and Eve faced separation from God. They had to leave the Garden and would never be able to return. As part of the consequences, the land would be cursed, and they would experience pain and sorrow. What had promised to be so pleasing only brought regret.

Eve was tempted by wanting great pleasure, wanting what was desirable to look upon, and wanting to advance her own cause (lust of the flesh, lust of the eyes, and the pride of life). Interestingly, Jesus was tempted the same way but didn't give in. (Matthew 4:1-11)

It would be sad if the chapter ended here, but it doesn't. Even in the midst of Adam and Eve's denial ("Don't look at me!"), God stepped in and said, "Yes, I know. Instead, look to *Me*." As they left the Garden, God promised He would provide a way for humans to enjoy a relationship with Him.

God did not abandon Adam and Eve. He made clothing for them to wear out of animal skins (the first animal sacrifice), which would serve as a constant reminder that there is a cost for sin.

exploring deeper

Open your Bible to Genesis 3:14-15. Part of the curse that came as a result of Adam and Eve's fall was a curse on the serpent. Read verse 14. What happened? Now, look at verse 15—there's a threat to Satan and a promise to man! The seed of the woman (Jesus) would crush the serpent's head (destroy the work of Satan).

Skill Time

Satan twisted God's truth to plant a seed of doubt in Eve's heart. He then challenged God's words and substituted them with a lie. This same process still happens today. Do you have doubts or confusion about God's Word? Write them down on a piece of paper, and tape it to the back inside cover of this devotional. Be honest, and tell God about your questions and/or hang-ups. Ask Him to help you with your doubts; then get ready for an exciting journey as you explore the Old Testament and learn about His truth!

HOW 'BOUT A SIGN OR TWO?

TAKEN FROM GENESIS 6-9

GETTING READY

Take a moment to pray. Even though you may be familiar with this story from the Bible, ask God to help you see beyond what you already know and teach you new things from His Word.

THE JOURNEY

Have you ever wished God would give you a sign that He really exists and is Who He says He is?

Noah looked about him and was sick at what he saw. Selfishness, violence, hatred, and sin were everywhere. Noah worried about their effects on his family. Ever since Adam and Eve disobeyed God and sin entered the world, evil had became more and more common. Instead of just yielding to outward temptation, people were being tempted by the wickedness in their own hearts. For example, one of Adam's sons harbored jealousy in his heart and desired personal gain. As a result, Cain killed his brother, Abel, committing the first murder. This was just the beginning.

Lamech, Cain's great-great-great-grandson (not the same Lamech who was Noah's father) didn't turn out so great. In his pride and arrogance, he took not just one wife, but married two—directly against God's plan for marriage. He also bragged about killing whoever displeased him. Such were the times in which Noah found himself living.

Although Noah was thankful he had found favor in God's eyes, he was bewildered at his assignment. *Build an ark? The earth and all that live on it will be destroyed? A worldwide flood?* he thought as he made careful measurements and began working. It was a job that would take 120 years to complete.

"Clean animals" were those to be sacrificed to the Lord. After the Flood, God also gave permission to eat them.

During this time, people came to question Noah. Some shook their heads in pity for a man they thought was insane. "This box is going to float?!" they laughed. "On what—dry ground?!" Noah faithfully went about his task. Many came by to mock; others simply ignored the 120 years of warning. Noah followed God's blueprints exactly. He knew he had heard the Lord.

When God's perfect timing had come, Noah was instructed to enter the ark with his wife, sons, and their wives. They gathered every kind of food that would be eaten and stored it away for themselves and the animals. Noah then loaded the animals God brought to him. He saw a male and female pair of every unclean animal, seven pairs of every clean animal, and seven pairs of every kind of bird. There were males and females of every living thing on the ark, as God had commanded Noah. Then the Lord closed the door. At that point, the fountains of the deep burst forth, and the floodgates of heaven were opened. God kept His promise!

For forty days the flood kept coming on the earth, but it was not over in forty days. The violent rush of water spouting from underground and the rain pounding down from the heavens covered the entire earth. The tallest mountains could not be seen. The swirling, violent waters flooded the earth for one hundred fifty days (five months!). But God had not forgotten Noah. He closed the springs of the deep and the floodgates of heaven and sent a wind over the earth to make the waters recede. After seven months of being in the ark, Noah felt it stop rocking. It had landed on Mount Ararat.

Three months later, the tops of other mountains could be seen. But the time of waiting was far from over. After another forty days, Noah sent out a bird each week to see if the water had dried up. After two weeks, a dove returned with a freshly picked olive leaf in its beak! Noah waited yet another week, released the dove, and it did not return. Only then did he remove the covering from the ark. He saw that the ground was safely dry! It had been a little over a year from the time he had entered the ark until now. God had kept His word.

Interestingly, almost all ancient cultures have legends of a flood. Some of these were written on cuneiform clay tablets, describing the same event we have recorded in our Bible.

After leaving the ark, Noah immediately worshiped the Lord and sacrificed some of the clean birds and animals on an altar he built. God blessed Noah and promised never again to destroy the earth and its inhabitants with a flood. As a reminder of that covenant, God placed a rainbow in the sky. It would stand as a reminder of the disaster and as a sign of His promise. That sign still stands today.

exploring deeper

Open your own Bible and turn to Genesis 9:28-29. How long did Noah live after the Flood? How long did he live altogether? Is that hard to believe? It shouldn't be. Before the Flood, the climate and atmosphere of the earth were very different from today. Life spans were much longer. During the Flood, the environment changed drastically, and the amount of time people lived began to decrease. The long life of Adam (930 years) meant that he could possibly have talked to Lamech, Noah's father.

CROSS ROADS

Every living thing on the face of the earth had been killed and rapidly buried in a watery, muddy grave. All had perished, but not without leaving a record. To this day, fossils and rock layers show proof of a worldwide flood. Fossils of sea animals have been found on every major mountain range in the world. Trees (sometimes upside down) have been found crossing into several different rock layers—layers that evolutionists believe took millions of years to form. This is another sign of rapid burial by a flood. God not only gave the sign of the rainbow, but also left fossils as a record of the actual event.

When you are wondering if God exists, will you accept His signs, or reject them?

MY WAY OR THE HIGHWAY!

TAKEN FROM GENESIS 9-11

GETTING READY

Don't skip this part! Every caver knows it's deadly to go caving on their own—they need at least one partner. So it is in exploring God's Word. You need a partner, and God stands ready to help and guide you. All you need to do is ask Him. Take a few minutes now to do just that. Give Him permission to be the one in the lead.

THE JOURNEY

Does it ever frustrate you when a good idea falls flat on its face, and a bad idea gains great acceptance?

What a deliverance! Noah's heart was humbled as he thought about the awesome power of God. Upon leaving the safety of the Ark, Noah built an altar to worship his Lord. Surely, God must have first place in everything! Starting all over, Noah and his family set out to obey God and live uprightly before Him. God told them to be fruitful, to multiply, and to fill the earth—and that is exactly what they meant to do. . . .

It soon became very clear, however, that although the fruit of sin had been destroyed with the flood, the root of sin still existed. This was evident in the life of Ham—one of Noah's sons.

One day Noah drank some wine from his vineyard and became drunk. His son, Ham, found Noah lying in his tent totally unclothed. Even though Ham knew it was wrong to look upon someone's nakedness, he ran to tell the juicy news to his two brothers. "Shem, Japheth," he called with a laugh, "you'll never guess what happened to Dad! Who would have thought it? Come, see for yourself!"

Ham's curse was to fall upon his son, Canaan. Canaan was the father of the Canaanites who would later prove to be very evil.

When Shem and Japheth arrived, they knew what had happened. Instead of sharing in the disgrace, they turned their heads away so as not to look upon their father. By putting a garment on their shoulders and walking backwards, they covered Noah. When Noah came out of his drunkenness, he knew what Shem and Japheth had done—and what Ham had *not* done. As a result, Shem and Japheth received a blessing, and Ham was cursed. This was just the beginning.

As Noah's descendants multiplied, people moved eastward and settled in the plain of Shinar where they became very comfortable. It was a good location. People from the tribes of Shem, Ham, and Japheth were getting along, and all were making a name for themselves. When they put their heads together, it seemed there was nothing they couldn't accomplish! Life was so great, they soon forgot about God and His plans for them to scatter and fill the earth. They decided they had a better plan of their own.

The tower was named "Babel" meaning "confusion"! It was very similar to a tower later built in Babylon called a ziggurat which functioned as an artificial mountain and center of idol worship.

Making bricks from mud and mortar from tar, the people began to build a tower in their own honor—a monument to their own strength. Steps led up the side to the place of worship at the top. But the worship was not for the one true God.

Seeing this evil intent and disobedience in Noah's descendants, God stepped in and confused their language so that His original plan might be carried out. Suddenly unable to communicate with each other, the people abandoned their plans and took to the roads—just as God had originally intended. God's plan would be accomplished even in spite of human rebellion. When in stubborn pride they boasted, "My way!" God stood firm and showed them the highway. . . .

exploring deeper

In your Bible, turn over to Genesis 11:6 and read it. What does it say? At first glance this seems to be a very strange statement God would make! Read it again. Does this strike you as odd? It shouldn't. God was not concerned that people would become too powerful—He made them, and He had the last word. Rather, God knew the danger and sad results of people becoming wise in their own eyes.

THINKING on your FEET

How will you respond when faced with the tempting choice of your own selfish ideas and desires?

TRUST ME

TAKEN FROM GENESIS 12-17

GETTING READY

Take a few minutes to prepare your heart. Ask God to help you know Him more, that you might better understand how very much He cares for you.

THE JOURNEY

Do you know people who make promises and never live up to them?

Abram trembled. He knew the seriousness of the matter that was now before him. Thoughts of his past filled his mind. It seemed just yesterday God had called him to leave the comforts of home and travel to an unknown place. "Leave your country and go to a land I will show you," God said. Then came the remarkable promise. "I will bless you and make you into a great nation. Your name will be great, and those who curse you I will curse. Those who bless you will be blessed. All people on earth will be blessed through you." How well Abram remembered those words. How easily he had forgotten them!

Out of faith, Abram had left his homeland and obeyed God by journeying to an unknown destination. Abram knew God had something special planned for him. God was going to raise up a nation of people who would live their lives as a testimony to the world of the one true God, *Yahweh*. Abram felt the depth of his own unworthiness as he remembered the scheme he had devised while journeying into Egypt.

Because his wife, Sarai, was so beautiful, Abram knew his own life would be in danger. Egyptian rulers often killed the husbands of beautiful women in order to take the wife for their own. So Abram posed as Sarai's brother. This way he would actually be honored, given gifts, and treated well by the ruler in hopes of striking a good arrangement for Sarai! Having momentarily forgotten God's wonderful promises and plan for him, Abram told a half-truth that Sarai was his sister. (He knew it wasn't *totally* untrue, since they both had the same father but different mothers. But he also knew it wasn't the total truth, since Sarai *was* his beloved wife!) When the ruler discovered the truth, Abram and Sarai were sent away. They could have been killed. Abram's lying had needlessly put both of their lives in danger.

God named Abram Abraham. Hebrew names carried great significance and often described a person's character or circumstance. In order to name someone, the namer would have to have both understanding of that person and authority over him.

Abram scolded himself. Why had he doubted God's protection? Didn't God say all nations would be blessed through his descendants? He should have known better than to fear for his life! Surely, God is capable of doing as He promised! "Yet, how can I be sure I heard God correctly? How can I know for certain He will give me a son to be my heir, and make my descendants more numerous than the stars?"

That question jarred Abram's thoughts back to the present where he stood trembling, watching.

Abram had done everything God said to do. He got a three-year-old cow, goat, and ram, as well as two birds—a turtledove and a young pigeon. Cutting the cow, goat, and ram down the middle, Abram laid each half on opposite sides of a ditch. This was the custom of preparing to make a covenant with someone else. It was the strongest binding agreement possible, and was an agreement made by friends, or people who were in relationship with one another. Abram knew the next step was to walk between the slain animals, saying: "If I break this covenant, may what was done to these animals be done to me." Abram was fearful, for God was asking him to walk before Him and be blameless. Abram knew he couldn't possibly keep his end of the bargain. What if he failed? What if his descendants would turn from God? A great fear and terror came over Abram.

> **Abraham didn't deserve to be chosen any more than we do. It was God's love reaching out to him. The New Testament talks of this as God's "grace."**

As Abram looked up into the darkness, he saw a most unusual thing! A smoking firepot and a flaming torch passed between the animals. Abram did not have to walk the ditch of blood! Yahweh God was doing it for him! God was taking full responsibility for both ends of the covenant. With the passing of the smoke and fire, God was saying, "I love you, and because I want to be in relationship with you, I will take care of your end of our agreement. I will cover the consequences of your inability to keep your part."

That night was one Abram would never forget. What he had seen and experienced would change him forever. No longer was he to be called *Abram* (exalted father), but *Abraham* (father of many). God was calling to Himself a people and a nation. Abraham was just the beginning. . . .

exploring deeper

In your copy of the Scriptures, turn to Genesis 15:6. An interesting statement was made about Abram—even in spite of his earlier weaknesses. What does it say?

Skill Time

Abraham is listed in the "Hall of Faith" in the New Testament Book of Hebrews (chapter 11). It has been said that faith is "walking to the edge of all the light that you have—then taking one more step." Faith in God is not a blind leap. Rather, it is based upon knowing and understanding who God (Yahweh) is. Just as God revealed Himself to Abraham, so He desires a relationship with us. He is the same yesterday, today, and forever. Do you have a relationship with the one true Creator God? Do you even know what that means? If you aren't sure, then please turn to the back of this book. (Go on!) There's a special message there just for you.

WHAT YOU SEE IS WHAT YOU...

TAKEN FROM GENESIS 13-19

GETTING READY

Don't forget to pray! Allow God to search your heart and show you any areas of weakness in your character. Take a moment to thank Him that He is the Author and Perfecter of your life. He knows and desires what is best for you.

THE JOURNEY

When given a choice, do you look out for your own needs first?

Lot couldn't believe it! This was too good to be true! Ever since Lot's father died, Lot and his family stayed and even traveled with his brother-in-law, Abram (later called Abraham). Now, however, Abram's and Lot's flocks, herds, tents, and possessions had grown too numerous. Their herdsmen began quarreling with one another, and Abram knew they could no longer stay together.

"Let's put a stop to all this quarreling and separate. Look, the whole land is before us! If you go to the right, then I'll go to the left. If you go to the left, then I will take the land on the right. You may choose first," Abram offered. Lot looked eagerly about him. Since he was given first choice, he could choose the best for himself!

As Lot stood there, he looked out over the vast land. He knew the importance of having fresh water available, and he directed his attention to the Jordan River and its surrounding plain. From where he stood, he could see lush green vegetation growing along the banks. Surely this would be the best land! *How foolish of Abram to let me choose first!* Lot thought. Lot pointed to the land he wanted, and then both men parted ways.

As Lot moved into the land he had selfishly chosen, he soon noticed that what he thought was fertile land was actually barren! The green "lushness" along the Jordan River was actually thickets! The watered part of the riverbed was too small for his flocks, and the plains along the river had such poor soil that nothing was able to grow! Lot knew his only solution was to move to the south by the Dead Sea or to one of the oases along the riverbanks. Little did he know the consequences he would suffer due to his choice.

A simple definition of "greed" is desiring to:

Get
Rapidly
Everything I
Encounter and
Desire

The people who lived in the oases were known for being evil. They worshiped idols and had no respect for God's laws. In spite of this, Lot settled among them and soon became a citizen. He rose to a position of leadership in government! Life went on as usual, and Lot became dull to the evil influences about him. They affected not only Lot, but also his whole family.

One day, two angels disguised as men came to the city of Sodom. Lot was sitting at the city gate and noticed them. "Come to my house," he offered the strangers. "You can clean up from your travel and get a night's rest." After some persuasion, the two men accompanied Lot home. That evening, men from every part of the city showed up and surrounded Lot's house. They had wicked thoughts and were consumed with desires that were neither God-honoring nor God-given. Lot stood in front of his door trying to reason with them, but the angry mob wouldn't listen. Instead, they almost crushed Lot in an attempt to break down the door. At that moment, the two visitors reached out and pulled Lot back inside the house. They struck the crowd with blindness so they could no longer see. Quickly, the two men instructed Lot to gather his family and immediately leave the city, for God was going to destroy it.

The "city gate" wasn't just a door on the fortified walls surrounding a city. It was a large buttressed area containing several rooms and stalls where people could pay taxes, talk to officials, or buy from merchants. To "sit in the city gate" meant a person was a ruler, judge, or official.

Lot hastily ran to warn his sons-in-law who were pledged to marry his daughters. "Hurry and leave this place for the Lord is about to destroy the city!" he urged. But they only laughed and thought he was joking. Returning to his house, Lot hesitated to leave his home. Finally, the two visitors grabbed his hand and led his family out of the city. "Flee for your lives! Don't look back, and don't stop anywhere in the plain!" they ordered. Everyone heard the orders, but not all took them seriously. Lot's wife looked back and was turned into a pillar of salt. Not only did Lot lose his wife and his home, his daughters lost their future husbands. As a result, they would later defile Lot in order to preserve the family line.

Their offspring became the Moabites and Ammonites—enemies of God's chosen people. What started as a selfish choice and greedy desire for the "best" only gave birth to a nightmare of consequences.

exploring deeper

Turn in your Bible to Genesis 19:16 and read it. What do the last few words of that verse say? Read them again. Now, skip down to verse 29 and read it. What do you learn about God from these verses?

DANGER AHEAD

In your life you will be tempted to make decisions the same way Lot did. Don't! Lot thought first of himself and his own greedy desires. In his haste, he had little regard for others, and even less regard for God's opinion. The result was a foolish choice that would end in painful consequences and disaster. What you see is not necessarily what you get! Don't be fooled. Don't make decisions based upon what *appears* to be best. Instead, ask God's counsel on the matter. Lot learned this the hard way; how will *you* learn?

THANKS! I NEEDED THAT!

TAKEN FROM GENESIS 22-24

GETTING READY

Take a moment to ready your heart by praying. Ask God to open your eyes so you might discover what He would have you learn. Thank Him that He is a God who is always near, no matter how your circumstances may look to you.

THE JOURNEY

Do you ever wonder if God is paying attention to your needs or difficult circumstances?

As Isaac stood in the field awaiting a bride he had never met, thoughts of his rich history flooded his mind. God had spoken to his father, Abraham, promising an heir and descendants more numerous than the stars! Isaac knew he was that heir, even though he had a half brother named Ishmael. He knew his parents hadn't trusted God to provide them a son and took matters into their own hands. Ishmael was the son of Abraham and a maid named Hagar. Isaac was later born—just as God had promised.

Isaac looked out over the horizon, remembering the long journey he took with his father when he was just a teenager. They had set out for the region of Moriah to worship the Lord. When they reached their destination, the two servants remained at the foot of the mountain. "Wait here until my son and I return," his father said with emotion in his voice. As they ascended the mountain, Isaac noticed something was missing. "Father, I'm carrying the wood, and you have the fire and knife, but we have no animal to sacrifice!"

"The Lord Himself will provide the lamb for the burnt offering, my son," Abraham said softly.

Upon reaching the top of the mountain, Abraham built an altar and laid the wood on top. Isaac felt relieved to have the burden of wood off his back. Little did he know the heavy burden weighing on his father's heart. When all was prepared, Isaac saw both a look of love and

> Ishmael gave birth to twelve sons whom God said would become a mighty nation. Ishmael's sons are today's Arabs.

sadness in his father's eyes. Yet a solid, unwavering obedience shone there that spoke of deep trust and faith in God. The next thing Isaac knew, his father was tying his hands and feet! What was going on here?! He felt himself being lifted onto the altar. Panic rose up and lodged in Isaac's throat! What started as a good day of worship had suddenly turned into a nightmare!

"The Lord will provide. . . ." Isaac kept hearing those words over and over in his mind, nearly drowned out by the noise of his own pounding, anxious heart. "The Lord will provide. . . ." Everything around Isaac seemed to move in slow motion. He saw the knife raised above his father's head, glimmering in the sunlight, poised to come plunging down. The silence was shattered not by a knife, but by a heavenly voice. "Abraham! Abraham! Don't lay a hand on him! Now I know that you fear God, for you have not withheld from me your son, your only son."

With a great sigh of relief, the knife fell limply from Abraham's hand. He grabbed Isaac with a hug, and they both wept. Upon looking up, Abraham saw a ram struggling in the thicket, temporarily caught by his horns. Isaac watched his father prepare the sacrifice and place it on the altar where he had lain only moments before. The Lord *did* provide. . . .

Isaac smiled to himself. Even though he was now a man, those words still came to mind—sometimes in the most desperate of situations! Suddenly, Isaac's eyes caught movement on the horizon. Could it be?!

Across the field came a small caravan. It was his father's servant returning from a long journey. He had left with ten camels and many gifts, and now returned with much less—yet, one special addition. Isaac walked toward them in the open field. As he drew nearer, he saw a young woman in a veil dismount from her camel. The servant had found him a wife. Isaac's heart rejoiced! He could tell Rebekah had not only outward beauty, but also inward beauty.

With great delight, the servant explained how he had asked God to give a special sign when the right woman came along. When Rebekah came to the well, she drew water for all of his ten camels. This was the sign for which he had asked the Lord. "When I found out her father was Sarah's brother," he went on, "I knew God had answered my prayers; He has provided!"

Isaac's heart rejoiced and he took Rebekah as his wife. Together, they had twin sons—Jacob and Esau—and God's promises continued to unfold.

Turn to Genesis 22 and read verses 7-8. Now quickly skip down and read verses 13-14. Look closely at verse 14. What did Abraham do in this verse?

Skill Time

YHWH-jireh is a name describing God. It means "the Lord provides." Do you have a need or a difficult situation you are facing? Take a moment and pray about it. After you've given it to God, write: "Genesis 22:14 ~ The Lord Will Provide" on a piece of paper and tape it up in a place you will notice it. In times of doubt, ask God to help your unbelief; then thank Him in advance for what He plans to do. He knows best what you need most.

TRICK OR TREAT!

TAKEN FROM GENESIS 25-35

GETTING READY

Begin your time in God's Word today with prayer. (By now, it should have become a habit!) Quiet your thoughts before God, and ask Him to help you understand the importance of honesty. Acknowledge that He is the source of all truth.

THE JOURNEY

Do you know people who trick others in order to get what they want?

"Jacob, I beg of you . . . give me some of that red lentil soup you cooked," Esau pleaded.

Wanting to benefit through the situation at hand, Jacob simply replied, "Only if you give me your birthright in exchange for it!" Jacob felt both clever and satisfied. Before he and his twin brother were born, God had given his parents a prophecy that the older son would serve the younger one. If Jacob could exchange places with Esau in the family will, he would gain the benefits and inheritance normally given to the oldest child. Jacob smiled at the thought. Obtaining Esau's birthright would make it all legal!

The birthright was a special honor given to the oldest son, entitling him to a double portion of the family inheritance and a position of leadership. If he chose to sell it or give it away, he would permanently lose those privileges.

"Yes! Anything—just give me some soup!" Esau hastily agreed. He cared little for his birthright and would gladly sell it for the price of a meal.

Everything seemed to be going Jacob's way until his mother brought alarming news. "Your father is now old and nearing death. Just this morning he sent your brother Esau to hunt and prepare his favorite meal. When he returns, your father plans to give him the blessing due the first-born—that blessing should be yours, Jacob! Listen to me, and follow my directions carefully. This is what you must do while Esau is gone. . . ."

It wasn't long before Jacob entered the room where his father lay. He was dressed in Esau's clothing and carrying the meal his father had requested. Jacob would use his father's failing eyesight to his advantage. "Is that you, Esau?" Isaac asked.

"Yes, Father," Jacob lied, "I have come with the meal you requested."

"You are back so soon, my son?" Isaac asked.

"Yes, Father. The Lord's hand was upon me," Jacob lied once more. When Isaac touched Jacob, he felt not the hair of Esau, but a cleverly placed goatskin to imitate Esau's hairy arms. Believing Jacob was Esau, Isaac gave his blessing. Jacob left the room satisfied and feeling he had gained much. It was a short-lived feeling.

When Esau returned from the field and discovered what Jacob had done, he was furious and sought to kill him. Rebekah devised a plan to send Jacob away to find a wife for himself among her family in Haran. This would put a safe distance between the two brothers. It was under these conditions that Jacob left his homeland and eventually met up with Laban, his mother's brother.

Now Jacob stood before his uncle in amazement. This couldn't be happening to him! Sure, he had tricked his brother and father, but that was entirely different—or was it?

"I worked seven long years for the privilege of marrying your youngest daughter, *Rachel*," Jacob said angrily. "And what do you do? You secretly disguise your oldest daughter to be your youngest! Instead of marrying my beloved Rachel, I find I have married *Leah!*" Disgust raised in Jacob's voice, and anger burned in his heart. Laban pretended innocence. "It's our custom for older daughters to marry first," he replied. "If you complete her wedding celebration week, I will give you Rachel's hand in marriage as well. You must then work for me an additional seven years!" Laban smugly replied. Jacob knew he had been tricked by one who was craftier than he was. It was a hard lesson to learn, for during those seven years, Laban cheated and stole from Jacob, but Jacob continued to work hard to fulfill his commitment.

Upon completing his obligations, Jacob fled from Laban for his homeland in Canaan. In spite of Laban's schemes and stealing, God had blessed Jacob. Not only did he have many possessions and livestock, but he now had eleven sons. Appearing to Jacob in a vision, God confirmed the covenant He made with Abraham, his grandfather, and Isaac, his father. It was now Jacob's turn to carry God's plan onward—but not until Jacob had learned his lesson fully. . . .

Before entering the land of Canaan, Jacob received word that his brother, Esau, was coming to meet him with 400 men. Jacob's heart filled with fear, and he divided his family into two camps hoping that if one were attacked, the other would be spared. He then sent messengers ahead bearing gifts and livestock in a desperate attempt to buy his brother's forgiveness. "Save me!" Jacob finally cried out to God, "even though I am unworthy of all the kindness and faithfulness You have shown me, Lord." When Jacob set down his pride, God acted on his behalf. It had taken him over twenty years to learn that simple lesson.

exploring deeper

Open your Bible to Genesis chapter 32, and look at verses 27-28. What question was Jacob asked? Do you think it caused Jacob to stop and think about his past? *Jacob* means "supplanter," or "trickster." The name *Israel* means "he fights with God," or "God fights." Because of Jacob's self-will, God fought against him. Jacob's twelve sons were later called the sons of Israel, or the Israelites. They would experience victory only to the degree that they allowed *God* to fight for them.

CROSS ROADS

Operating under our own steam and efforts usually yields disappointment because we don't have the total picture—God's perspective. Rather than rely on God to work, we run ahead of Him with our own plans and schemes—often manipulating people or circumstances to get what we desire (or believe we deserve). God wants us to put things into His hands. If we try to work out the details ourselves, we will either miss God's blessing or become disappointed in the results. God leaves the choice to us: Trick . . . or treat? Which one will you choose?

WHY ME?!!

TAKEN FROM GENESIS 37-50

GETTING READY

Take a few minutes to search your heart and be quiet before the Lord. Ask Him to point out any people in your life you need to ask forgiveness from—or give forgiveness to. Bow your head and thank God for His provision and forgiveness in your life.

THE JOURNEY

Do you ever find it difficult to forgive those who wrong you or cause you harm?

Joseph's heart skipped a beat as he recognized who stood in front of him. What should he do? Loneliness . . . suffering . . . hard work . . . pain—all of these he had experienced since his brothers sold him as a slave. That was twenty long years ago. Oh, how he missed his father—was he still alive? Joseph remembered Jacob's last words spoken to him, just as if it were yesterday. . . .

"Joseph, my son," Jacob had said, "Please find your brothers who are grazing the flocks and return to me with news of how they're doing."

What started out as a simple errand ended up a nightmare!

When Joseph's brothers saw him approaching, anger and resentment burned in their hearts. They despised him for being the favorite son and hated his nonsense dreams. "Imagine!" they scoffed. "Us bowing before our little baby brother? Never!" To get rid of Joseph forever, they threw him into a pit and planned to leave him there to die. When a traveling caravan of merchants drew near, their plans changed. Joseph was sold as a slave and taken to Egypt. The brothers returned home with Joseph's robe in hand and reported their brother had been killed by a wild beast. They held up his robe (which they had torn and dipped in goat's blood) as evidence. In their eyes, Joseph was as good as dead.

Joseph was sold to Midianite merchants for twenty shekels of silver. The Midianites were descendants of Ishmael.

Now sitting on a polished throne, Joseph swallowed hard, forcing his emotions down. Obviously, his brothers didn't recognize him. Why should they? The Joseph *they* knew was a teenage brother they sold into slavery. Now, twenty years later, Joseph was the second most powerful man in all of Egypt! But it hadn't been easy getting there.

When he reached Egypt, Joseph was sold to Pharaoh's captain of the guard, Potiphar. Potiphar noticed that the Lord was with Joseph, granting him success at every turn. As a result, Joseph found favor in the eyes of his master and was given care over Potiphar's entire household. Unfortunately, Joseph also found favor in the eyes of his master's wife, who thought him handsome and desirable. One day, she cornered Joseph while her husband was away, but Joseph escaped from her advances. Angered, she devised a tale that Joseph had attacked her. Potiphar's anger burned, and Joseph was thrown into prison—innocent and misjudged.

One day in prison, Joseph interpreted the dreams of Pharaoh's cupbearer and baker who were also prisoners. The cupbearer promised to present Joseph's case before the king when he was released. It wasn't until Pharaoh had a disturbing dream (two years later!) that Joseph was remembered. Finally brought before the king, Joseph interpreted his dream which predicted seven years of bountiful harvest in the land followed by seven years of famine. "Let the Pharaoh take action and appoint a man who is discerning and wise, setting him up as an overseer over the land," Joseph suggested. Seeing the wisdom God granted Joseph, Pharaoh gave him the job. A ring was placed on his finger and a royal robe on his back. Adorned in this fashion, Joseph now stood before his brothers who had no idea to whom they were bowing! Joseph weighed his options.

Should he treat his brothers harshly, as they had treated him? Should he reveal himself with an "I told you so" attitude, reminding them of his dreams they ridiculed? Perhaps he would simply deny their request for grain, sending them home empty-handed to suffer, just as he himself had suffered. Joseph's emotions rose within him, and he could no longer contain himself. "I am your brother Joseph, the one you sold into Egypt!" he exclaimed. His brothers stood speechless; terror and guilt etched painfully upon their faces. Joseph's next words caused them even greater shock; for his words weren't full of anger and bitterness. They were words full of forgiveness!

exploring deeper

Through Joseph the whole family line was preserved. Pharaoh even gave the best land in Egypt (an area called Goshen) to his brothers and father to settle upon and raise their livestock. Joseph's forgiveness to his brothers had far-reaching effects. However, an unusual thing happened when their father died. Turn to the last chapter of Genesis (chapter 50) and read verses 15-21. Do you think Joseph's brothers understood the depth of true forgiveness?

Skill Time

When offended (either deliberately or by accident) you will be tempted to get even. Don't. Anger and bitterness in your heart don't make you the winner, they make you the victim. That's why God commands us to forgive one another in Colossians 3:13: "Bear with each other and forgive whatever grievances you may have against on another. Forgive as the Lord forgave you."

Asking and giving forgiveness goes deeper than just saying, "sorry" or "that's O.K." and "no problem." It is saying (and meaning) the words: "I forgive you." Those words are hard to say unless you truly mean them (that's why we usually say, "that's O.K." and "no problem"). True forgiveness is impossible without God's help! The next time you're offended, put into practice these simple steps: 1) Give your anger over to God. 2) Check your heart to make sure you aren't falling prey to bitterness. 3) Say the words, "I forgive you" as soon as possible.

GETTING YOUR BEARINGS:
THE BOOK OF EXODUS

Exodus is the second book in what we call the Pentateuch (*penta*, "five" and *teuchos*, "scroll"). It is the second book out of five written by Moses, and part two of Genesis. As you explore Exodus, notice an immediate change in the terrain. Genesis ended with Jacob's family of seventy moving to Egypt and living favorably under the Pharaoh. Exodus opens 350 years later with the Hebrews living not as guests of a Pharaoh, but as slaves! In Genesis we saw families; in Exodus we see the beginning of a nation. Keep alert as you make your way through this book, and don't assume you already know what's ahead. Exodus is loaded with neat surprises and a fresh look at who God is. Are you daring enough to explore it and find out? Then read on. . . .

I PLEDGE ALLEGIANCE...

TAKEN FROM EXODUS 1-2

GETTING READY

Before you begin your journey today, pause and ask God to direct your thoughts and your heart. God is all-knowing and wise. Everything you encounter in this life must first pass through His hands.

THE JOURNEY

Have you ever struggled with obeying God when someone in authority tells you to do something wrong?

"There are too many Israelites for us to control," the new Pharaoh stated one day. It had been a little over 400 years since Joseph's family was invited to live in Egypt. During Joseph's lifetime, Egypt was ruled by a group of people called the Hyksos (who were descendants of Shem). Since they were not fully Egyptians, they accepted foreigners in their land. Now, however, the Egyptians were back in control. Joseph and his brothers were no longer alive, and the Hebrew people were almost two million strong! Political powers had changed, and so would the Israelites' lives!

"If I don't do something about all these Hebrews," the Pharaoh muttered, "they could easily rise up against us, siding with our enemies if we were to go to war!" The Pharaoh knew the danger of enemies trying to take the land. He also knew that the Hebrews had once lived peacefully under the Hyksos people. The more Pharaoh looked about him, the more insecure he felt. He soon became angered at the ever-increasing Hebrew nation, and came up with a wicked plan to stop its growth.

Pharaoh called for the two head midwives (Shiphrah and Puah) who helped deliver babies in Egypt, "When the Hebrew women are giving birth," he said, "check to see if the baby is a boy or girl. If it's a girl, let the baby live. If it's a boy, kill it." A fiendish smile curled on Pharaoh's lips, and he felt quite pleased with himself. "That will put a quick stop to these detestable Hebrews," he muttered under his breath.

Shiphrah and Puah, however, feared God and didn't carry out the Pharaoh's wicked command. Pharaoh soon noticed the number of Hebrews had not decreased, and questioned the two head midwives. "The Israelite women are so strong, they give birth before we can get there to help!" they lied. The king was furious. Now his secret plan would have to go public and would come in the form of a decree.

The name Moses sounded similar in both the Egyptian and Hebrew language. When the princess gave Moses his name, it meant "son" or "is born." In Hebrew, the similar sounding name meant "to draw out"—a constant reminder of God's provision and Moses' rescue from the Nile River.

"Every Hebrew boy who is born must be thrown into the Nile River," he ordered. "Only the girls may live." This time it would be law, and it would be *enforced!*

Upon hearing this decree, a Hebrew couple named Amram and Jochebed hid their newborn son. Choosing to follow a higher law—God's law—they could not, and would not follow the law of the land. However, three months had passed, and it now became difficult to conceal their son in their home. Not knowing what else to do, Jochebed made a water-tight basket from the reeds that grew along the Nile River. With loving hands and a breaking heart, she placed her son in the basket and left him there among the reeds. Her daughter, Miriam, stood watch to make sure no harm came to the baby.

When Pharaoh's daughter went down to the Nile River to bathe, she saw the basket floating in the reeds and had one of her attendants fetch it. Seeing it was a Hebrew boy, Pharaoh's daughter had pity for the baby. Miriam stepped out from behind the reeds. "The baby appears hungry," she said. "Would you like me to find a Hebrew woman who could nurse the baby?" When the princess nodded, Miriam hurried off to find her mother. She couldn't wait to tell her that her baby brother had found favor in the eyes of Egyptian royalty!

Upon seeing his daughter's attachment to the baby, Pharaoh had little choice but to allow the boy to grow up within the royal courts. It was against his better judgment, but denying his daughter was something he could not do. Little did he know what the future would bring!

As the years passed, Moses grew from a baby boy to a strapping young man. Although he had the best education possible and enjoyed all the benefits of Egyptian royalty, Moses' heart grew heavy. Looking about him, he noticed the poor treatment and suffering the Hebrews experienced at the hands of the Egyptians. Although he was Egyptian raised, Moses never forgot he was Hebrew born. Perhaps someday . . . in some way . . . he could help his people. Moses looked for that opportunity.

exploring deeper

Open your Bible to Exodus 1, and read verses 20-21. Does this strike you as unusual? Is God rewarding the midwives for not telling the truth? Take a closer look! Especially focus on the first half of verse 21. Shiphrah and Puah had things in their proper order—they feared (and obeyed) God first—regardless of personal cost to themselves. The Lord saw their hearts and rewarded them.

THINKING on your FEET

In our society, there are many instances where the "law of the land" conflicts with the law of God. Just because something is legal doesn't mean it's moral or right. God allows challenges to come across our path so that we might have opportunities to stand up for Him. The next time you are faced with such a decision, where will your allegiance be?

YOU MEAN, ME?!!

TAKEN FROM EXODUS 2-4

GETTING READY

God is a God who desires to know and have a relationship with you. He created you—your life is not a mistake. He also has a purpose and plan for your life. Take a moment to thank Him for that fact. Ask Him to help you discover what He wants you to learn through your time in His Word today.

THE JOURNEY

Do you ever not do something because you feel you aren't good enough, or you might fail?

Moses looked down and couldn't believe what he had done! His hands trembled, and he nervously looked around him to see if anyone had noticed. The sight of an Egyptian beating an Israelite—one of his own people—angered him beyond control, and Moses reacted violently. Now, the lifeless body of the Egyptian lay at his feet. Moses glanced around again and quickly covered the Egyptian's body with sand.

The next day, Moses saw two Hebrew men fighting. "Why do you hit your fellow Hebrew?" he asked the man who was in the wrong. The man sneered angrily, "Who made *you* ruler and judge over *us?* Do you plan to kill *me* like you killed that Egyptian the other day?" Like a sharp dagger, the words cut deep into Moses' conscience, threatening to reveal their truth. The wrong Moses had done in a moment of anger became known. When word reached the ears of Pharaoh, Moses' life was in danger. Not liking any Hebrew person in the first place, Pharaoh now had a good excuse to do away with Moses forever.

Fleeing for his life, Moses left Pharaoh's court for the desert dunes 300 miles east of Egypt. When he arrived in Midian, Moses sat down near a well to rest. Drops of perspiration rolled off his brow as he looked around and noticed how much different and harsher the desert was compared to the fertile land of Egypt. Where would he go? How would he eat? What would he do? Even though Moses was Hebrew born, he was raised by Egyptians and knew nothing of a shepherd's life-style. As Moses pondered his options, he noticed seven girls drawing water from the well to give drinks to their father's flocks. Some shepherds came along and drove them away, but Moses came to their rescue and watered their flock.

"A kind Egyptian came to our rescue!" the girls breathlessly reported to their father, Jethro, who was a Midianite priest. Upon hearing his daughters' report, Jethro sent for Moses to come as a guest and stay with them. A friendship of respect and trust began between the two men, and soon Moses was given the hand of Jethro's daughter Zipporah in marriage. Moses spent the next forty years of his life as a shepherd and became very familiar with the desert land in the Sinai Peninsula area. Little did he know how God was preparing him for a future task of leading more than just sheep through this barren land. . . .

Mount Horeb is another name for Mount Sinai—the place where God would later give Moses the Ten Commandments.

Having journeyed to the far side of the desert with Jethro's flocks one day, Moses saw something strange on Mount Horeb where the sheep were grazing. It was a bush that was on fire, yet not burning up or even being scorched! When Moses took a closer look, the voice of God called out from the flames. "Moses! Moses! Come no closer!" He commanded. "Take off your sandals, for you are standing on holy ground! I am the God of your father, the God of Abraham, the God of Isaac, and the God of Jacob." Upon hearing these words, Moses knew in whose presence he was standing, and was overcome with both fear and awe. With his face to the ground, Moses listened carefully to every word God said.

God had seen the Hebrews suffering as slaves at the hands of the Egyptians, and He had a plan. Moses would return to Egypt and go to Pharaoh to demand the release of the Hebrews. Then he would lead them to the land that God had promised to give them! Panic rose up and caught in Moses' throat. "You mean, *me?!*" he managed to choke out. Knowing his own past and failures, Moses listed reasons why he would only fail at the task given him.

"Who am *I*, that *I* should go to Pharaoh and bring the Israelites out of Egypt?" he said, calling attention to his own unworthiness. God simply replied, "I will be with you," and gave Moses a sign that would happen in the future to prove it. "What if the Hebrews ask who sent me?" Moses countered. God answered, "Tell them, I AM has sent you." Moses grew quiet; never before had the Lord identified Himself with a name, indicating His character. He grew restless and desperate. When Moses brought up his fear, his poor public speaking, and even his own cowardice, the Lord answered each and every objection. God would give him the ability to perform signs and wonders so the people would know he was God's messenger. His brother, Aaron, would speak for him. Above and beyond all else, God Himself promised to be with Moses. When Moses cried, "You mean, *me?!*" God simply replied, "Yes, and I also mean *Me*."

exploring deeper

Turn in your Bible to Exodus 4 and read verses 10-13. What was Moses' problem? Notice what he says in verse 13? (Go on, read it!) Are those words you have ever felt or said? Now skip down to verse 17. What did God tell Moses to do? Notice the word "miraculous." God takes us where we're at, and *He* works the miracles in and through us.

Skill Time

When Moses gave his list of excuses, God responded by revealing a part of His own character: "I AM." In effect, God is saying, "I am the One who designed you; I am the One who gives you life; I am the One who desires to use your life in a significant way; I am all you need; I am God, and there is no other; I am that I AM—any questions?" In your own life, think of three excuses or weaknesses why you feel you can't serve or obey God. Now, give those weaknesses to God. Start by saying, "Lord, You know that I am (*say your weakness*). I know You are (*give the opposite of that weakness*). Please help others to see Your power in my life because of my weaknesses. Let them see You as the One they truly need. Amen."

IS THIS REALLY NECESSARY?!

TAKEN FROM EXODUS 5-14

GETTING READY

Stop and pray about your time in God's Word. Ask Him to open your eyes and heart, that you might discover what He wants to show you today. He is never far off or unconcerned about you.

THE JOURNEY

Have you ever been blamed for a bad day someone else is having?

Cries of pain and anguish rose up from various houses in the land as a dark shadow passed by each and every home. It was a terrible night, and one that would be remembered forever. This was God's last plague and final message—a message of deliverance for some, a message of destruction for others.

Moses stayed in his home as God instructed, waiting and watching. The stillness of the night seemed heavy and quiet, only to be interrupted by sudden screams and crying outside. Moses stood in silence, as experiences of the past weeks and months flooded his mind. He knew he had been sent by God to rescue the Israelites from their slavery in Egypt, but it had not been an easy task.

"The Lord is concerned about us and has seen our misery!" the Hebrews rejoiced when Moses came with a message of deliverance from the Lord. With excitement, they waited as Moses pleaded their case before Pharaoh—it was an excitement that would quickly fade. "Who is this God, that I should obey Him and let my slaves go?!" Pharaoh answered arrogantly. Serving all the gods of Egypt, he had little interest in hearing about the God of Israel. "If these slaves have time to think about worshiping their God, they must not have enough work to do!" he scoffed. As a result, the workload on the Israelites was doubled. Instead of rescuing his people, Moses had only brought more hardship! In despair, the people revolted and would no longer listen to him. "Why don't You deliver Your people as You promised?" Moses asked the Lord. God answered by explaining what was to be done and what would happen. God had a plan, and He had His reasons. . . .

Each plague was a targeted attack on one of the many (false) gods of Egypt.

A scream suddenly echoed through the streets and briefly caught Moses' attention. He knew another firstborn child had died—as would many more children and even firstborn cattle. It had been a long road up to this point in time, and God had given many signs and warnings in the form of plagues. In the beginning, the plagues caused only discomfort, such as when all the water in Egypt turned to blood and killed the fish, causing a stench. Then the frogs came, and the gnats and swarms of flies. Slowly the plagues increased in intensity. All the Egyptians' livestock were killed, while the Israelites' remained untouched. Painful boils came upon the Egyptians, and hail destroyed most of their crops. What little remained was soon totally consumed by a plague of locusts. All of Egypt was devastated—except for Goshen, where the Hebrews lived.

Time and again, Moses appeared before Pharaoh, but Pharaoh remained unwilling to completely release the Israelites and turned a deaf ear—at least until tonight. Tonight would be God's final sign of His power. It would be a lesson that would cut close to home and deep into the heart of Pharaoh. Moses had warned Pharaoh, and had helped the Israelites to prepare. For the Hebrew people, tonight would be a night they would see God's deliverance from bondage.

> The blood on the doorposts symbolized much more than the Israelites' obedience to a strange command! It was the sign of a sacrifice. One day, God would provide the Perfect Sacrifice—a Lamb without spot or blemish. We find this fulfillment in the New Testament.

More wails rose from the valley. Those who did not obey God's command of slaughtering a lamb and placing its blood upon the top and sides of their doorframes experienced the angel of death visiting their home and taking the lives of all the firstborn within. But those who sacrificed a lamb in exchange for the life of their firstborn, were not harmed. The angel saw the blood and passed over their homes.

A rap on the door and a summons by the Pharaoh brought Moses out into the night air. The only sign the angel of death had come and gone was the trail of sorrow and despair left behind. One of those despairing was Pharaoh; he too lost his firstborn—his only son and heir to the throne. "Go, and leave my people!" he whispered through clenched teeth. Because of the many plagues, all the people in Egypt had come to stand in fear and awe of the God of the Hebrews. As a result, the Israelites were given whatever they requested, and thus plundered Egypt. Taking with them articles of silver, gold, and clothing, the Hebrew people left Egypt and its worries behind— or so they thought.

exploring deeper

Do you know what happened at the height of the Israelites' victory? Turn in your Bible to chapter 14 of Exodus. It's the exciting conclusion of today's lesson and is worth reading on your own. For now, skip down and read verses 10-12. Then, compare it to verse 31. Who was the lesson of hardship for this time? Do you think it was necessary?

THINKING on your FEET

When hardship or difficult circumstances come into our lives, we often become discouraged. Sometimes we blame others, while at other times we are being blamed! When fingers are being pointed, lessons are often being missed. As a result, we fail to see God at work in our daily lives. God might desire to do a miracle in and through us, or He might allow our suffering to point others to Him. The next time you face a difficult circumstance, how will you respond?

IS THIS A TEST?

TAKEN FROM EXODUS 15-18

GETTING READY

Take a moment to prepare for your time in God's Word today. Examine your heart, and ask God to show you areas that are not honoring to Him. Give Him permission to change those areas.

THE JOURNEY

Do you need to know all the "whys" before you obey certain rules?

Fear. Excitement. Relief. Curiosity. These emotions and many more filled the hearts and minds of the Hebrews as they set out on their journey following Moses. "Free at last!" they exclaimed joyously, their eyes aglow with the promise of a better future and a new land they could call their own. Knowing the fragile condition of their hearts, God didn't lead them by the shortest route to the Promised Land. Traveling along the Mediterranean coast would only put the Israelites in danger of a war with the Philistines, and they were not ready for that. Instead, God took them to the southeast past Mount Sinai. Many lessons were yet to be learned, and the three-month journey would provide opportunities for both the teaching and testing of God's people.

"Who among the gods is like You, O Lord? Who is like You—majestic in holiness, awesome in glory, working wonders?" the Israelites shouted with joy. Tambourines shook, and even the very young and old danced in celebration, for they had all seen God miraculously deliver them from Pharaoh and his chariots that had pursued them. Hemmed in by mountains on one side and the Red Sea on the other, the Israelites were delivered from certain defeat when the Lord parted the Red Sea and allowed them to pass through—nearly two million of them! Once the Israelites were safely over, the Egyptians charged forth—only to be defeated in a watery grave. It was a time of great rejoicing for the Israelites, and the young nation knew God was with them.

After their great victory at the Red Sea, the Israelites traveled three days in the desert without finding water. Finally coming to an oasis at Marah, they found the water totally undrinkable and bitter! The Israelites complained, and God instructed Moses to throw a designated piece of wood into the water, and the water would become drinkable. Although it didn't make sense, Moses obeyed. Instantly, the water turned sweet and was able to satisfy the needs of all. It was at that point God gave the Israelites a command. "You must listen carefully to Me and do what is right. Pay close attention to what I say and keep the rules I give," God commanded. Filled with the sweetness of the water, the Israelites easily agreed . . . and readily forgot.

The word "manna" comes from the Hebrew words *man hu* which mean, "what is it?" This bread from heaven came in thin flakes, looked white like coriander seed, and tasted like honey wafers.

As days passed into weeks, God faithfully led the Israelites from oasis to oasis. He guided them with a pillar of cloud by day and a pillar of fire by night. When the cloud stopped, the Israelites would stop and camp. When it moved onward, they did too. Now, however, it was a month and a half since they had left Egypt, and the excitement of the adventure had worn off. They became hungry and irritable. "It would have been better for us to stay in Egypt and die as slaves," they complained. "At least *there* we had food to eat!" Soon, all the people were grumbling and blaming

Moses for their discomfort. "Your grumbling isn't against me, but against the Lord. God has heard your complaining and will show you that *He* has brought you out of the land of Egypt. He will give you meat in the evening and bread in the morning. Then you will know that He is the Lord, your God," Moses said. Moses then relayed the specific rules God wanted the people to know. "You are to go out each morning and collect what God provides," he said. "No one is to keep any for the next day. However, on day six, you must collect a double portion, for the next day is the Sabbath—a day of rest—and there will be no manna to collect." The rules were simple and easily understood, however, they weren't completely followed.

"That's a strange rule! Why should I only collect for today? There's plenty here, and who knows what tomorrow may bring!" some Israelites said to themselves. As a result, they paid little attention to God's rules and stored away extra manna. When the next morning came, they discovered their manna spoiled and crawling with maggots! Others forgot God's words of instruction and went out on the Sabbath hoping to collect manna, but found none. Returning with empty arms because of the missing manna, the Israelites were faced with the truth of God's words. If they listened to Him closely and obeyed what He said, they would be blessed. If they didn't, they would experience His judgment. Life in the desert would provide a testing and training ground for their careful obedience to God and His rules.

exploring deeper

God wanted the Israelites to depend upon Him daily—a reason He commanded them not to store up manna. However, in Exodus 16:4, God tells Moses *another* reason for His rule. What does He say? (Turn there in your Bible and find out!)

DANGER AHEAD

As you go through life, you will encounter some rules that appear to make no sense at all. Be very careful how you react! You will be tempted to search for a reason in your own mind, only obeying the rule after it has met with your personal approval. Such an attitude is one of arrogance and sets you up for a fall. God wants us to be dependent upon Him, and that includes allowing Him to be the source of our strength to help us obey rules we might feel are unnecessary. Sometimes rules are there for a test of our obedience. When faced with rules, don't give in to the temptation to challenge them—instead, accept them as a challenge.

PLEASED TO MEET YOU

TAKEN FROM EXODUS 19-24

GETTING READY

Take a moment to quiet your heart and be still before God. Think about His power. Think about His creation and all that you see about you. Ask Him to open your heart and eyes to His greatness, and to help you appreciate Him more.

THE JOURNEY

Do you ever feel that the Ten Commandments are just a list of "dos and don'ts"?

It had been three months—three months of journeying since they had left Egypt and entered the desert. Already the Hebrews had seen God's faithfulness, and they had been tested by His simple instructions. Now, they would witness an awesome demonstration of His power and love.

The ground trembled as the Israelites stood in fear and awe. They had spent three days preparing their hearts and cleansing themselves in preparation for this day, but were not prepared for all they would see and feel. Having been led outside of the camp by Moses, the Hebrews stood at the foot of Mount Sinai. They knew that to touch the mountain would mean certain death, for God had given specific instructions that no one was to come near. Barricades were even set up to keep both man and animal at a safe distance. The Israelites looked on, ready to meet God.

Lightning ripped across the sky and thunder rumbled in the valley below. A thick cloud hovered over the top of the mountain, signaling a loud trumpet blast. Then Mount Sinai became covered with smoke as the Lord descended upon it in fire. The earth shook, and smoke billowed from the mountain like a furnace. All the Israelites stood in silence, gripped by what they saw before them. "Speak to us yourself, Moses, and we will listen," they cried out, "but don't have God speak to us, or we will die!" They knew what they looked upon was just a glimpse of God's power and majesty. As they watched, Moses approached the thick darkness where God was, for God had a message He wanted delivered to the people.

A covenant is an agreement between a greater party (such as a king) and a lesser party (his subjects) in how they can live in relationship to one another. Only the one in greater authority has the right to initiate it. The other has the opportunity to either accept or reject it.

"Tell this to the Israelites: I AM the Lord your God, who brought you out of Egypt and out of your slavery," the Lord spoke to Moses. "You shall have no other gods before Me. You shall not make for yourselves any idols or show dishonor to the name of the Lord. Keep the Sabbath day separated as a special and holy day. Honor your parents, so that you may live long as a nation in a covenant relationship with Me. Do not take another person's life by murder. Find delight only in the husband or wife who is yours. Do not steal. You shall not ruin someone else's reputation with lies about him, and do not long for, or desire, anything that belongs to another person." Moses listened as God continued His instructions. They were God's ground rules for how the people could live in a covenant relationship with Him.

When the Lord finished, Moses came down from the mountain and made his report to the people. "This is what the Lord says. . . ," he began, and carefully detailed all that God had spoken to him. He described not only (what we call) the Ten Commandments, but also a total of 613 separate commands and instructions on how they were to live and govern themselves as a nation.

Standing in the shadow of Mount Sinai, the people heard God's conditions and readily accepted them. "Everything God says, we will do!" they proclaimed with a loud voice.

"You are to be My holy people," God said, desiring that the Israelites would live differently than the pagan nations in the land to which they were traveling. Surrounding nations worshiped false gods and constantly lived in uncertainty. How would they know if they pleased or angered their god? The Lord God of Israel, however, lovingly drew His people into a specific relationship with Himself. They would not be left guessing or uncertain about where they stood, but would know exactly what God required of them. God, the Creator of the universe, had revealed His power and holiness and the conditions necessary for keeping His covenant. To be in relationship with Him was an awesome and unique privilege—one that would enable the Israelites to experience both security and trust.

exploring deeper

In your Bible, turn to Exodus 20:20. What was God's purpose in displaying His power to the Israelites? Notice Moses' first words, "Do not be afraid." Being afraid is based on a lack of trust in a person or situation. The "fear of God" is a respect for His power and a true understanding of who He is. This brings a basis for trust and confidence.

Skill Time

God desires to be in a relationship with you. Because of who He is, He has given you guidelines as to what pleases and displeases Him. Because there is such a great chasm between His holiness and our sinfulness, we immediately see where we fall short and "miss the mark." Even though the Ten Commandments were just the "summary" of the entire covenant with Israel, we find them nearly impossible to keep! The fact that God gave them is His way of saying, "I love you and want you to know Me." The fact that we can't keep them should cause us to respond with, "I need You!" Have you ever said those words to God—and meant them? If not, and if it is the desire of your heart, bow your head right now and pray: "Lord, I see Your holiness, and I see my sinfulness. Please forgive me for my shortcomings. I want to be in relationship with You, but I need Your help. I can't live a good enough life on my own." Now turn to the back of this book and discover the special provision God has for you!

BLUEPRINTS? FOR WHAT?

TAKEN FROM EXODUS 25-31

GETTING READY

Stop and pray before beginning your time in God's Word today. Ask Him to be the teacher of your heart, and to help you understand more about Him.

THE JOURNEY

Do you ever secretly wonder if there's more than one way to God?

"Tell the Israelites to bring Me an offering of gold, bronze, silver, precious gems, and fine linen," the Lord told Moses. These were the riches the Egyptians handed over to the Israelites as they departed Egypt—riches that God provided for a reason. "You are to receive it from each man whose heart prompts him to give," God instructed Moses. "Have them use these items to make a holy place for Me, and I will dwell among them. My tabernacle is to be exactly like the pattern I will show you," He said, listing the exact supplies of what they were to use. Moses would spend forty days on Mount Sinai meeting with God and receiving all His instructions. Careful note was made of each item that was to fill the tabernacle, for through it God would reveal more of Himself, and a word-picture that would stand as a blueprint for all time.

"Make a chest out of acacia wood—the strongest wood that grows in the Sinai peninsula," God instructed, "and then cover it inside and out with pure gold. The lid is to be very special—of pure solid gold, with two gold angels facing each other and spreading their wings across the cover to protect it."

The first thing God described to Moses was the most important. It would be called the ark (container) of the covenant (God's agreement with Israel). Choosing to use something from their culture they could understand, God initiated a relationship with the Hebrew people by use of a covenant agreement. It was an agreement between two people or groups that would help them live together peacefully. The greater person (God) was the only one who could draw up the terms. The lesser person (the Israelites) could then accept or reject those terms. Each person was to keep a short, easy-to-read summary of the agreement in his most holy, sacred spot. For Moses, that spot would be the ark of the covenant. Little did he know, the ark would also be *God's* spot as well! "There, above the cover between the two cherubim that are over the ark, I will dwell and meet with you," God announced. This relationship with His people would be founded upon God's faithfulness to His covenant.

> The word tabernacle means "to abide." Its ability to be disassembled and moved reminded the Hebrews that God was not contained within four walls or one location.

"Next, make a table of the same type of wood, and overlay it with pure gold," God said to Moses. On this table would be stacked twelve loaves of bread (a loaf for each tribe of Israel) as a reminder of God's provision. Each week the loaves would be replaced with fresh ones by a priest. Not far from the table and also in the Holy Place (where only the priest could go) was to be a golden lampstand. Having seven branches, it was to burn at all times and never go out, providing the only light in the Holy Place.

A huge veil and an altar of incense blocked the entrance to the Holy of Holies. Inside this room were the ark of the covenant and the mercy seat where God dwelt between the two gold cherubim. Just outside was a vessel made of bronze where the priest could wash and become "ceremonially clean." In front of that was an altar where animals were to be sacrificed as a reminder of the covenant and the penalty of sin.

Moses kept careful note of everything the Lord said, right down to the specific measurements and exact descriptions. He knew God had a purpose and a plan. Coming to worship God—the Almighty Creator of the universe—would have to be on His terms, not man's.

Moses had no idea as he set the tabernacle in place that each piece represented and pointed to the coming Messiah and would find its fulfillment in the New Testament. God's provision of the perfect sacrifice, once for all, was already being foretold. God's plan and blueprints were in place. The only way to God was through God's way, and He was pointing to it through the picture of the tabernacle.

Josephus, a Jewish historian, explained the veil separating the Holy Place from the Holy of Holies. It was four inches thick, and horses pulling in opposite directions couldn't tear it apart! Interestingly, the moment Jesus died on the cross, the veil in the temple tore from top to bottom.

exploring deeper

Look up Exodus 25:8-9 in your Bible. Who is speaking here? Pay close attention to verse 9. Why do you think that was so important?

CROSS-ROADS

The tabernacle is not an outdated blueprint for the way we must approach God; it is a fulfilled one. When Jesus (the Lamb of God, and God's provision for the perfect sacrifice that would end all sacrifices) died on the cross, the veil in the temple miraculously tore—not from the bottom up, but from the top down, by God's own hand. The tabernacle, which was just a blueprint, was no longer needed because what it pointed to had come. Still today, the only way we can come to God is through what He has provided; there is no other way. Coming to God must follow God's plans—not ours. Whose blueprints will you follow—your own or God's?

TABERNACLE BLUEPRINT

Bread on the table
Golden candlestick
High priest representing people
Brass water basin to wash in

Animals without defect
   —sacrificed on the altar
Veil, keeping people from God

GOD'S FULFILLMENT—JESUS

"Bread of Life"
"Light of the World"
"Great High Priest"
We are "washed" through
   God's Word.
Jesus, perfect "Lamb of God"
   —sacrificed on the cross
Torn veil, God accessible to all
   through Jesus

HOW COULD YOU?

TAKEN FROM EXODUS 32

GETTING READY

You may be tempted to skip this part, but don't! Take the time to stop and pray before going any further. Tell God what is on your mind right now, and allow Him to tell you what is on His.

THE JOURNEY

When you trust somebody with a job, and she lets you down, do you have a hard time trusting her again?

It had been a long time—over a month—since Moses went up Mount Sinai to meet with God. "What could be taking so long?" Aaron wondered as he looked up the mountain. From the valley below, it looked like a consuming fire on the mountaintop.

"Hey, Aaron," the Israelites said one day as they gathered around him, "this Moses who led us out of Egypt—we don't know what's happened to him!" Aaron could see the people were becoming concerned and discontent. It was a hard thing to have left the comforts of Egypt (before they became slaves) and all that was familiar. Sure, they had seen

God miraculously deliver them from Pharaoh in the crossing of the Red Sea. He had also guided them through the wilderness and provided manna for them to eat. Yet, Moses was the only one who had ever communicated with God. He was their spokesman to the God they were just getting to know! Without Moses, the Israelites were uncertain and questioning. At least in Egypt, there was the comfort of seeing images of gods and knowing they were there. *Perhaps that is what they needed!* Aaron thought.

"Make us gods who will go before us!" they said, gathering around Aaron. Aaron hesitated and then sighed as he looked back up the mountain. No sign of Moses—still. *Will Moses even return? What am I to do with these people?* he thought. He knew about as much as they did, for although he could speak well, he himself had never spoken with God. Aaron felt torn. He knew the Israelites were working themselves up, and his own heart wasn't far behind! Aaron glanced back up the mountain and then slowly looked away. There's no harm in giving the people what they desire. After all, it's only a little thing.

"Take off all the gold jewelry you are wearing and bring it to me," Aaron suggested. The people did as they were told. Taking what they handed him, Aaron used a tool and worked with the gold. When finished, he presented an idol to them that was cast into the shape of a calf. The people rejoiced, for now they had a god fashioned into something they were familiar and comfortable with. "These are our gods, O Israel, who brought us up out of Egypt!" they shouted. Seeing this celebration, Aaron built an altar in front of the calf and announced, "Tomorrow there will be a festival to the Lord!"

> **Trust is based on:**
> Truthfulness
> Respect
> Understanding
> Sincerity
> Tenacity (sticking with something)

Everyone was in the mood for a good time, but things had soon gotten out of control. "To our gods!" the people cheered as they became drunk and danced wildly about. They did not see Moses approaching from Mount Sinai, carrying the stone tablets containing the terms of God's covenant with them. The closer Moses came, the angrier he became with Aaron. Upon reaching the camp, Moses' eyes caught sight of the golden idol. With anger in his heart, he threw down the stone tablets. The pieces that lay at his feet represented Israel's broken covenant relationship with God.

With anger and disappointment Moses later sought out Aaron. "How could you do this?! What did these people do to you, that you led them into such great sin?" he demanded. Aaron remained quiet for a moment, realizing the seriousness of what he had done and how he provided a bad example and bad leadership to God's chosen people. "Don't be angry, my lord," he stammered, hoping to cover his wrong. "You know how prone these people are to evil. When they said to me, 'Make us gods who will go before us, since we don't know what happened to Moses,' I simply told them to take off their gold jewelry. When they handed it to me, I threw it into the fire, and out came this calf!" Aaron lied. Moses diverted his attention from Aaron and looked at the scene before him. Because of the Israelites' behavior, they would become a laughingstock to their enemies—that is how far Aaron allowed them to get out of control. That is how far he had led them into sin.

"Everyone who is for the Lord come stand by me," Moses yelled above the chaos. All the Israelites from the tribe of Levi came forth. At that point, Moses instructed them to go throughout the camp, killing all who claimed loyalty to the golden calf. In all, 3,000 people were killed. The remaining rebellious people were killed by God through a plague because they had worshiped the calf Aaron made.

exploring deeper

It would be sad if the story ended here, but it doesn't. Moses took his disappointments to the Lord and prayed for God's forgiveness of the people. Because of this, God would give the remaining Israelites—and Aaron—another chance. In your Bible, turn over to the last chapter in Exodus (Exodus 40). Now, look at verses 12-13. What job did God give Aaron? Do you think that was an important statement to Aaron about God's forgiveness? What about to Moses?

DANGER AHEAD

In this life, you will experience people you trust letting you down. Your first reaction could be one of explosive anger, "How could you!" Or perhaps you could choose the route of ignoring that person, giving him the "silent treatment" to show your personal disapproval of him. Still another reaction could be "stuffing it" and ignoring it even happened. Even though these are all common responses, they are deadly ones. Moses didn't choose to hold a grudge, but gave his disappointment over to God and even prayed for Aaron and the remaining Israelites. He knew God could take something bad and turn it around; only God could restore broken trust. Be careful how you react to those who break your trust.

GETTING YOUR BEARINGS:
THE BOOK OF LEVITICUS

Feasts, festivals, offerings, sacrifices, and laws—all of these are detailed in the Book of Leviticus. At first glance, Leviticus seems strange and quite boring to read. It's like reading a highly detailed instruction manual on a subject you aren't even familiar with! But that's just the first glance. By stepping back and taking a look at the *big* picture, we come away from this book with some pretty important lessons in life.

Leviticus was given to Moses by God on Mount Sinai. Now that the tabernacle was built, God needed to teach the Israelites how to worship. Having been slaves in Egypt, the only worship the Israelites knew was that of pagans worshiping false gods and idols. Bringing the Hebrews out of Egypt, God would now have to get Egypt out of the Hebrews. Many of the rules and regulations found in this book are to keep the Israelites "separate" and different from the nations surrounding them. They are a safeguard to keep the people from sinking back into the practices of the other godless nations.

As you explore Leviticus (we will explore it only very briefly), understand that each law or regulation in this book served a purpose. Many laws protected the Israelites' physical health—forbidding them to eat scavenger animals which often carried diseases. Other laws protected their spiritual health by keeping them from slipping into their old lifestyle and forcing them to depend upon God for their forgiveness. Although we won't explore all the rules and regulations of Leviticus, this book points loudly and clearly to one thing—God's holiness and our need to respect it.

POOF

TAKEN FROM LEVITICUS 8-10

GETTING READY

Begin your time in God's Word today by talking to Him (what we call prayer). Be honest with God, and express to Him your desires to know Him more. Ask God to give you a greater understanding of His power and holiness so you might learn to truly worship Him.

THE JOURNEY

Do you know people who treat God casually?

It was a day of great celebration and rejoicing! The tabernacle had been built and even dedicated according to God's specific instructions. Now, the high priest—Aaron, chosen by God Himself—would stand before God and represent the Israelites. His sons would serve as regular priests under his authority.

"This is what the Lord commands to be done," Moses proclaimed loudly to all. Aaron and his sons, Nadab, Abihu, Eleazar, and Ithamar, stood at Moses' side. Before them stood the entire assembly of Israel—all gathered at the entrance of the Tent of Meeting, waiting and watching with great expectation.

Aaron and his sons had already been washed with water, dressed in their priestly garments, and anointed with oil. Now they stood silently watching as Moses' hand moved with skill, preparing the animal to be sacrificed as God commanded. It was a solemn moment, for Aaron and his sons understood the symbolism of the bull taking their place and paying the penalty for their sin. They reached out and placed their hands upon the animal's head just as it was about to be slain—totally identifying with that bull as their personal substitute.

"Stay here at the entrance of the tabernacle for seven days and so do what the Lord requires," Moses instructed. For those seven days, Aaron and his sons did exactly as they had been told—careful to obey everything the Lord had commanded through Moses. On the eighth day, Aaron offered his first sacrifices as high priest on behalf of the people. When he finished, the Lord made His presence known through a fire that came down and consumed the remainder of the sacrifice being offered. Seeing this, the people shouted for joy and fell facedown in worship. Having only seen God's glory from a distance before, they now experienced being "close to God." As Aaron went about his priestly duties, he respected God's holiness and knew it wasn't to be treated casually. Unfortunately, that was something his two oldest sons lost sight of.

Even though all of the tribe of Levites were dedicated to serve as priests, only descendants of Aaron could hold the office of high priest.

Nadab and Abihu (Aaron's two oldest sons) had a very important job. Their job was to take a piece of coal from the altar of the Lord and place it in the bottom of their incense burners. Only fire from this altar was considered holy. Special incense was then to be sprinkled on top of the hot coal, causing a pleasing aroma to go up before the Lord's presence. The burning of incense was only to happen at specific times in the morning and the evening, all according to what God had commanded. Nadab and Abihu knew these things, yet with incense burners in hand, they completely disregarded God's clear instructions on how it was to be done. Casually entering the Holy Place, the brothers disobeyed God and offered Him a different kind of fire than He had commanded. *A fire is a fire*, they thought. To them, it might not have mattered where they got the piece of coal, or the exact timing of carrying out their duties—but to God it did. Coming before God was a privilege, not a right.

In a split second a hot fire came out from the presence of the Lord and consumed Nadab and Abihu. It was not the same fire that gave approval and acceptance to Aaron's sacrifices. Instead, it was an act of judgment and punishment. God put a quick end to such careless treatment of His holiness, and provided a lesson for anyone else who would follow in their steps. God Himself had said, "I will be treated as holy by those who come near Me. Before all people, I will be honored." Nadab and Abihu had carelessly forgotten that fact, and paid for it with their lives. What they did (and didn't do) stands as a lesson for all time: treating God's holiness casually only results in casualties.

exploring deeper

W here did Nadab and Abihu first see a glimpse of God's holiness? Turn in your Bible to Exodus 24 and look at verse 1 and then verse 9. This was no ordinary occurrence, but a special treat. Note that when they "saw God" it was not meeting God face-to-face, for no man can see God face-to-face and live. Instead, God chose to reveal a part of Himself to them in a way they could picture and always remember. For Nadab and Abihu, there was no excuse.

Skill Time

Right now, take a quick inventory of your life and ask yourself these questions:

How big is God in my eyes?

Have I reduced Him to something I can comfortably handle?

Do I feel He is there to serve me, or do I serve Him?

Do I treat God's holiness lightly?

Do I use His Name in an empty way?

Over and over in Scripture, we are reminded of the holiness of God. Much like Nadab and Abihu, we too are without excuse. Spend a few minutes and wrestle this through in your heart. God is the same holy God now as He was back then. He is still to be highly respected. Want proof? Just remember how Nadab and Abihu went "poof."

Lord, please forgive us for how casually we treat Your holiness. The miracle of a relationship with You is more than we can understand. Help us to know more clearly all that You are, that we might honor You better through our attitudes, our words, our actions, and our very lives. Amen.

HO-HUM

TAKEN FROM LEVITICUS 23

GETTING READY

Stop! Don't just skip over this part. When you pray, be sincere, and really commit this time to God. Ask Him to help you notice things you've skipped over before. Invite Him to show you how He is a God of purpose and nothing in His Word is there by mistake.

THE JOURNEY

Have you ever read something in the Bible that seemed boring, so you skipped over it?

When we read about the feasts God commanded the Israelites to celebrate, we are tempted to skim the page to something we feel has more meaning to us. If this is what you have been tempted to do, then read on—you're in for a great eye-opener!

"Tell the Israelites they are to worship Me and celebrate these seven feasts as a reminder of all I have done for them—and all I will do," the Lord commanded Moses. The feasts were not huge meals the Israelites would eat (like we think of Thanksgiving), rather, they were times of celebration, remembering, and drawing their hearts toward God. Each feast carried an important message and meaning—everything was done as God had commanded. Why? God would use these days not only as a reminder of what had happened, but also as a picture of what was to come.

When God set up the feasts, He divided them into two seasons. The first four came in the spring, and the remaining three came in the fall.

SPRINGTIME FEASTS
Passover
Feast of Unleavened Bread
Feast of Firstfruits
Feast of Weeks (Pentecost)

FALL FEASTS
Feast of Trumpets (*Rosh Hashanah*)
Day of Atonement (*Yom Kippur*)
Feast of Booths (or shelters)

Do the feasts still sound ho-hum? Remember: God is a God of purpose! Not only did the feasts help Israel to remember all that God had done in the past, they laid a groundwork for something He planned to do in the future. What God commanded the Israelites to begin celebrating, He Himself would one day bring to completion.

To fully understand this, let's jump to New Testament times, around 1,400 years after Moses died. The time is the Passover season in the spring—Jesus' last days on earth. The place is Jerusalem. During this particular time, the Passover fell on a Friday, the Festival of Unleavened Bread began on the next day (Saturday), and the Feast of Firstfruits the day after that (Sunday).

Jesus' very life and ministry happened to fulfill the springtime feasts. The fall feasts will be completely fulfilled when He returns, according to Scripture.

On Friday, the day of Passover, one lamb was offered up for the whole nation. In the middle of the afternoon, the priest would climb to the highest part of the temple, and at the precise moment of 3:00 P.M., he would blow on a trumpet made from a ram's horn. At the sound of this blast, everyone in the city would briefly stop what they were doing and look toward the temple, knowing at that exact moment one lamb was being offered up for the whole nation. It was at this same moment that Jesus, the "Lamb of God," said "It is finished" and offered up His life on the cross to redeem all mankind.

Sundown on Passover day started the Feast of Unleavened Bread. During this feast, the people recognized their dependence upon God to bless their wheat-growing season (which began at this time). They would seek God, asking Him to give them bread (or life) out of the ground. On this day, Jesus was buried. Only one week earlier, Jesus had said, "Unless a grain of wheat falls into the ground and dies, it cannot give life."

The Feast of Firstfruits came the next day and celebrated the barley harvest. During this feast, the people picked the first few barley grains beginning to ripen in their fields and brought them as an offering to God. They were saying to God, "Just as You have given us these firstfruits of the harvest, we trust You to bring about the rest of the harvest." It was during this very feast that God chose to raise Jesus from the dead. In 1 Corin-inthians, Jesus' resurrection is called the "firstfruits" of what is to follow. It is God's proof and promise of eternal life for all who accept His provision—a provision pictured through the feasts and fulfilled in Christ.

exploring deeper

In your Bible, turn to Leviticus 23:4 and see what it says. What do the first six or eight words of that verse emphasize? Who came up with the idea of the feasts? Did it matter if they followed a special schedule, or appointed time? When God does something, He does it with purpose; His ways are so much higher than ours!

CROSS ROADS

The next time you read something in Scripture that appears to be boring or of no purpose, will you simply skip it and say "ho-hum," or will you explore it and say "hmmmm"?

GETTING YOUR BEARINGS:
THE BOOK OF NUMBERS

Before you explore Numbers, it's important for you to know where this book got its name. At the very beginning of the book, a census is taken where all Israelite men of military age (twenty years old and older) were counted, or "numbered." Forty years later, at the close of this book and just before finally entering the Promised Land, another census is taken. To us, taking a census may seem unimportant, but to the Israelites it was of great significance. As you read through the Book of Numbers, you will find out why.

Reading through this book is like exploring the lowest level of a dark cavern. In this book we see the nation of Israel at its worst. Of the many thousands of Israelites who left Egypt in Exodus, Caleb and Joshua end up as the only two adults permitted to enter the Promised Land. Even Moses was denied! What happened to everyone? That is what the Book of Numbers is all about, and something we will explore together.

As we go through the dark tunnels of Numbers, don't lose your way—and don't try to shortcut! There are important lessons in here we all need to learn, and definitely something each of us can identify with! So grab your gear, and let's go. The Book of Numbers isn't as boring as you might think! Just watch your step. . . .

IF ONLY...

TAKEN FROM NUMBERS 11

GETTING READY

Pause for a moment to look around you and think about things you can be thankful for. If you're having a hard time, ask God to show you what you should be thankful for. If you're still having a hard time, ask God to give you the desire to even want to be thankful.

THE JOURNEY

When you're not happy with your circumstances (or feel you've gotten the raw end of a deal), do you complain?

The initial excitement had now died down. Mount Sinai was far behind, and it seemed like the distance to their destination—the land of Canaan—lay forever ahead. When would they reach this new land? No one seemed to know! Each day the Israelites traveled brought them one day closer, but they never knew how long their journey would be. Only God knew, and He was divinely guiding them with His presence.

As long as God's presence (in the form of a cloudlike pillar by day, and a column of fire by night) rested above the tabernacle, the Israelites would stay where they were. When it lifted, they'd pack everything up and set out. It didn't matter if they had camped there for a whole month, or just one day. When the cloud moved, they knew it was time to follow. At the Lord's command they encamped, and at the Lord's command they set out. There was no advance notice, no warning, no planning, and no

Quail were residents of Egypt and the Holy Land, but also migrated north in the springtime (March). They would often pass over narrow portions of the sea and become exhausted. God used a strong wind to blow them over to the Israelites' camp.

pattern! All they knew was that God was with them, guiding and comforting them with His presence and providing for their every need. To some, this personal attention from God didn't seem good enough. . . .

"Manna! Nothing but manna to eat! I'm getting tired of this stuff all the time!" some began to mutter under their breath. Others nearby heard the complaints. "You're right," they chimed in, "the food was much better in Egypt." "If only we had stayed there," some others murmured as they looked out across the barren land. "I remember how we ate fish in Egypt for free! We even had cucumbers, melons, leeks, onions, and garlic! If only we hadn't left Egypt," they sighed. The Israelites ignored all that God

had done for them, and forgot the slavery they suffered while in Egypt. One man voiced what they were all thinking, "I would do *anything* for a taste of meat right now—anything to stop eating this *manna!*"

And so the complaining continued. It didn't take long for the craving of their mouths to become the desire of their hearts. It took even less time for a rebellious, ungrateful, complaining, and bitter attitude to develop among them. This thankless spirit soon reached Moses.

"What am I to do with these people—Your people—Lord?" he asked in frustration. "They're becoming too much for me to deal with! They say they would be happy if only they had meat to eat! Where am I supposed to get meat in this barren land?! There wouldn't be enough even if all the fish in the sea were caught for them!" he added impatiently.

God heard Moses' complaints and answered him. "Their desire for what they left behind in Egypt is their rejection of Me and what I have provided for them," He said. "I've heard their thankless and bitter complaints, and as a result, I will give them what they crave. Only it will not be meat for one meal, or even one day. Instead, I will give them meat to eat for a whole month—until it comes out of their nostrils and they detest it! This is because they have rejected My provision for them, saying, 'If only we hadn't left Egypt!'"

At that point, God caused a strong wind to blow some migrating quail off course so that they flew only three feet from the ground and were easily caught. All that day and night and even into the next day the Israelites gathered quail. "So long, manna; hello, *meat!*" the Israelites said as they eagerly collected, cooked, and prepared the quail. "Now this is more like it!" they agreed among themselves.

However, in the middle of their meal, God brought judgment upon them. Those who turned their backs on God and traded His provision for something they craved, received the consequences of their choice. What they thought would bring life and fulfillment only brought death.

Before moving onward, the Israelites named that place *Kibroth Hattaavah* (which means "graves of craving") and buried all those who had died from eating the quail. Unfortunately, they didn't bury their root of complaining. That was one of their first mistakes. . . .

exploring deeper

In your Bible, turn to Numbers 11. Now, look at verses 4-6. In each verse, there are "key" words we tend to use even today when we complain. Can you pick them out? *(Hint: the key complaining words in verse 4 are the same as the title of today's devotion. Verse 5 has something to do with comparing to the past, and the key complaining word in verse 6 is the opposite of "always.")* Are you guilty of frequently using any of these words in your vocabulary?

Skill Time

God doesn't expect you never to complain, but He does expect you to bring your complaints to Him. Moses complained directly to God, whereas the Israelites just complained. God wants you to tell Him what you are experiencing. Don't be afraid to admit to God your deepest feelings, failings, angers, and hurts. (He already knows them anyway and is only waiting for you to bring them to Him.) Next, thank Him for who He is—He is much bigger, stronger, and more powerful than you think. Ask Him to help you with your attitudes, circumstances, and problems. Tell, Admit, Thank, and Ask (TA-TA). Stop right now and do it. Whenever you catch yourself slipping into a "complaining" mode, you have the power to say "so long!" (ta-ta) to it—if only you will take it to God.

NO WAY!

TAKEN FROM NUMBERS 13-14

GETTING READY

Before journeying onward with today's devotion, give your day to the Lord. Ask Him to help you see things from His perspective.

THE JOURNEY

Do you ever feel discouraged or tempted to give up when others say you won't accomplish what you're trying to do?

"It's great! What a perfect opportunity!"

"No way! Are you crazy?!"

It had been forty days—more than a month of anxiously waiting—and now that word had finally come back, there were different opinions. Who should they believe? Only moments ago there had been excitement as the returning Israelite spies appeared over the horizon. Their assignment had been to enter "enemy territory" (also known as Canaan—the Promised Land) to see what the land, people, and towns were like, and to return with a sample of the fruit in the land.

Everyone marveled over the size of the grape cluster brought back as well as the pomegranates and figs. "What fertile soil!" some shouted. "What wonderful land! Truly it does flow with milk and honey as God said!" others agreed. "Imagine! This is the land to which we have been journeying!" others added with delight. However, the excitement and eagerness that filled the air slowly died out as one after another of the men gave their reports.

"We went into the land, and it *does* flow with milk and honey as you say! Here is the fruit to prove it!" one reported and then grew quiet, searching for the right words to say next. "But the people who live on this land are very powerful," another spy added. "Their cities are all like large fortresses!" One by one, ten of the twelve men spoke badly of the land. With each comment, the hearts of the Israelites became distracted, pulling away from their faith and trust in God. Caleb and Joshua stood by, watching in both amazement and disbelief.

"Flowing with milk and honey" is a term meaning the land was very rich and fertile—able to supply both rich pasture for cattle (which would then produce an abundance of milk) and hosting a large variety of flowers (a source of food for honey-making bees).

Having been one of the twelve sent out, Caleb's voice rose over the confusion. He and Joshua both knew the words the others spoke were true, because they had seen it with their own eyes. Yet, the recommendations given by the others were all wrong! They had their eyes on the wrong thing! "We should go up and take possession of the land; we can do it!" he urged.

"No way!" the others quickly shot back, trying to silence Caleb. "The land we explored devours those living in it. It's full of large people—descendants of Anak. We couldn't possibly defeat the Amalekites, the Hittites, the Jebusites, the Amorites, *and* the Canaanites! We'd all be killed!"

That night, all the people raised their voices and wept aloud. "Why is the Lord bringing us to the edge of this land, only to let us die by the sword?" They began grumbling against Moses and Aaron. It wasn't long before their fear led them to rebellion. "Our women and children will be taken captive! Wouldn't it be better for us to go back to Egypt? We should choose a leader and go back!" they shouted. Disregarding all that God had done for them and promised to do, the Israelites were ready to turn their backs on Him and walk away.

Sensing this, Caleb and Joshua urged again, "The land we explored is exceedingly good! If the Lord is pleased with us, He will lead us into that land and will give it to us. Only do not rebel against the Lord, and do not be afraid of the people of the land. Their protection is nothing, but the Lord is with us. Don't be afraid!"

But the Israelites didn't see that the obstacles ahead were opportunities for God to show His power through them. No one would listen. In fact, the whole assembly even talked about stoning Caleb and Joshua to put an end to the nonsense. It was at this point the glory of the Lord appeared at the tent of meeting in front of all the Israelites.

"How long will these people treat Me with contempt?" God said to Moses. "How long will they refuse to believe in Me, in spite of all the miraculous signs I have performed among them?" The Lord's anger burned against the Israelites. "As surely as I live," He declared, "not one of you will ever see the land I promised. Instead, I will do to you the very things I heard you say: your bodies will drop dead in the desert, but I will bring your children in to enjoy the land you have rejected. No one over twenty years old will live to enter the land—except for My servants Caleb and Joshua. They will enter the land because they follow Me wholeheartedly."

God continued to explain to the Israelites the terms of their punishment. For forty years—one year for each day the spies explored the land—the Israelites would suffer for their sin and not be permitted to enter the land until that generation died off. As for the men who spread the bad report about the land and made their fellow Israelites turn against God, they were struck down and died of a plague before the Lord.

exploring deeper

Believe it or not, this isn't the end of the story! Turn in your Bible to Numbers 14:39-45 and read it aloud. What were the Israelites trying to do here? Did God honor it? Why or why not? Now, back up and read verse 24 of this chapter and compare it. God desires faithfulness and obedience the first time around.

DANGER AHEAD

When you are faced with a difficulty, you will be tempted to "reason it out" by looking first to your own abilities and resources— often leaving God completely out of the picture (or at least on "standby" to refer to when "all else fails"). In so doing, you are actually turning your back on God's faithfulness to carry you through difficult situations. That's what the Israelites did—and they missed out. Don't play the game. Instead, say "no way!" when your circumstances or friends begin to influence you away from your faith and trust in God. Dare to be a Caleb.

STEP ASIDE, PLEASE

TAKEN FROM NUMBERS 16-18

GETTING READY

As you begin today, stop and pray. Ask God to help you change any bad attitudes you might have hiding in your heart.

THE JOURNEY

Do you ever feel it's not fair when others are chosen for a job you believe you could do better?

"You've gone too far!" Korah told Moses and Aaron with arrogance in his voice. Being a Levite, Korah didn't like the fact that he had to help take care of the tabernacle, yet never had any special privileges in it. He didn't think it was fair that Aaron (the high priest) got special treatment. "Why do you set yourselves above everyone else?! We are all holy—every one of us—for God is with us!" Korah challenged.

Why does Aaron get to be high priest anyway?! Korah secretly thought. *I could do just as well—if not even better than him! The only reason Aaron gets to be high priest is because he's Moses' brother, not because he's the most qualified,* he scoffed. Korah glanced at Dathan, Abiram, and On standing by his side. They were from the tribe of Reuben but had readily joined him in revolt. Behind them stood 250 men—well-respected leaders—and all brought together in rebellion under Korah's influence. Korah had his army, and this was a winnable battle—or so he thought. With a smug attitude, he awaited Moses' reply.

Censer literally means "firepan" and was a bronze container used to burn incense (which represented prayers being offered up to God). Incense was made from a pale yellow resin called frankincense, shells from the fragrant mollusk, and two types of gums taken from plants—one resembling the fragrant juice from the myrrh tree.

Taking a deep breath and looking at the situation before him, Moses sighed. He knew he and Aaron had their positions because God had chosen them for the task. It didn't mean they were better; they were just being obedient. As a result, Korah's rebellion against Moses and Aaron was really rebellion against God. With a steady voice, Moses met Korah's gaze and answered the large group. "You Levites have gone too far! Isn't it enough that the Lord brought you near to Himself to work in the tabernacle? You stand before all of Israel and minister to them! But now you are trying to get the priesthood as well! In the morning, the Lord will show who belongs to Him and who is holy. Along with Aaron you, Korah, and all your followers are to take your offerings of incense and present them before the Lord. The man the Lord chooses will be the one who is holy."

The next morning, Korah and his men gathered in front of the tent of meeting. When the glory of the Lord appeared to the entire group, so did judgment. What Korah, Dathan, and Abiram thought would be their moment of triumph was actually a moment of doom.

God instructed Moses to tell the people to back away from the tents of these men and to touch nothing of theirs. Then He caused a great earthquake to split open the ground, completely swallowing up the three men and their families. A great fire then came from the Lord and consumed the 250 men who were offering the incense. Only the censers were left in the smoldering remains.

"Take the censers," God instructed, "and tell Eleazar, son of Aaron the priest, to hammer them into flat sheets to overlay the altar. Let it remind the Israelites that no one except a descendant of Aaron should come to burn incense before the Lord, or they will become like Korah and his followers."

The next day, the whole Israelite community grumbled. "You've killed the Lord's people!" they accused Moses and Aaron. Already, their hearts were slipping into an attitude of rebellion and revolt. Seeing this constant rebellion, God began to strike the Israelites with a plague, but Aaron grabbed his censer and stood between the Lord and the people, praying for God's mercy. The plague ended, but not before 14,777 of the Israelites had lost their lives.

This problem of rebellion was getting out of hand. God determined to show the people that Aaron was the one He had chosen as high priest. "Speak to the Israelites and get twelve staffs from them, one from the leader of each of their tribes," God said to Moses, "Aaron is also to have a staff to represent the tribe of Levi. Write the name of each man on his staff, and place them in the tent of meeting in front of the ark of the covenant. The staff belonging to the man I choose will sprout, and I will rid Myself of this constant grumbling against you by the Israelites." God would settle this matter of who was in charge once and for all.

Moses entered the tent of meeting the next day, and went into the Holy of Holies. Before him were all the staffs—just as they had been left the day before. None had sprouted except one. It was Aaron's. Not only did Aaron's staff sprout, it had budded, bloomed, blossomed, and produced almonds! God was leaving nothing for the Israelites to question concerning His choice. Aaron was the high priest. Gathering up the staffs, Moses brought them out for all the Israelites to see. Each man took his own staff, but all eyes were on Aaron's staff. Not a word was spoken—no words of explanation were necessary. God had chosen, and they knew God was the One who chooses best.

exploring deeper

Turn in your Bible to chapter 18 of Numbers and read the first verse. What is God telling Aaron about his job? With privilege comes responsibility and accountability. Now, skip down and read verses 5-7. Pay attention any time you see the word "gift" or a similar word (hint: it's in verses 6 and 7). What did God want Aaron and the others to understand?

Skill Time

Doing what God calls you to do is very important; so is letting others do what God has called them to do. It's not a matter of "either serve, follow, or lead"; it's a matter of choosing to "serve, follow, *and* lead!" Serve others; follow God's guidance; lead the kind of life that points others to Him. That is the responsibility God has given you—regardless of the job you are (or are not) doing. Sometimes it's just a matter of saying, "step aside, please" to your pride and trying to see things from God's perspective. Fill in the words below, and pray this prayer from your heart:

Thank You, Lord, that I can do (name a task) very well, and perhaps even better than (name of a person). I know, however, You haven't given me that job right now. As an act of my will, I give this up to You. You gave me the abilities, and You have a perfect plan for how they can best be used. Please keep me from being jealous of others or puffed up with pride. I want to use what I think I'm good at to serve You, not myself.

Is This For Real?

TAKEN FROM NUMBERS 21-25

Getting Ready

Before reading on, quiet your heart before God. Simply take a moment (or several moments) to pray and ask God to still your thoughts and help you block out any distractions. Ask Him to help you understand what He wants you to learn today. (Don't read on until you've done this.)

THE JOURNEY

Have you ever been around someone who seems to be one way, but in the end, turns out to be completely different than you thought?

Balaam listened to the messengers who stood before him. They brought word of how King Sihon and all the Amorites attacked a nation called Israel and were soundly defeated. Now, the Israelites were nearing the land of the Moabites, and King Balak knew the Israelites were too powerful to defeat. That is why he sent his messengers to seek Balaam's services.

"These people seem to cover the face of the land and have settled along the plains next to me. Now come and put a curse on them because they are too powerful. Perhaps then I will be able to defeat them and drive them out of the country. For I know that those you bless are blessed and those you curse are cursed," the king had said.

Balaam studied the messengers who held out money to pay for his services. Of all the magicians in the land, he was the best. Because his reputation as a sorcerer was well known, he was not surprised that King Balak would send princes to pay him to work his magic and win the favor of the gods. Balaam knew that a people's own gods held the most power over them—be it for good or bad—so he sought to make contact with the God of Israel. To him, the God of Israel was no different from any of the gods of the land. Little did he know . . .

Balaam has been compared to Judas in the New Testament. Both men came close enough to truth to seem sincere. Both seemed to serve God—for a time. However, motivated by their own ambitions and greed, they turned against God.

"Spend the night here," Balaam told the messengers, "and I will give you the answer the Lord gives me." That night, God spoke to Balaam and told him not to go with the men. "You must not put a curse on these people because they are blessed," the Lord said. As a result, Balaam refused to go and sent the princes away. Not one to be turned down, King Balak sent other princes even more numerous and distinguished than the first. He also offered to richly reward Balaam and do whatever Balaam said. Such an offer sounded good to Balaam, so he would once again seek the God of the Israelites. "Even if Balak gave me his whole palace filled with silver or gold, I could do nothing to go beyond the command of the Lord," he cautioned the messengers, then advised them to stay the night.

That night, God came to Balaam and said, "You may go with these men, but do only what I tell you." Balaam became excited. Perhaps the Israelites' God was giving in! He would go with these men with the intent of doing as the king asked and getting his reward. The next morning Balaam saddled up his donkey and went with the princes of Moab. On the way, however, his donkey began acting strangely. At first she went off the road into a field—then up against a wall, crushing Balaam's foot. When the donkey finally sat down and refused to move ahead, Balaam beat her angrily with his staff.

The Lord opened the donkey's mouth, and she said, "What have I done to make you beat me?"

"You've made a fool of me!" Balaam responded. "If I had a sword, I'd kill you!" Then the Lord opened Balaam's eyes to the angel standing with sword in hand, blocking the donkey's way. "If it hadn't been for your donkey turning away from me these three times," the angel said, "I would certainly have killed you by now, but I would have spared her." Realizing the Lord had sent the angel to oppose him, Balaam admitted his wrongful motives. "I have sinned. If you are displeased, I will go back and not continue," he answered. Stepping aside, the angel told him to continue, and warned Balaam to speak only what God told him.

King Balak's name means "destroyer; emptier" and describes the very thing he tried to do to the nation of Israel through the help of Balaam.

The next morning, King Balak took Balaam to a high point where he could see part of the Israelites' army. In a solemn ceremony, Balaam told the king to sacrifice up seven bulls and seven rams, then wait beside his offering. "Perhaps the Lord will come to meet with me. Whatever He reveals to me, I will tell you," Balaam said over his shoulder as he went aside to a secluded place. God did meet with Balaam and put a message in his mouth—but it wasn't one king Balak wanted to hear. Instead of cursing the nation of Israel, Balaam gave a blessing! Unhappy with the results, the king whisked Balaam to another spot hoping he would be more inspired to curse the Israelites. Again, Balaam only blessed the Israelites. When this happened a third time, King Balak was angered.

"I brought you here to curse the Israelites, but you wouldn't! Now, leave and go home! I said I'd reward you richly, but the Lord has kept you from being rewarded," the king snapped. Turning to go, Balaam said, "Let me warn you what the Israelites will do to your people in the days to come. . . ."

exploring deeper

It seems on the outside that Balaam had a change of heart and decided to follow the Lord. In your Bible, turn to Numbers 22:18 and read it. What does he say when he mentions the Lord's name? Coming from the lips of a sorcerer, does this seem odd to you?

DANGER AHEAD

The story of Balaam doesn't end in chapter 25 (although that seems to be the last we hear from him). In Numbers 31:16 we learn that Balaam, after failing to manipulate God, later offered advice to the enemy on how the Israelites could be lured into sin. Having come so close to the truth, and having even "talked the talk," Balaam quickly returned to his old treacherous ways. He wasn't for real.

You will come across some "Balaams" who seem genuine on the outside but really aren't. Their motives aren't to serve God, but to use God to serve themselves. Watch out for them. Just because someone looks like a believer or talks like one doesn't mean he truly is a believer.

It's Close Enough

TAKEN FROM NUMBERS 32

Getting Ready

Stop and pray. Use this time to allow God to examine your heart. Ask Him to give you courage not to settle for anything less than His perfect plan for your life.

The Journey

Do you know people who like to "play it safe"?

First the Amorites had been defeated, then the Midianites. What victories God was giving the nation of Israel as it continued on its journey toward the Promised Land! In preparation for entering the land, a census had been taken to number the people, and a new leader was chosen. Joshua would be the captain, and Moses would be laid to rest, just as God had told Moses. Moses knew his days would soon be coming to a close. Having brought the Israelites up to the land, he would not be able to bring them through it. Moses knew there was a lot to accomplish between now and then.

"Moses!" a group of men called, pulling Moses' thoughts to the present. Moses looked over and saw men from the tribes of Reuben and Gad approaching. These two tribes ranked ninth and tenth in size, but were blessed with large herds and flocks. "The land we conquered from the Moabites and the Midianites is perfect for our flocks," they said. "If you please, we would like to have this land as our portion. Don't make us cross the Jordan River into the Promised Land," they pleaded. Moses, as well as Eleazar and the leaders of the community, fell silent at the shock of the request. It was Moses who finally spoke up.

The census wasn't just "counting heads"; it was much-needed information! It not only measured Israel's military strength, but also helped determine how the Promised Land would be divided— since land was given according to the size of the tribe. Lastly, the census provided accurate genealogical records.

"Shall your countrymen go to war, conquering the new land while you sit here?" he challenged. *Did we come this far only to have you refuse to enter the land the Lord has promised to give us?* Moses thought. *Isn't this the same type of rebellion that happened forty years ago?* Moses cleared his throat and spoke his mind. "Why are you discouraging the Israelites from going over into the land the Lord has given them? This is the same thing your fathers did when I sent them from Kadesh Barnea to look over the land! After viewing the land, they discouraged other Israelites from entering it. As a result, God's anger burned, and no man twenty years old or more who came up out of Egypt would be allowed to enter the Promised Land. No one, that is, except Caleb and Joshua—for they were the only ones who trusted God. Because of this great sin, the Lord caused us to wander in the desert forty years— until the whole generation of those who had done evil in the Lord's sight was no more."

Moses paused, allowing his words to have their full effect. "Now, here you stand before me, Eleazar the priest, and all the community leaders—standing in the place of your fathers—making the Lord even more angry with Israel. If you turn away from following the Lord,"

Moses cautioned, "He will again leave all these people in the desert to die, and you will be the cause of their destruction!" With those words, silence fell upon the group. They could see the Jordan River and the land on the other side, full of unknowns and uncertainties. They also knew the land on this side of the Jordan was perfect for their needs. Their hearts were torn as they wrestled with the issues before them. In no way did they want to rebel against God or cause harm to fall upon their fellow Israelites.

"We would like to build pens here for our livestock and cities for our women and children, but we are ready to arm ourselves and go across the Jordan with you until all the other tribes have taken possession of their land. We won't return here until that is done, but while we're gone, our women and children can live in fortified cities and be protected from any enemies in the land. For the land here on the east side of the Jordan is the land of our inheritance," the Reubenites and Gadites responded.

Moses looked at them thoughtfully. He knew God's perfect will was to bring the entire nation of Israel into the land of Canaan. This was God's purpose and plan. It was also a promise given to their ancestors, Abraham, Isaac, and Jacob. He looked solemnly into each of the faces before him and gave them permission with a condition. "If you will do this—if you will arm yourselves before the Lord for battle and go across the Jordan, staying with your fellow Israelites until they have driven out all the enemies of the land and claimed their portion—then you may return here and keep this land as your possession. Your obligations toward your fellow Israelites will be completed. If you do not live up to your end of the bargain however, you will be sinning against the Lord," Moses warned. "And you may be sure your sin will find you out." The Reubenites and Gadites responded to Moses' challenge. "We will do just as the Lord says. We will cross over into Canaan armed, but the property we inherit will be on this side of the Jordan."

exploring deeper

In your Bible, turn to Numbers 32:16-17. It may seem like a generous offer the Reubenites and Gadites are making, but look again more closely. In verse 16, what do they plan to do? Now, compare that to verse 17. Does it seem they want to help the cause, but not totally identify with it?

Skill Time

Trust is a hard thing, for it often demands we step out of our "comfort zones" and away from the "playing it safe" mode. God has a perfect plan, and we need to trust Him that it is just that—perfect. Unfortunately, we are often too willing to settle for second best. We get as close to following God's will as we can, while still trying to keep our foot on the other side of the Jordan—just to be sure. This only sets us up for future struggles—something the Reubenites and Gadites later discovered. What keeps you from following the Lord wholeheartedly? What compromises do you come up with to make yourself feel better about what you're doing? Take a moment to think about it. On a slip of paper, write down what God brings to your mind. Then, across the top of the paper, write: "This is the Jordan I must cross." Give it to God in prayer, and ask Him to help you look up (to Him for strength) and move out. Don't settle for "close enough," for it will eventually pull your heart far from Him.

GETTING YOUR BEARINGS:
THE BOOK OF DEUTERONOMY

Deuteronomy is the last of the first five books of the Old Testament. It acts like a bridge between the Pentateuch (*penta* meaning five) books of Law and the History books (starting with the Book of Joshua).

Deuteronomy is made up of three speeches Moses gives to the Israelites as they are poised to enter the Promised Land. In these three speeches, Moses does three things:

1. He gives a history of God's past dealings with them.

2. He restates the rules for maintaining that relationship.

3. He gives the list of curses and blessings that depend on whether the Israelites break or keep their covenant with God.

What Moses does in the Book of Deuteronomy is very similar to how a covenant is laid out. For our purposes, we'll only look at a couple of the issues Moses addresses.

NOTE: If for some reason you've skipped around in this devotional, now would be a good time to go back and read what you missed in Genesis, Exodus, Leviticus, and Numbers. Reading these passages will give you a better understanding of what the Old Testament is all about. There's important information you'll need to gain and carry with you as part of your gear during the rest of your time exploring in the Old Testament. (Trust me. It's really worth your time to take a brief detour and then come back—there's great stuff back there!)

If you're going back, enjoy the journey, and we'll see you shortly. If you're heading on, then let's go. . . .

WHO?

TAKEN FROM DEUTERONOMY 7-11

GETTING READY

Stop and pray. Allow God to open your eyes to areas in your life that draw your heart away from Him or cause you to lose your focus.

THE JOURNEY

Do you find it easy to forget about God—especially when things are going well in your life?

The Israelites looked up and followed Moses' gaze out to the horizon. How easy it was to think they were better than others; to think they deserved what God was going to give them; to think they had somehow earned it.

"After the Lord drives out your enemies and you take possession of the land, don't say, 'Look what I've done for myself!' Don't let the success you experience turn your head from God," Moses warned. He knew all too well the Israelites' tendency to forget the Lord their God. "Walk closely with God, that it might go well with you," he advised.

Moses paused, thinking of the right words to express what was on his heart. He knew his life would soon end, for God told him he would not enter the Promised Land—the land just on the other side of the Jordan River. Moses looked at the sea of faces before him. They had suffered wandering in the desert forty years because of their parents' disbelief and disobedience to the Lord. Now that God had raised up this new generation of Israelites, would they follow in the footsteps of their forefathers? Would they, too, disobey and forget God and His promises? Would they turn their backs on God, or would they worship and honor Him?

An idol is anything you cherish in your heart more than God. It is something that knocks Him from His place of honor and importance in your life.

Moses watched as everyone nodded agreement to the fact that God had worked wonderful miracles and signs on their behalf. They all cheered as they remembered how God divided the waters so they could pass safely through, then closed them upon Pharaoh and his army. The people smiled at how God fed them with manna and provided water for them in the desert. There was no denying the fact that God had just helped them defeat the Amorites and the Midianites—giving them the land they were now standing upon. "Moses, don't worry! We'll have faith in the Lord. Haven't we done so in the past?" the Israelites responded confidently.

Moses continued, reminding the Israelites about the dangers ahead and their tendency to turn from the Lord their God. He could see their smiles of triumph fade as they remembered some of their past actions and the painful consequences. One by one, Moses brought them to mind so they might never forget them. One by one, the words hit home, like carefully placed nails hammered into wood: "making a golden calf and worshiping it" . . . "complaining and murmuring" . . . "lacking faith and trust in God" . . . "rebelling against God's command for you to take possession of the land He was giving you." Several in the crowd shuffled their feet uncomfortably. Others simply glanced down at the ground, embarrassed at the truth of Moses' words. As a nation, they hadn't been

Moses spells out the key to the Israelites' success in Deuteronomy 11:22-23. By observing God's commands and loving Him, by walking in His ways and holding fast to Him, the Israelites would experience success. Success would come from the hand of God, not from their own efforts.

the most obedient group of people. Success in the new land would come only because God was faithful to carry out what He had said He would do for them. It would not come because of their own great accomplishments.

"And now, O Israel," Moses challenged, "what does the Lord God ask of you but to fear Him?" Moses knew the Israelites must never lose sight of God's awesome and mighty power. "Walk in all His ways and enjoy a relationship with Him. Love Him; serve Him with all your heart and soul, and obey His commands. No matter how well it goes in the land, never forget the Lord your God."

Moses knew his days with the Israelites were drawing to a close. The mantle of leadership would soon be handed over to Joshua, who had proven himself faithful and wholehearted. *These people will be in good hands, Lord,* Moses thought to himself, *as long as they never forget about You.*

exploring deeper

Open your Bible to Deuteronomy 11:16 and read it. What does it say? It is interesting to note that the gods worshiped in the land of Canaan all dealt with success. (For example, there was a god of rain so that the crops might be successful and produce plenty.) Take a look at verse 17, the very next verse. Knowing what you know about the false gods in the land, what is the significance of what God says He will do? Finally, continue reading down from verse 18 through verse 21. (Go ahead! Reading in God's Word for yourself is vital for your own personal growth.) Do you see the reason behind this "plan of action"? How do you think it will help the Israelites not forget God as easily?

DANGER AHEAD

Moses warned the Israelites to be careful or they would be enticed to turn away and worship the false gods of the land. To be "enticed" means to be lured into something—much like a fish that is drawn to a hook with bait dangling on it. By getting too close or even "sampling" a taste of the bait, the fish finds itself hooked. So it is with us. Our culture tries to entice us away from God using bait such as success in life, approval from others, wealth, recognition, materialism, pride, and even busyness with activities that keep us constantly moving so we don't have time for God. These are the "gods" of our land—beware of them and don't be fooled whenever they come dangling into your life.

WHAT ARE MY OPTIONS?

TAKEN FROM DEUTERONOMY 30

GETTING READY

Take a moment to quiet your thoughts before the Lord. Tell God what is on your heart, and then give Him a chance to tell you what is on His. Ask Him to give you the courage and strength to choose wisely in your life.

THE JOURNEY

Ah, that's no big deal—don't worry; it'll all work out.

Loosen up and give yourself a break!

No one said anything to me, and I didn't follow those rules.

You can always worry about that later.

Go for it! You only live once!

Do you sometimes struggle with listening to the world's advice?

"Choose this day which path you will take," Moses advised.

The words of Moses rang true and clear in the ears of all who were present. They were solid, firm, and sure. There would be no misunderstanding of the last words and important advice Moses desired to leave with the Israelites. Moses knew each and every face before him represented a choice. Together, those choices would have an effect on the well-being of the nation as they ventured into the new land. Obedience to God wouldn't be a mere option; it would be a matter of life or death. Moses knew the Israelites needed to understand this important matter.

"What I'm commanding you today is not too difficult or beyond your reach," Moses declared. "It's something you've already known about since your time in the wilderness," he reminded them. "Therefore, don't look for someone to tell you the right thing to do, because God has already told you." Moses looked into as many faces as he possibly could. He met their gazes, encouraging and challenging them with words both spoken and unspoken. Only moments ago he had explained the curses that would fall upon the nation if they turned their backs on God.

"Carefully follow the terms of this covenant so you will do well," Moses challenged. "Today, all of you are standing in the presence of the Lord your God. You are here to enter into a covenant the Lord is making with you this day and sealing with an oath," Moses added. The Israelites nodded in agreement. They knew God had called them to be a nation set apart as an example, that through their influence the world might know that the Lord is God.

> The purpose of the Law was to point the Israelites to God's holiness. Romans 3:20 states: "No one will be declared righteous in [God's] sight by observing the Law; rather, through the Law we become conscious of sin."

Moses continued, "The covenant is this: the Lord will give you success only if you obey Him and keep His commands and decrees written in this Book of the Law, and only if you turn to Him with all your heart and soul. However, if you choose not to do so, you will experience the same death and destruction your enemies face."

Having heard their options, the Israelites needed no further explanations.

Moses became quiet for a moment. These words would be God's marching orders and his closing advice to the Israelites. "This day I call heaven and earth as witnesses against you that I have set before you life and death, blessings and curses," he challenged. "Choose life so that you and your children may live and that you may love the Lord your God, listen to His voice, and hold fast to Him. The Lord is your life."

The Israelites considered the seriousness of Moses' advice. Clearly a line had been drawn in the sand. To choose obedience would be to choose God's blessings. To choose disobedience would mean destruction. Either way, the choice was theirs. Moses had given his advice, and now God would give the Israelites what they chose.

exploring deeper

In your Bible, turn to Deuteronomy 30:15-18 and read it. Specifically look for the words "if," "but," and "then," and carefully read what follows them. Does this seem harsh to you?

THINKING on your FEET

Today, it's hard for us to believe what we do or don't do has a life-or-death consequence. That's because we have lost sight of the holiness of God. From the Old Testament times to now, God has not changed. He is still a holy God, and the line is still drawn in the sand. The only difference is the conditions. Instead of living and dying by theLaw, we have a different option. God has provided a sacrifice for ourguilt of not living up to His laws. To accept God's provision is tochoose life. To reject it. . . . The choice is yours. On which side of the line will you take your stand?

GETTING YOUR BEARINGS:
THE BOOK OF JOSHUA

The Book of Joshua is the first of the "Historical books" in the Old Testament. This doesn't mean everything up to now wasn't historical or didn't really happen. It simply means that the focus will shift to the Israelites as a new nation in a new land—their exciting victories . . . and their deadly mistakes.

Joshua is an exciting book, but not without its difficulties. Reading through this book often raises the question of why God would have the Israelites wipe out entire cities—killing even innocent women, children, and animals—when He Himself said, "Thou shalt not kill," in the Ten Commandments. Because of this question, we are tempted to overlook what doesn't feel comfortable to us and never come to understand the purpose behind it all. If you've personally struggled with this, brace yourself and read on! This is an area we're going to explore together! (You *were* warned this book could be *dangerous!*)

Before we explore Joshua, you need to know that the Law has been given and everything is in place. Moses and Aaron are no longer alive, and Joshua is now in charge. Aaron's son, Eleazar, is high priest. You also need to know something about God's character. Even though God brings judgment upon people and nations, He also gives ample opportunity for people to turn from their wickedness. Those living in Canaan (with the exception of Rahab) chose to continue to live in wickedness and to suffer God's judgment through the hands of the Israelites. So, what about the commandment not to kill? Didn't God cause the Israelites to break one of His rules? When God gave the Law, He didn't say, "Thou shalt not kill," as we commonly quote. God said, "Thou shalt not murder." There is a difference. Murdering is killing for your own selfish reasons.

By journeying through Joshua, you'll have other opportunities to learn about God's character. See how He answers the cry for help and changes someone's life around. Explore how He shows His power and love at the cost of commitment and makes His wisdom available—even when it is ignored.

As you can see, Joshua is far from historical ho-hum! It's a book packed with life lessons just waiting to be discovered. Enjoy your time exploring.

HELP

TAKEN FROM JOSHUA 1-2

Getting Ready

As you begin exploring the Book of Joshua, ask God to search your heart and help you change how you view others. Thank Him that He never gives up on you—or anyone else who truly wants to know Him.

THE Journey

Have you ever looked at certain people and assumed they would never be interested in God?

The large walls of the city of Jericho loomed ahead, daring anyone to be foolish enough to attack. Cautiously, the two Israelite spies entered the city and looked for a place they could gain information with no questions asked. Their eyes went to a house on the city wall. It looked like it belonged to a woman who had little honor. "No one will ever think of asking for us there!" they thought, "not with the whole town used to seeing strange men coming and going from that place!" The spies knew the importance of the mission Joshua sent them on, and the need for information drove them onward. They would go to Rahab's house. . . .

Having been informed that Israelites were in Jericho to discover the best way to attack, the King sent orders to Rahab to bring out the men who had reportedly come to her house.

"Yes, there were men here—but I didn't know where they came from," Rahab lied. "They left at dusk, and I don't know which way they went. If you hurry, though, you might be able to catch them!" The door closed and Rahab let out a sigh of relief. It was good the soldiers hadn't searched her home, for she had hidden the two men on the rooftop amid the bundles of flax that were drying. Assuming a woman like herself would not have any interest in the God of Israel, the soldiers quickly left in hot pursuit of two men they would never find.

Flax is a plant which is turned into linen from which clothes can be made. Bundles were often hung on rooftops to dry. The three to four foot lengths provided an ideal hiding place for the spies.

Climbing to the roof, Rahab yearned to talk with the two men she had risked her life to save. She knew they were Israelites who served the One True God. "I know that the Lord has given our land to you. We have heard how the Lord parted the Red Sea so you might pass, and how He has given you victory over your enemies. Because of what God has done for you, all who live in this country are melting in fear," Rahab confided. Then, in a moment of quiet reflection, Rahab stated what she knew in her own heart to be true. "The Lord your God is God in heaven above and on the earth below." The two spies looked at each other, shocked at what they heard.

"Now then," Rahab continued, "please swear that you will show kindness to my family and spare our lives since I have shown kindness to you."

"Because you risked your life for a God you barely know, we will see that your life is spared—and those of your whole family—so you might come to know Him better," the spies proclaimed.

"Please give me a sure sign that what you say will come to pass," Rahab asked of them.

"Our life for your life," the men assured her.

With that, Rahab let the men down by a rope through her window. Since her house was on the city wall, it would make their escape easier. "Go to the hills so those pursuing you

Rahab and her family were spared as promised, and lived among the Israelites. In Matthew 1:5 we learn that Rahab married an Israelite named Salmon and had a son named Boaz. It was through this line that King David, and later Christ, would come.

116

will not find you. In three days—after the soldiers return, it will be safe for you to go on your way," she advised.

Before slipping over the edge, the two spies cautioned Rahab. "The promise we have made to you will be fulfilled only if this scarlet cord remains on this window. If you or anyone in your family leaves this house during the time of our attack, they will not be spared." Rahab nodded in agreement and sent the spies on their way.

"Let it be as you say," she whispered. While watching the two men disappear over the horizon, Rahab securely tied the red cord in the window. She would watch and wait.

exploring deeper

Turn to Joshua 2:11 in your Bible and look at the second half of that verse. Coming from the source that it did, these words were totally unexpected! What do they say? Rahab was able to make the statement she did because of what she saw God do in the lives of the Israelites. Even though she had a bad past, she didn't let that stop her from coming to God.

Skill Time

Take a moment and think about the people in your life. Is there someone who seems "unlikely" to ever come to know the One True God? Put their name on an index card and write Joshua 2:11 across the top. Keep this in your Bible and use it as a reminder to pray for that person. Then live your life in such a way that it points others to God's greatness. Don't assume people aren't interested in God; the cry for help is often heard in the least expected places.

WHAT'S THE MEANING OF THIS?

TAKEN FROM JOSHUA 3-4

GETTING READY

Before reading today's devotion, stop and pray. Ask the Lord to help you conquer any fears and concerns you have that keep you from following Him wholeheartedly.

THE JOURNEY

Do you sometimes find it difficult to make a total commitment?

The water roared swiftly past, slamming against rocks in a frothy foam and crashing against the banks. The fast-moving Jordan River was at its peak in flood stage. Just beyond it lay the fortresslike city of Jericho, secure and confident. The people there worshiped Baal, a god they believed controlled wind, storms, rain, and the depth of the river. Knowing the Jordan was at flood stage, they felt protected and shielded by their god. They had nothing to worry about—or so they thought.

"Come and listen to what the Lord your God says," Joshua yelled

118

over the noise of the river. For three days the Israelites had camped along the banks of the Jordan, watching its sheer power and force carve through the gorge. The river was a barrier standing in the way of the mission God was calling them to. They could go no farther until they crossed that barrier.

"This is how you will know that the living God is among you and will help you accomplish what He has for you to do," Joshua continued. Looking at the priests, Joshua signaled them to carry the ark and go ahead of the people. "The ark of the covenant of the Lord—the Lord of all the earth—will go before you into the Jordan. As soon as the priests carrying it set foot in the river, the waters flowing downstream will be cut off." The Israelites became quiet upon hearing Joshua's words. Only the thundering of the fast-moving water could be heard, threatening to swallow up anything crossing its path. This would be an extreme test of their faith. The Israelites all watched as the priests neared the banks of the river.

Now positioned directly in front of where they were to cross, the priests carrying the ark stopped. There was no gentle slope where they could stick their feet in to test the waters and see if God would do as He promised. This would be an all-or-nothing commitment. Once they stepped off the bank, the priests would either be in water over their heads or on dry ground as God had promised. With a lurch, the ark moved forward, and they took their first step—the step of faith God was waiting for them to take.

Suddenly, the air fell silent. The mighty roar that once brought a challenge to the Israelites' faith was gone. There, in the middle of the riverbed stood the priests—completely dry and standing on firm ground!

The use of "standing stones" or *masseboth* was a way of remembering. They caused travelers passing by to stop and ask, "What happened here? What's the meaning of this?" They were places to remember, like the Lincoln Memorial in Washington D.C., or the war memorials in Russia. Seven different times in the Book of Joshua they are set up in order to point the attention of the world to God's power.

With excitement and newfound faith, the Israelites passed in front of the ark, ever mindful of God's presence with them.

The Jordan River (meaning "to descend; to go down") was named because of how rapidly it drops in elevation. Being only 50-75 feet across in most places, the Jordan runs along a ridge in the earth's crust. The place the Israelites crossed was very near to where Jesus was later baptized.

Joshua then gave specific orders to twelve men God told him to choose—each representing one of the tribes of Israel. "Go over to where the ark of God is in the middle of the Jordan and select a large stone. Carry this stone out on your shoulder and to the place we will camp," he commanded. "These stones will serve as a sign. When your children ask you, 'What happened here? What's the meaning of these rocks?' tell them the great thing God has done on your behalf, and how He stopped the flow of the Jordan River—a large obstacle that stood before you," Joshua explained.

Once the Israelites had accomplished all God instructed them to do, Joshua commanded the priests to come up out of the Jordan. The moment they set their feet on the land, the waters returned and raged at full flood level.

Taking the stones that had been carried out from the middle of the river, Joshua stacked them together as a standing memorial to God's power in their lives. There they would remain for all the world to see.

exploring deeper

In your Bible, look up Joshua 4:24. What does it say? (Go on, look it up!) What two reasons are given for the barrier set before Israel and how the Lord delivered them? What effect do you think this had on the people of Israel? How about the people of the land?

Skill Time

God's promise to the people of Israel couldn't be fulfilled until they were willing to trust Him and take the first step. Once they did, God was able to work powerfully on their behalf. What barriers do you face that keep you from the mission God has called you to? Take a moment and search your heart. God desires to use your life as a "standing stone" or memorial to His power and love, but He can't do anything until you are willing to make a total commitment to Him. When faced with challenging obstacles, realize they are only opportunities for Joshua 4:24 to be fulfilled in your life. Memorize this verse and keep it handy.

LET THIS BE A LESSON TO YOU!

TAKEN FROM JOSHUA 5-6

GETTING READY

Find a quiet spot and take a moment to reflect on all that God has done and provided for you in your life. Ask forgiveness for the times you've taken the Lord for granted or neglected to thank Him.

THE JOURNEY

Does it ever bother you when people take credit for a job they didn't do?

Joshua looked out toward the horizon to the fortified walls of Jericho. Because word had gone out about the miraculous crossing of the Jordan, fear of the Israelites and their God reigned in the hearts of those living in the land. As a result, Jericho was tightly closed up—allowing no one to enter or exit. *This will make attacking Jericho all the more difficult,* Joshua thought to himself while drawing closer to the fortress for a better view.

Joshua looked back over his shoulder to where the Israelites were encamped at Gilgal. During the past forty years of wandering in the wilderness, neither the celebration of Passover nor circumcision had been observed—not until now. Now, the Israelites could be a nation that would walk obediently before its God. They were an army poised for battle.

A movement suddenly caught Joshua's eyes and caused him to look up. There, standing before him, was a soldier with a drawn sword in his hand. *If this is an Israelite,* Joshua thought to himself, *he is out-of-bounds. If this is the enemy, I'm ready to fight!* "Who are you?!" Joshua demanded. "Friend or foe?!"

"Neither one," came the powerful reply. "I am the commander for the army of the Lord." The meaning of those words struck Joshua, and he fell facedown to the ground in respect. "I am at your command," Joshua replied, shaken. "What do you want your servant to do?" he asked humbly, suddenly realizing the battle plan had little to do with the Israelites and everything to do with God. "Take off your shoes, for the ground you are standing on is holy," came the answer. Joshua did as he was told, then listened carefully to all the instructions the Lord had for him.

When did the manna stop? Joshua 5:12 tells us God didn't stop providing manna for the Israelites until the day after they ate of the fruit of the land in Canaan!

When he returned to the men who were armed and ready for battle, he shouted, "God has promised to fight for us and deliver Jericho into our hands!" The soldiers listened intently, waiting to hear Joshua's words of wisdom and his plan of attack. They weren't prepared for what they heard next! "This is what we are to do," Joshua told them. "Take up the ark of the Lord and have seven priests in front carry their ram's horns and blow them as we march. An armed guard will go in front of the ark, and one behind. The rest of you soldiers will follow. We'll march around Jericho once, then return to camp." When Joshua finished giving instructions, no one said a word. *What kind of battle plan is that?!* they wondered.

The Israelite army did as it was told and marched around Jericho once before returning to camp. The whole process took no more than about thirty minutes. The next day, the Israelites rose at dawn and repeated what they had done before. Each day for six days straight the Israelites did this—just as God commanded. Each day they carried the ark before them and encircled Jericho one time while blowing on the ram's horn trumpets. When the seventh day came, however, the orders changed." Today we will march not just once, but seven times around the city!" Joshua proclaimed. "After the seventh time around, the priests will sound a blast on the horn, and you are to shout, for today the Lord has given you the city!"

Joshua's curse (Joshua 6:26) was fulfilled in 1 Kings 16:34 when a man named Hiel tried to rebuild Jericho in the days of King Ahab. Hiel lost both his oldest (firstborn) and his youngest son in the process.

Obediently, the Israelites picked up the ark and marched. In their hearts they knew such an act would never deliver the city into their hands—not unless God was behind it. For every lap they marched, the Israelites endured the laughter and ridicule of the soldiers on the wall above. Marching around seven times seemed like an eternity. Suddenly, the Israelites heard the long blast on the ram's horn. Lifting their voices to the heavens, they gave a great shout. Panic suddenly replaced the laughter they had heard from their enemies. With a loud rumble, the walls began to crumble and explode outward! Screams and cries of terror rang out as the Israelites ran in. According to God's instructions, they were to completely destroy anyone and everything that remained—sparing only Rahab and her family. "Take nothing for yourself," Joshua warned, "for this city is to be totally devoted to the Lord!" Joshua knew the victory had come from the Lord alone; therefore, the Lord alone deserved the rewards and the credit.

exploring deeper

Turn to Joshua 6:26 and read what it says. Does this make sense to you? What do you think is the reason behind what Joshua says here? The destruction of Jericho was God's way of saying, "Let this be a lesson to you." For the people of the land it would stand as a monument of God's power and ability—so that the world might know He is God. To the Israelites, it would also stand as a promise of more to come.

THINKING on your FEET

When you are handed a success by the Lord, do you give the credit to God, or do you bask in the rewards as if you accomplished it yourself? How do you acknowledge the "Jerichos" of your life?

OUCH

TAKEN FROM JOSHUA 7

Getting Ready

Don't explore this devotion until you've stopped to pray. God made you and knows what you struggle with. Take a moment and examine your life, then confess (agree with God) any areas that are holding you back from being all God wants you to be.

THE JOURNEY

Have you ever taken or kept something for yourself that really didn't belong to you (even if it was something small)?

Excitement buzzed in the camp at Gilgal. It had been a great day of victory for the Israelites as they watched God deliver the city of Jericho into their hands. Just as God commanded, all the Canaanites had been slain, and nothing was taken for personal use—well, almost nothing.

"Joshua, we've just come back from spying out the city of Ai," Joshua's men reported excitedly. Joshua looked out to the horizon. The city of Ai lay only eleven miles away from Jericho and directly in their path of travel. It would be an important city to capture. "Taking the city should be easy for it's only guarded by a few men!" Joshua was informed.

Joshua listened to the report and knew only a portion of the Israelite army was needed to accomplish the task. As a result, only 3,000 soldiers were sent, allowing the rest of the army to stay back at camp. Excitement from the recent Jericho victory and promise of success followed the soldiers out of camp. A spirit of defeat and retreat followed them back in. Thirty-six Israelite soldiers had been killed, and the army had been forced to retreat. The conquest of Ai was a disaster! What happened?! There was no reason for them to have been defeated! Something was definitely wrong.

After Achan's sin had been dealt with, the Israelites re-attacked Ai and won. Because God had not put a "ban" on Ai, the Israelites were permitted to loot the city and take the spoils of war for themselves.

In confusion and frustration, Joshua fell facedown to the ground before the Lord and questioned God. "Why did you even bring us across the Jordan just to be destroyed at the hands of our enemies?" he cried out. Joshua agonized in his heart, *When our enemies hear how we were defeated at Ai, they'll come to attack us and wipe us off the face of the earth! What will happen to us? What will happen to the honor of God's name? What happened?!*

"Joshua, what are you doing?! Stand up!" the Lord commanded. Joshua stood up. "The reason the Israelites suffered defeat at Ai is because they have broken My covenant. They took things that they were forbidden to take from Jericho. They have stolen, lied, and placed some of these forbidden items with their own possessions," God continued. Joshua felt sick. He listened silently as God described what had to be done. "You cannot stand against your enemies until you remove these things from among you," warned the Lord of Israel.

The next morning, Joshua did as God directed. First he called all the tribes to come forward. When God pointed out which tribe it was, each clan of that tribe then came forward. God was narrowing down the suspects, and Achan began to break out in a cold sweat. *It was only a*

little thing I took, he consoled himself. *It seemed such a waste to let those things lay buried in the rubble and ruins! They were valuable!* Achan looked up and into the strong gaze of Joshua, who now stood before him.

"Tell me what you've done," Joshua ordered. Achan's heart melted.

"It's true! I stole from the Lord and sinned against Him," he confessed. "When I saw the beautiful robe from Babylonia, the silver coins, and the wedge of gold, I took them for myself. They are hidden under my tent."

> Sin isn't just "doing wrong things"; it is a heart attitude. For an easy definition of sin, look at its spelling: S-I-N. What's in the center of the word? I. Simply put: sin is any time I become centered on myself.

Joshua grieved in his heart. Although Achan might have felt his sin was too small and personal to hurt anyone else, he was wrong. Achan's sin didn't affect just him, it affected the whole nation of Israel. It not only caused the Israelites to suffer defeat at Ai, but also caused Joshua to question God. Something that seemed so small and promised such pleasure only caused grief and destruction. Achan's sin came at a high cost to many. Achan not only lost his life, but his entire family as well. They were burned and buried with the things Achan had stolen.

exploring deeper

Turn in your Bible to Joshua 6, and read verses 17-19. "Devoted to the Lord" meant the items were under God's judgment and thus strictly forbidden for the Israelites to have. Take a close look at verse 18. What does it say? What does this tell you about the type of person Achan was?

DANGER AHEAD

In our society, it's easy to think our sin affects only us and is harmless. Don't believe it. Life is full of opportunities to disobey God's direction. As Achan learned, disobedience (even in things that seem small) brings disaster down the road. Giving in to temptation only allows Satan to have a foothold in your life. Once that happens, you won't be able to stand or have victory. Worse yet, your life will affect others around you. Don't go down that path.

BUT I THOUGHT—

TAKEN FROM JOSHUA 9

GETTING READY

Take a moment to pray. Quiet your thoughts and heart before the Lord, and ask Him to teach you what He wants you to learn.

THE JOURNEY

Do you ever act first, and *then* think later?

Joshua looked suspiciously at the group of men. Their clothes were old and the sandals on their feet well worn. A quick glance at the donkeys showed heavy loads of worn-out sacks and old wineskins, cracked and mended. "We've come from a distant land seeking to make a treaty with you," one of the men spoke up. Joshua met their gaze, wondering about this odd group of men. "Who are you and where are you from?" he questioned. The band of men looked at each other quickly but answered Joshua without hesitating. "We've come from a very distant country," they offered. "We know all that God did for you in Egypt and even how He helped you defeat two kings on the east side of the Jordan." They carefully did not mention what they knew of the recent battles at Jericho and Ai. "We desire to make a treaty with you and live in peace," they finished.

Joshua and his men thought about the words they heard. Clearly, God had commanded them not to make any treaties with the inhabitants of the land of Canaan. All cities and their people were to be completely destroyed and conquered by the Israelites. If these people truly were from a distant land, there would be no problem in making an agreement to live in peace together. The band of men watched Joshua closely, seeing him silently weigh his options. "How do we know you're from far away and not one of our neighbors?" Joshua challenged.

The people living in Gibeon were called "Hivites" and were descendants of Ham's son, Canaan.

"Look," the leader stated as he walked toward the donkeys, "here's proof we are speaking the truth." Joshua followed and watched the stranger pull out some bread. "Upon leaving our country, we packed these provisions to bring along. The day we set out, they were fresh from the oven—look at them now!" he said, pointing to the dry and moldy bread. He then directed Joshua's attention to the wineskins. "When we left our country, these were full and new. See how cracked they are!"

"And our clothes—," another joined in, "our clothes are all worn out from the long journey!"

Joshua looked at the evidence before him—it all seemed to back up the words of the strangers. Just to be sure, however, Joshua and his men asked to sample the provisions—everything checked out. Joshua then signed a treaty promising to live in peace with these people and not destroy them. The Israelite leaders all agreed and backed it up with an oath. They had no idea they were all being deceived.

"But I thought—," Joshua later stammered in anger, unable to finish his sentence.

"We even sampled their provisions—what more could we have had as evidence?!" one of the leaders offered. It had been only three days since the signing of the treaty—three days to find out the strangers with whom they had signed a treaty were really from the city of Gibeon only twenty-five miles away! Joshua felt frustrated. They had been tricked into signing a treaty with Canaanites—the very ones God had said to destroy! When the people in the camp heard the story, they were angered in their hearts. Many soldiers grumbled, expressing a desire to kill off the Gibeonites anyway—treaty or no treaty! Joshua reminded them that an oath before the Lord had been made, and God held them accountable to keep it. The Gibeonites couldn't be touched.

During the reign of King David (2 Samuel 21:1-2) there was famine in the land for three years because Saul broke a standing treaty and oath that had been made before the Lord. That treaty was the one Joshua had made with the Gibeonites, guaranteeing the Gibeonites would not be killed.

"Why did you deceive us?!" Joshua demanded of the Gibeonite leaders. The leaders remained silent for a moment and then responded. "We were told how the Lord your God promised to give you this land, commanding you to destroy all who live in it," they replied. "We feared for our lives; that is why we tricked you into signing a treaty with us. Now do with us as you see fit."

Joshua made the Gibeonites become slaves with duties of cutting wood and carrying water. By associating their work with the tabernacle, Joshua made sure the Gibeonites would be exposed to the worship of the one true God.

exploring deeper

Look up Joshua 9:14 and read what it says. According to this verse, what wise thing did Joshua and the leaders do? What one vital mistake did they make? (Hint: it's something they did *not* do.)

THINKING on your FEET

Often we are tempted to rush ahead and make decisions based on our own wisdom. Leaving God on the sidelines, we operate on our own understanding—and suffer. God wants us to use our heads, but He also wants us to use His wisdom. That can only be gained by checking in with Him. Whose wisdom are you operating on?

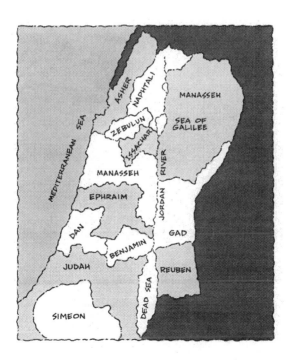

The next devotion tells us how Joshua conquered the land of Canaan and divided the land among the tribes. This map shows you how that land was divided up.

GIVE ME A CHANCE TO *EXPLAIN!*

TAKEN FROM JOSHUA 22

GETTING READY

Come to your time of exploring today with a ready, willing heart to learn. Ask God to remove any distractions or thoughts that battle for your attention—including wrong thoughts or attitudes you have toward others. Dedicate this time to Him.

THE JOURNEY

Does it ever frustrate you when others assume they know what you're thinking—and they're wrong?!

Joshua let out a sigh of satisfaction. With the Lord's help, thirty-one kings and their cities were conquered! The battles were over, the land was divided up, and each tribe received what God had promised it would inherit. *Thank you, Lord,* Joshua breathed, and then turned his attention to the tribes of Reuben, Gad, and half of the tribe of Manasseh.

"You have been mighty warriors and faithful to help us conquer the land of Canaan," he commended. "You've done all that you promised to do and completed the mission the Lord our God gave you. Now that the battles are over and the land is divided, you are free to return to the land you requested as your inheritance—the land just outside of Canaan on the other side of the Jordan." The soldiers looked into the eyes of Joshua with equal satisfaction. It had been seven long years of fighting. Now they would be returning to their families with great wealth—large herds of livestock, silver, gold, bronze, and iron, and a great quantity of clothing. All this God had provided from the cities they had helped to conquer. Finally being able to return to their families, they would share and divide up the wealth.

Joshua met their gaze and blessed them before sending them away. "Be very careful to keep the Law of the Lord. Love Him and walk in His ways," Joshua reminded them. "Obey God's commands and hold fast to Him—serve the Lord with all your heart and soul." Each of the men knew the importance of Joshua's words and vowed to do just that. With a heartfelt good-bye, they left Joshua and the ten-and-a-half tribes in Canaan and headed east to Gilead.

Having arrived at the banks of the Jordan, the men remembered how God miraculously allowed the Israelites to cross and gave them victories in the land of Canaan. Looking up, they saw the mountain ranges on each side of the Jordan River with heights of over 2,000 feet. Between these mountains lay the Jordan Valley like a large trench with the river running through it. The separation between them and the rest of the Israelites suddenly hit them. "What if, in the future, the ten-and-a-half tribes say, 'You have nothing to do with the Lord our God. See, the Jordan stands as a boundary line between us.'—What will happen then?" the men asked each other.

Shiloh was in a central location for all the tribes in the land of Canaan. By having the Tabernacle and altar of the Lord there, it became the central place of worship for the Israelites.

"Let's build an altar on the border of the land of Canaan," one of them suggested, "to remind us of the God we share with all the tribes of

Israel." The men agreed this was a good solution and built a huge altar that could be seen from a great distance.

The Israelites on the other side of the Jordan saw the altar and became enraged. Why had the eastern tribes built an altar when they were supposed to offer sacrifices only at the tabernacle in Shiloh? "How could they do this?!" they asked. "How could they forget the Lord their God so easily and build their own altar?"

According to Leviticus 17:8-9, if an Israelite offered a sacrifice on any altar other than the one at the tabernacle (tent of meeting), he must be cut off from his people. Building an altar was also something only a priest could do.

"They are rebelling against God!" someone shouted.

"Are they now taunting us to bow down to idol worship by placing this altar on our side of the Jordan?!" another added. Having gathered together at Shiloh, the whole assembly made plans to go to war against the eastern tribes of Gad and Reuben, and the half-tribe of Manasseh. Appointing one man to represent each tribe, a delegation of ten leaders quickly left Shiloh with Phinehas (son of Eleazar the high priest) to go and confront the matter. Anger in their hearts drove them onward.

Having arrived at Gilead, the ten leaders fired their accusations against the men who had built the altar. "How could you break faith with God?" they demanded. "Don't you know your rebellion will bring God's anger down upon us all?!" Reuben, Gad, and the half-tribe of Manasseh listened in stunned silence. "May that never be!" they quickly answered. "This altar isn't for us to worship at or offer sacrifices upon. Rather, it is a memorial to remind you of our right to offer our sacrifices at the one true altar of the Lord in Shiloh. We feared that one day your descendants would say to ours, 'You have no share in the Lord with us,'" the men explained.

When Phinehas and the leaders heard what the men had to say, they no longer talked about going to war against them. Instead, they rejoiced in their hearts and praised God.

exploring deeper

In your Bible, take a look at verse 28 in Joshua 22. Now, drop down and read verse 30. What does it say? Do you see an important connection between the two? Notice the words "when" and "heard" in verse 30. They are critical!

Skill Time

When there's a conflict, we are tempted to react before we hear the whole story. Sometimes we assume we know what the other person is thinking and don't take time to listen to his side. Busy trying to prove our point, we don't "hear" the other person and often misunderstand what he's said or done. God is not honored by those actions. Everyone deserves a chance to explain and the opportunity to be heard. When you come in conflict with someone today or in the next few days, make a point to practice the art of listening! Use this as your guide:

L - Let the other person express himself.
I - Ignore the urge to interrupt or cut in.
S- Seek to understand.
T - "Tune in" to what's being said.
E - Examine the facts.
N - Never assume you know what's going on in the other person's heart.

GETTING YOUR BEARINGS:
THE BOOK OF JUDGES

When you think of the word "judge," the idea of a courtroom comes to mind. This is not what the Book of Judges is about! Many people look at this book and think of heroes such as Gideon, Deborah, and Samson who came to rescue the Israelites. Even that is not what Judges is all about. So, exactly what is this book about?

The Book of Judges (which spans approximately 350 years) is all about what happens when people turn from God and make their own rules. It graphically shows the lowest levels to which people can sink when they neglect the Lord. The very last verse of Judges sadly states: "Every man did what was right in his own eyes . . ." Having just come from the victories of obedience in the Book of Joshua, how could the Israelites change so much? What happened?! That is what you'll discover as you go through Judges!

As you explore this book, look for a pattern in behavior. The Israelites' sin causes them to suffer at the hands of their enemies. When they call out to God, He sends someone to rescue them. After a while, the nation forgets about its relationship with God and starts sinning again. So the cycle continues: sinning, suffering, asking, receiving, forgetting . . . sinning. This sad cycle is repeated not just once or twice, but over and over.

As you crawl through the dark passages of this book, take notice of one bright light penetrating through—God's patience. God never gives up on His people or abandons them. Despite major flaws in their character and mistakes they make, God patiently works with what He has, desiring to draw them back to Himself. Judges is a book of second chances and opportunities for new beginnings.

THAT'S GOOD ENOUGH FOR ME!

TAKEN FROM JUDGES 1-2

GETTING READY

Before you explore, ask God to help you be more willing to obey Him all the way (rather than halfway). Allow Him to speak to your heart and show you areas in your life that need to change.

THE JOURNEY

When faced with a hard task, do you quit early?

Joshua was gone, and now it was up to them—each tribe—to drive out the enemy from their own territory. Although only pockets of Canaanites lived here and there, the job of conquering the enemy was still a task to be finished. It was an important job that needed to be done.

"Remember, God will fight for you," Joshua had said. "As you rely on Him, He will help you accomplish the task. Only be very careful not to associate with those living in the land. You must drive them out completely, or they will become a snare to you," Joshua had wisely warned. Having remembered the words of the Lord through Moses, Joshua faithfully reminded the Israelites of God's rules. While Joshua was still living, the Israelites obeyed those rules. When he died, however, they were easily forgotten. One compromise led to another, and instead of finishing the job God had given them to do, the Israelites looked for easier alternatives. They wanted to follow a path of least resistance.

In Deuteronomy 7:2-6, God had given three rules for when the Israelites entered the land: 1) Totally destroy the enemy. 2) Don't marry the inhabitants of the land. 3) Don't follow after their false gods. The Israelites ignored all of these.

"Come up to our territory and help us fight the Canaanites," those in the tribe of Judah asked the tribe of Simeon. "In turn, we will then help you in yours." A deal was made, and the two tribes fought side by side. When they conquered the city of Bezek, however, they didn't kill the king. Instead, they cut off his thumbs and big toes, making sport of him. No longer would he be able to hold a weapon or lead his troops in combat. This was not something God commanded or approved of.

Continuing on in battle, the two tribes gained control of Judah's hill country but stopped short of gaining control over the valley. "We're no match for such weapons!" they cried out in fear as the Canaanites' iron chariots bore down upon them. Backing away from the challenge of completing the job, the tribes limited their fighting to where the chariots couldn't go.

The Canaanites lived in city-states governed by separate kings. This made conquering the land more difficult, for a captured king could not surrender for the rest of the land. Each city had to be conquered individually.

While all this was happening, the tribes of Joseph (Ephraim and half of Manasseh) were making compromises of their own. "If you tell us how to get into the city," they bargained with a man from the Canaanite city of Bethel, "we'll see that you are treated well." The Canaanite man agreed, and even though the entire city was destroyed, he and his family were allowed to live. This was only the beginning. Ephraim and

Manasseh soon found it difficult to drive the Canaanites from the land, for they were a strong and stubborn people. "Why should we get rid of them," they began to reason in their hearts, "when we can force them to serve us and benefit from their skills and trade?" Rather than struggle to finish the job of conquering the land, the tribes of Joseph decided to allow the Canaanites to live alongside them. It wasn't long before the other tribes did the same.

The very thing Moses and Joshua warned the Israelites about doing had finally happened. Rather than loving and following God with their whole hearts, the Israelites were influenced by their enemies and began to bow down to pagan idols. Because they hadn't fully obeyed the Lord's rules, their compromising actions would lead to their own downfall.

> **After Joshua died, so did most of the generation who had originally entered the Promised Land. The task of finishing the job was now in the hands of an entirely new generation who neither sought the Lord nor knew what He had done for them (Judges 2:10).**

exploring deeper

In your Bible, look up Judges 3, and read verses 5-6. (Don't worry about pronouncing all the "ites" in verse 5 correctly—the main point is in verse 6!) According to these verses, what next steps did the Israelites take? Did you see this coming?

Skill Time

Many of us are no different from the Israelites. Instead of obeying God fully, we come to the halfway mark in our wrestling with sin. Feeling like we've done a good enough job, we look for an easier standard to reach, or a partial compromise. Because we've come partway, we say, "That's good enough for me!" and pat ourselves on the back. Unfortunately, "that's good enough for me" isn't good enough for God. Doing something halfway is just as bad as not doing it at all in God's eyes.

Take a moment and think about your own life. What difficult task has God called you to do that you've given up on? Tell Him about it right now. Ask for His forgiveness, then make a point to make it right. Use today as a starting point to live wholeheartedly for Him.

Lord, I've only followed You halfway and have grown comfortable living with sin in my life. I want that to change. Right here, right now, I dedicate my life to following You. Help me to obey You completely so I'll have no retreats and no regrets.

Signed _____ date _____

YOU'RE *SURE* YOU'RE SURE?

TAKEN FROM JUDGES 3-7

GETTING READY

Start this time by thanking God for who He is. Thank Him that He is not limited in His power or ability. Thank Him that He knows you well and chooses you anyway. God can be fully trusted, for He always keeps His word.

THE JOURNEY

Have you ever doubted God's ability to work in or through you?

A sense of panic filled the air. The Midianites were everywhere! Once again they came at harvest time, stealing for themselves and completely destroying the land and crops in their path. Sheep, cattle, and donkeys were brutally killed, and the Israelites were left with nothing. Once again, as at other times in the past, the Israelites were being crushed by their enemies. Once again, they first cried out to their idols who couldn't help them, then they cried out to the living God. Once again, God answered their plea for help and raised up someone to deliver them and redirect them back to Himself . . .

Gideon looked over his shoulder to make sure no Midianites—or anyone else for that matter would see him! He quickly threw his grain down into a winepress and began working it. Under normal conditions he would have an abundance of grain to be threshed in a large open area—but these weren't normal conditions. Because of the Midianites, grain was scarce, and any threshing had to be done in secret to keep it from the invaders.

Threshing was the process of removing the outside coating of the grain to get at the more useful inside kernel.

"The Lord is with you, mighty warrior," a voice said, as Gideon jerked his head up in fear. To his relief, it was the voice of a stranger sitting under an oak tree and watching him—not that of a Midianite's tauntings.

"But sir," he sighed, briefly stopping his work to reply, "if the Lord is with us—the Israelites—why is all of this happening?" As of yet, Gideon didn't realize he was talking to the angel of the Lord. He continued working while talking to the stranger. "Where are all the miracles and wonders we heard our fathers describe?" he said in frustration. "God has abandoned us and given us into the hands of our enemies!" Gideon stopped to look up and see the effects of his words on the stranger. He wasn't prepared to hear the response he got.

"Go in the strength that you have, and save Israel from the Midianites," the angel of the Lord instructed. "I am sending you!" The words had a numbing effect on Gideon. *Perhaps I didn't hear correctly, or this stranger doesn't know me very well,* Gideon thought to himself. He looked at the angel doubtfully and commented, "How in the world can I save Israel when I'm the least in my family, and my clan is the weakest in the tribe of Manasseh?" Gideon knew the words were true. He certainly was a coward if ever there was one. He would rather run from trouble than fight it. "I will be with you," came the reply, "and you will destroy the Midianites as easily as if you were fighting only one man."

Suddenly, Gideon wondered if God were speaking to him. He needed to be certain in his heart. Wanting some kind of sign, Gideon asked the angel of the Lord to wait while he gathered supplies to bring as an offering. The angel agreed. When Gideon returned, the angel instructed, "Place the meat and unleavened bread on this rock and pour out the broth." Gideon did as he was told. Taking the staff he was holding, the angel touched the tip of it to the offering, and fire came out of the rock and consumed the meat and bread. The angel of the Lord then disappeared. Gideon stood both speechless and terrified.

That same night the Lord spoke to Gideon and gave him a test. He was to tear down the family altar to the false god, Baal, and build a proper one to the Lord. He was also to take his father's choice bull (which had been dedicated to Baal) and offer it up to God instead. Knowing the altar was large, Gideon took ten of his servants and did just that. He worked at night, however, in fear of being discovered.

Although reluctant, Gideon was the fourth "judge" God raised up to help Israel. The others were Othniel (who saved the Israelites from the Mesopotamians); Ehud (who delivered them from the Moabites); and Deborah (who directed the defeat of the Canaanites).

"Lord," Gideon prayed after hearing that the Midianites had joined forces with others and were coming to attack, "You said You'd save Israel from the Midianites by my hand. If this is true and You'll do as You promised . . ." Gideon hesitated a moment, grabbing a piece of fleece that had been recently shaved from a sheep. "If what You say is true," he continued, "then give me a sign. See, I will place this piece of wool on the ground. If in the morning there is dew on it, but none on the ground, I'll know what You say is true." The next morning Gideon found the fleece soaked but the ground dry. Still fearful in his heart, he then asked God for yet another sign. "Don't be angry with me Lord, but if I am to do what You say, make the fleece dry and the ground wet!" Just like the first time, God patiently met Gideon's conditions—waiting for Gideon to finally obey.

exploring deeper

Look up Judges 6 and read verses 14 and 16. What do they say? Chapter 7 contains the rest of the story and the "famous battle." At the beginning of this chapter, God reduces Gideon's army from 32,000 down to 300 men, so the Israelites would understand it was God who fought for them. Then, in verses 8-11, God allows Gideon to do one more thing. What is it? What does this tell you about Gideon's character?

DANGER AHEAD

Like Gideon, we pretend to be seeking God's will when really we are doubting Him! Constantly looking for signs only shows our lack of faith in God's character to guide and provide as He promised. It also focuses our attention on the wrong thing and can easily get us away from the Bible. Signs don't make us better believers; they make us weaker ones. Watch that you're not tempted to chase after them.

GIVE ME LEADERSHIP, OR GIVE ME DEATH!

TAKEN FROM JUDGES 8-9

GETTING READY

Take a moment to stop and pray. Tell God about the things you struggle with in your heart and mind, and what you desire most with a passion. Ask Him to help you keep those in perspective.

THE JOURNEY

Do you know people who will do just about anything to be the one in control?

Abimelech scoffed in his heart as he remembered how his father, Gideon, turned down the opportunity to rule over the Israelites. "Rule over us as king!" they had begged after seeing Gideon deliver them from the Midianites. "Not only you, but also your sons and their grandsons!" they offered.

"No," Gideon had replied, "neither I nor my sons will rule over you, but God will." Abimelech spat on the ground in disgust as he remembered those words. . . . *Neither I nor my sons will rule over you*, he mocked in his heart. *Speak for yourself!*

147

Now that Gideon had died, Abimelech determined in his heart to move in and fill that position. He felt it was his right. Abimelech's only problem was his seventy half-brothers. *That's seventy threats to my becoming King*, he realized. *I'll have to come up with a way to eliminate the competition!* Abimelech knew if anyone was going to stand in his way, it would be one of them. Abimelech had a plan, and that plan would involve traveling to his mother's relatives in Shechem for help.

"Who would you rather have rule over you?" Abimelech charged the people of Shechem. "All seventy of Gideon's sons, or one man?! Remember, I am your relative!" Deciding to support Abimelech, the people took seventy silver coins from their temple and gave them for his cause. With this money Abimelech hired reckless adventurers who became his followers and journeyed back with him to Ophrah. There, they put to death all of his brothers—except one. Jotham, who hid, had escaped. *This will guarantee my ability to rule!* Abimelech said to himself, satisfied over what he had done. Little did he know . . .

Just because Gideon was a hero in battle didn't make him a hero in daily life. Gideon not only married many women, he also had a concubine through whom Abimelech was born.

On the day Abimelech was to be crowned king in Shechem, Jotham climbed to an overhang and shouted out his warning to all who would hear. He drove at Abimelech's unworthiness to rule, telling how he killed his brothers. He then pointed out that only worthless people seek to lord it over others. "Those worthy to rule are too busy doing useful things to seek places of honor for themselves," he stated. Jotham then accused the people of crowning Abimelech king only because he was their relative—not because he deserved it. Finishing his speech, Jotham jumped down and escaped to Beer to live. He was afraid of Abimelech—and rightly so!

After three years, the Shechemites weren't so happy with their new king. "Who is this Abimelech, and why should we citizens of Shechem serve him?" Gaal, a newcomer, ridiculed. "If I were in command . . ." Things were turning sour, and the people were turning against

Abimelech. Already Gaal's boasting had won the confidence of the people—something Abimelech knew he would need to stop.

Gathering together a small army, Abimelech journeyed with his men at night to take positions around Shechem. At sunrise, they planned to advance upon the city and kill Gaal and his men. *We'll see where all his boasting gets him now,* Abimelech hissed through clenched teeth.

When Abimelech defeated Gaal and his men, the victory neither satisfied him nor relieved his fears. *What if others in Shechem become disloyal and rise up against me?* he worried. Wanting to protect his self-claimed authority, Abimelech returned and brutally killed the people of Shechem while they were out working in their fields. He then pressed his attack against the remainder of the city, causing nearly a thousand people to run into the stronghold tower of Shechem for safety. Driven by his rage, Abimelech took branches and set them on fire near the tower entrance, causing all within to die of suffocation. He then took salt and cast it about the city, proclaiming it a destroyed area, worthless to be built upon again.

> It was not uncommon during a battle for women to join the men at the city wall and drop heavy objects down upon the enemy. A heavy millstone, being a simple farmer's tool one-and-a-half feet in diameter, became an excellent weapon!

Just northeast of Shechem lay another town, named Thebez. Not sure how far Gaal's influence had spread, Abimelech attacked that city, too, trying to kill anything and everything in sight. Fearing for their lives, people ran screaming for safety and locked themselves in the tower at Thebez and climbed out upon the roof. Abimelech advanced upon the tower with the intent of burning it down as well. As he drew near to the tower door to set it on fire, a brave woman dropped a heavy millstone on his head, and he was struck down. Seeing Abimelech's life had ended, his followers disbanded and simply went home.

Abimelech's desire to be in charge drove him to the point of doing anything to accomplish it. "Give me leadership, or give me death!" Abimelech sadly managed to accomplish both.

exploring deeper

Turn in your copy of the Scriptures to Judges 9:53-54. When this happened, what did Abimelech request of his armor bearer? Even on his deathbed he was consumed with his own pride!

DANGER AHEAD

Although this chapter in Israel's history is gruesome, it holds an important warning for us! The desire to be "numero uno" lies within us all. It's called the sin nature, and we each come fully equipped with it! If left unchecked, the desire for control becomes consuming. Don't get drawn into its clutches. When you have the urge to "control" others, use that as a signal to remember Jotham's words: those truly worthy to rule don't get caught up in seeking places of honor for themselves. Guard yourself and don't fall into the same trap Abimelech did.

CAN WE ERASE THAT?

TAKEN FROM JUDGES 10-12

GETTING READY

Pray, asking God to help you deal with old habits and quick actions that tend to get you into trouble. Thank Him that He is able to give you the power and strength to change.

THE JOURNEY

Have you ever gotten so "caught up in the moment" that you made rash statements without really thinking?

"You stole our land!"

"Did not!"

"Did too! Now give it back peacefully—or else!"

Jephthah knew he had a decision to make. For 300 years the Israelites had lived in Gilead, and there had never been a dispute over the land—until now. Suddenly claiming the land was his, the Ammonite king threatened to attack.

Jephthah thought about his options. The people of Gilead had come to him asking for his help. *How strange,* Jephthah thought to himself, *my own brothers living in Gilead drove me away, saying I'm not worthy to have an inheritance with them. Now, when there's trouble, they come for my help!*

The Amorites were the original inhabitants of the land of Canaan. Amorite means "westerner." The Ammonites were a race descended from Lot's youngest daughter and often teamed up with other nations against Israel.

Jephthah's father was the one for whom the area was named—Gilead. Unlike his brothers, Jephthah wasn't born through Gilead's wife, but rather from a Canaanite woman of little honor. Regardless, Jephthah was a child of Gilead's, and that had caused a problem with the rest of the family. Being half-Israelite and half-Canaanite, Jephthah was considered worthless—until now. Now his help was needed, and he had been offered the reward of being head over all of Gilead if he would help fight the Ammonites. Agreeing to do so, Jephthah now faced the task before him. Seeking to solve the problem peacefully, he first sent a message to the Ammonite king.

"Gilead was never yours in the first place," Jephthah corrected. "It was taken from the Amorites, not the Ammonites. Further, God gave this land into our hands, and we have the right to possess it, just as you have the right to possess any land given to you by your god." Jephthah smiled to himself at that thought. "Lastly, no one has ever challenged Israel's ownership of this land since it was conquered 300 years ago! We have not wronged you, but you are wronging us by waging war against us." The king of Ammon, however, paid no attention to Jephthah's message and prepared to attack. God then empowered Jephthah to lead his army against the Ammonites.

As he marched his troops across the land, Jephthah had some time to reflect on the events in his life. *I was cast off as worthless, and now I hold command over an Israelite army!* he thought with wonder. Living outside of Gilead as he did, Jephthah knew he had gained valuable leadership experience by heading up a band of adventure-seeking men. *But this is totally different!* he told himself. *This is much bigger, and the stakes are much higher!* Even though the people of Gilead had a ceremony for Jephthah making his leadership official, he felt the heavy load of responsibility. The people of Gilead were counting on him—and he had been counting on himself to pull this off. In a moment of emotion, Jephthah blurted out, "Lord, if You give me the victory . . . then when I return home triumphantly, I will sacrifice to You as a burnt offering whatever first comes out of the door to meet me!" Jephthah felt better that he had included God in his plans and went on to defeat the Ammonites, conquering twenty towns. What a victory it had been!

A simple definition of acting out of impulse (impulsively) is:

I
Mistakenly
Plunge ahead,
Underestimating
Long-term
Side effects on
Everyone and
   everything in my life.

Word of Jephthah's success quickly reached Gilead, and everyone began celebrating—especially Jephthah's household. As Jephthah strode up to his home, the door flew open, and Jephthah's daughter ran out to meet him, dancing to the sound of tambourines. Jephthah froze in his tracks. It was at that moment his rash and unwise vow fully hit him. His face suddenly changed from celebration to grief. *Oh, that I could go back and erase what I vowed,* he groaned. Jephthah's daughter, his only child, sensed something was drastically wrong. How would he explain it to her?

exploring deeper

Open your Bible to Judges 11 and read verse 30. (Although verse 31 completes the thought, stop after you read verse 30.) Now, closely look at the first two words Jephthah says to the Lord in this verse. What are they? Have you ever spoken those words to God?

THINKING on your FEET

Many struggle with this event in the Bible. "How could God allow Jephthah to make such a vow when He knew Jephthah's daughter would be the first to greet him?" The real point is, how could Jephthah make such a vow?! God is not impressed nor honored when we act impulsively without stopping to think about our actions. Through God's mercy, we do have an "eraser"— His forgiveness—but often we suffer the consequences of our action. Jephthah acted impulsively (in the emotion of the moment) and made a foolish vow. The next time you are tempted to do the same, how will you respond?

Those who act out of IMPULSE show . . .
I - Inability to stop and reason
M - Misplaced confidence
P - Poor self-control
U - Underestimating the consequences
L - Love of quick pleasure
S - Slowness to consider other alternatives
E - Emotionally based decisions

GOTCHA!

TAKEN FROM JUDGES 13-16

GETTING READY

Spend a moment talking with the Lord. Admit to Him areas in which you are prone to be tempted. (He already knows them and is simply waiting for you to agree.) Thank Him that He is available to rescue you from temptation—if you let Him.

THE JOURNEY

Have you ever been tempted to play around with temptation?

No problem, Samson smiled to himself, *it's not that big of a deal. I'm still in control.* Samson felt he was big enough and strong enough to handle just about anything. *After all, didn't I kill a lion with my own bare hands?* Samson reflected on all that had happened in his life, and how easily he had gained what he wanted. He remembered demanding his parents get him a Philistine wife whom he had desired. He remembered discovering bees had made a hive in the carcass of the lion he killed and the riddle he made out of it.

Out of the eater,
Something to eat;
Out of the strong,
Something sweet.

If his bride hadn't nagged him for the answer and secretly told the Philistines, they would never have guessed it. *Even so,* Samson recalled, *I easily killed thirty men, stripping them of their possessions to pay my loss of the bet. Indeed, is there anything that can ensnare me or keep me down?* he challenged.

Samson remembered the Philistine woman from Timnah who had briefly been his wife and how angry he had been when he lost his bet. He was so furious he left the wedding party and went to live with his parents. Believing Samson had rejected her, the Philistine woman married Samson's best man. When Samson discovered this, he took revenge on the Philistines and played a damaging prank on them—one they would feel the effects of for a long time. Samson caught 150 pairs of foxes and tied them together by their tails—fastening a torch to each. He then lit the torches and set the foxes loose in the Philistines' fields, destroying not only their grain, but also their vineyards and olive trees. When the townspeople saw what Samson had done, they killed his former bride and her family. In return, Samson attacked them viciously. *No one defeats Samson!* he thought to himself.

Most Nazirite vows were temporary, but Samson's was lifelong. Under this vow, a person was not permitted to touch anything dead, drink wine, or cut his hair. One by one, Samson broke all three restrictions.

Samson's actions caused concern for the Israelites, who wanted to avoid trouble with the Philistines. A group of men from the tribe of Judah went to the cave where Samson was staying.

"We're here to take you captive, Samson," they replied, "and hand you over to the Philistines. We promise not to kill you ourselves, but will tie you up and deliver you to them, as they demand." Looking at the men, Samson replied, "I'm only doing to them what they did to me." He then allowed himself to be bound up, knowing he'd be able to escape—one way or another.

Upon approaching the Philistine camp, Samson felt the Lord's strength and easily snapped the ropes which bound him. Then, picking up the jawbone of a donkey, he used it to strike down and kill a thousand Philistine soldiers. "With a donkey's jawbone, I've made donkeys of them. With a donkey's jawbone, I killed a thousand men!" he boasted triumphantly. Samson felt confident about his ability to escape danger, not knowing this would one day lead him to his own destruction.

Grain, grapes, and olives were major crops for people living in this area.

Samson was strong, brave, unstoppable, and in control. Although full of power, Samson wasn't always full of wisdom. For twenty years he fought with the Philistines, rescuing Israel from their oppressive rule, yet he couldn't fight his desire to play around with temptation. . . .

One day Samson visited a woman of little honor in the Philistine town of Gaza. When word got out Samson was there, the city gate was surrounded in an effort to attack him. Samson, however, left earlier and surprised the Philistines by removing the city gates and carrying them off with him. Because of this, the Philistines wanted to do away with Samson even more. Knowing he had a weakness for Philistine women, they knew it would be only a matter of time before Samson could be trapped.

Delilah stroked Samson's head, asking for the third time the secret of his strength. Already Samson had lied twice about how his strength could be taken away. Knowing that Philistine soldiers waited in the next room, Delilah was determined to have success this time. "If you really love me, you'd tell me," she demanded. Unable to resist Delilah's charms and her continual asking, Samson told his secret. While he rested in her lap, Delilah cut Samson's hair —breaking his Nazirite vow. When she said, "Samson, quick! The Philistines are upon you!" he shot up and tried to break the ropes binding him but could not. He then realized what had happened. *Gotcha!* the enemy sneered with delight.

exploring deeper

Quickly turn to Judges 16:20 in your Bible. (Go on! Look it up!) Read it, then read it again. It's a sad commentary on the effects of temptation—and the results! Thankfully, this isn't the end of Samson's story. In verses 21-30 we see God's mercy and second chance for Samson. It makes for some exciting reading.

CROSS ROADS

The strongest man in the world couldn't handle the snare of temptation. (Temptation comes in many forms.) Like Samson, if we relax our standards—"playing with" temptation and falsely believing we're in control— we too will fall victim. Take this moment to reflect on your own life. What are temptations you face? Do you run from them, or do you play with them?

GETTING YOUR BEARINGS:
THE BOOK OF RUTH

After finishing Judges, Ruth is a breath of fresh air and a glimmer of hope! Interestingly, the story of Ruth takes place during the time of the judges—somewhere around the time of Gideon.

Another interesting thing to keep in mind while exploring Ruth is to understand that Ruth wasn't from the nation of Israel—yet she becomes the great-grandparent of King David! How does all this happen? (You'll just have to read on to find out!) The story of Ruth is a beautiful picture of God's love and faithfulness.

I'M WITH YOU

TAKEN FROM RUTH 1-4

GETTING READY

As you begin your time with God, start it with prayer. Thank Him for what you've seen Him do in your life and for how He's provided for you—not just the big things, but also the small things.

THE JOURNEY

Do you ever feel concerned about your future?

"Please don't try to keep me from going with you," Ruth pleaded. "Wherever you go, I have determined to go. Your people, the Israelites, will become my people; your God will become my God," she stated. Seeing Ruth would not back down, Naomi could only think of their uncertain future together.

"Is that Naomi?!" women from Bethlehem whispered to one another as Ruth and Naomi entered town. "What happened to her? And who is that with her?" they questioned.

Naomi's only response was, "I left Bethlehem full—with a husband

and two sons—but now I am returning empty handed. Therefore, no longer call me Naomi (which means "pleasant") , but call me Mara (which means "bitter"), for God has made my life very bitter."

After speaking these words, Naomi grew quiet. Memories flooded her mind of leaving Judah because of a famine in the land and moving to the land of Moab east of the Jordan River. Her husband desired to stay there only until the famine passed, but ended up dying in that foreign land—not only he, but also her two sons. Now, ten years later, she was returning—without them.

Naomi looked silently about her, noticing how full the fields were with grain and barley. She could tell it was the beginning of the barley harvest. *Such a difference from when we left,* she observed quietly. Ruth looked into the sorrowful eyes of her mother-in-law and followed her gaze out into the fields. What would the future hold? Would they be able to survive without husbands to provide for them?

"Let me go into the fields and pick up the leftover grain behind anyone who will allow me," Ruth said to Naomi. "Go ahead, my daughter," Naomi replied, watching Ruth go out the door. How thankful she was for God's Law that permitted the poor to glean in the fields after the workers. *Even if Ruth returns with little,* she told herself, *at least it will be something—and that something could mean the difference between life and death!* Little did she know what Ruth would bring back.

A "kinsman-redeemer" was a close relative (brother) who would buy or "redeem" a piece of property being sold due to poverty in order to keep it in the family. If there was a widow involved with the property, he was to marry her and raise up a son so his brother's name might live on.

"Who is that young woman?" Boaz asked his foreman as he noticed Ruth hard at work, gleaning behind the harvesters. "She's the Moabitess who came back from Moab with Naomi," the foreman replied. "She's been working steadily from morning until now except for a short rest," he added. Boaz pondered the foreman's words, then approached Ruth to speak with her. "Don't go and glean in another field and don't go away from here," he offered kindly. "Follow along after my servant girls, and whenever you become thirsty, get a drink from the water jars my men have filled."

Ruth looked up into Boaz's kind eyes. "Why are you so kind to me, a foreigner?" she asked.

"Because I've been told what you've done for your mother-in-law since the death of your husband—how you left your father and mother in your homeland and came to live with a people you didn't know," he answered. "May you be richly rewarded by the Lord, the God of Israel."

Boaz was the son of Salmon, the husband of Rahab (from Jericho). When Boaz married Ruth, they had a son named Obed who later became the grandfather of King David!

With those words, Boaz invited Ruth to eat along with his workers. He then secretly instructed his men to purposefully leave behind stalks of grain for her to pick up. By the time evening came, Ruth had more than enough grain to last several days—almost thirty pounds!

Returning home, Ruth showed Naomi all she had gathered and told her about Boaz's kindness.

"Boaz?" Naomi suddenly repeated, hardly able to believe what she heard. "Boaz is one of our close relatives! He is one of our kinsman-redeemers!" Delighted to see how God was already providing, Naomi became hopeful. Perhaps their future wasn't so dim after all.

exploring deeper

Do you want to know what happens next? Then turn to chapter 4 of Ruth and read verses 13-17. You won't want to miss it! Clearly, God was watching out for Ruth and Naomi's future—and much more.

Skill Time

Take this time to think about some of the fears you have concerning your future.

Perhaps it's a great opportunity you're afraid you'll miss, or a task you think you might fail at—especially when it counts the most. Whatever it is, take this moment right now and tell God about your fears. Allow yourself to be comforted by the fact that He says, "I am with you." God is a God who is in control—even over the little things in life.

Deuteronomy 31:8 states: "The Lord himself goes before you and will be with you; he will never leave you nor forsake you. Do not be afraid; do not be discouraged." Memorize this promise, or copy it down on something you can easily carry with you this week. Use it as a daily reminder to trust Him with your future.

GETTING YOUR BEARINGS:
THE BOOK OF 1 SAMUEL

The Book of 1 Samuel is full of exciting adventures, sharp corners, and definite contrasts! As you explore this book, you will notice three main people: Samuel (for whom the book is named), Saul, and David. Samuel was the last of the judges, and the judge who came after Samson. He was also a priest who had the privilege of anointing Israel's first king, and one of the first prophets. (No wonder he had a book named after him!) It has been thought that Samuel wrote most of this book, but the last seven chapters were finished by the prophets Nathan and Gad.

Saul was the first king over the nation of Israel. Starting out well, he finished poorly. As you read about his life, see if you can discover where he went wrong. David is introduced in this book as the king-to-be who God would use to replace Saul. Follow David's life and crawl with him into the dark corners and difficult situations he faced. Would you have made the choices he did?

Originally, 1 and 2 Samuel were written as one book, but in our Bible they are divided up into two. As you explore 1 Samuel, you'll see that little things really do matter. If you're careful, you'll pick up on at least eight things not to do as you read about the lives of the people within these pages. (There are also a few bright spots here and there which provide terrific examples to follow! See if you can find them.) Enjoy your time exploring! I'll see you at the other end of the tunnel. . .

IT'S JUST A LITTLE THING

TAKEN FROM 1 SAMUEL 1-3

GETTING READY

As you begin your time in 1 Samuel, start with prayer. Ask God to show you what He would have you to learn. Ask Him to help you be more faithful to the little things.

THE JOURNEY

Have you ever gotten tired of doing ordinary tasks, thinking no one really notices anyway?

Samuel looked about him. Day in and day out, he did the same thing: opening the Tabernacle doors each morning, cleaning the furniture and sweeping the floors. Even though they were ordinary tasks, he knew he needed to be faithful to them. Eventually he would be able to help Eli the High Priest perform some of the sacrifices, but for now this was his job. Samuel became lost in thought, remembering how his mother said she prayed for him—even before he was born. . . .

"Oh Lord," Hannah wept bitterly, whispering the words through clenched teeth and parched lips. Her heart grieved, for she loved her husband but wasn't able to bear him a child. Although Elkanah was understanding and loved Hannah nevertheless, Hannah couldn't bear it. She thought in her heart that the inability to have a child announced to everyone she was a failure—and it was a social embarrassment to her husband as well! The jeers and snide remarks of Peninnah only made matters worse. *No,* Hannah said in her heart, *I won't give in to bitterness. Instead, I will ask the Lord to grant me a son—and that son will be brought up to serve Him all the days of his life.* With that, Hannah laid her prayer out before the Lord. Eli, the High Priest, saw Hannah's lips moving, but heard no sound. Thinking she was drunk, he went to reprimand her, only to find she was pouring her heart out before the Lord!

"May the God of Israel grant you the request you ask of him!" he told her kindly.

God in His mercy did grant Hannah's request and she gave birth to a son. When he was three years old, Samuel was brought to the Tabernacle and presented to Eli. "Remember the prayer I prayed several years ago?" Hannah said softly. "God answered it and gave me a son. I am now going to keep my promise to the Lord by dedicating Samuel to His service." Eli looked down at the young lad. He remembered Hannah and would honor her vow before the Lord. From that day on, Samuel lived with Eli in order to be trained in the ways of a priest.

> Elkanah had two wives, and this only caused grief in his family. Peninnah was Elkanah's other wife.

A loud noise startled Samuel and brought his thoughts back to the present. *What's going on in there?* he wondered to himself. Finishing his task, Samuel went to investigate. He found Eli's sons, Hophni and Phinehas, threatening one of the worshipers. "Give us the portion of the sacrifice we deserve," they demanded, "or we'll take it by force!" Daily, Eli's sons showed disrespect toward the Lord and His offerings. They would demand their cut of meat before it was sacrificed to the Lord—taking the best for themselves and leaving the leftovers for God. This made a mockery of the worshiper's offering, and brought disgrace upon the office of priest. Hophni and

Phinehas had little regard for God or others. They thought what they did in their personal lives was a little thing, and little things didn't matter.

Samuel watched their actions, but didn't allow them to influence his own. He was dedicated to God's service—not just by his parents, but through his own choice. He would do his best to live for the Lord and not selfishly for himself. He determined in his heart to be faithful to whatever task God called him to do—even if it was little ordinary stuff for now. Little did he know the great plans God had for him.

"Did you call me, Eli?" Samuel asked one evening. Eli looked over at Samuel in surprise. He hadn't called Samuel's name all night, yet this was the third time Samuel had gotten out of bed and came to him! *Could it be God calling him?* Eli wondered. "Go back to bed and if the Lord calls out your name again, say, "Speak Lord, for your servant is listening," Eli instructed. Samuel did exactly as he was told.

The next morning, Eli called for Samuel, but Samuel didn't have happy news. The message the Lord had given Samuel was about Eli and his sons. God was going to send his judgment upon them, and upon Eli, for not correcting his sons' bad behavior. The job of High Priest would eventually be stripped from Eli's descendants—and as proof of this, both of Eli's sons would die on the same day. Eli's heart was saddened. He had allowed his sons to act unfaithfully in the little things, and soon they became unfaithful in the big things. All those "little things" added up to chunks of character—bad character—and that's a big thing in God's eyes.

Because God didn't give land to the Levites, He met their needs through the offerings people brought to the Tabernacle. It was a common practice to allow a priest to stick his fork into the pot of boiling meat and keep for himself whatever his fork speared. Eli's sons took advantage of this by using a Tabernacle tool that had a special meat hook.

exploring deeper

Open your Bible to 1 Samuel 3:19-20 and read it. Does this sound different from the descriptions of Eli's sons you just read about? What do you think made the difference?

THINKING on your FEET

Little things add up and shape our character. Samuel must have known that, for he remained faithful in the little "daily stuff" of life. Interestingly, what we consider a "little thing" is often a big thing to God! Eli's sons had no respect for the Lord or for their duties as priests. Being faithful in the little things is often a test to see if we will be faithful with the big things in life. (It's much easier to be faithful with the big things than the little!) God evaluates our actions—and our motives! Little actions do speak louder than words! This week, what will your actions say about you?

THIS IS NOT WORKING. . . .

TAKEN FROM 1 SAMUEL 4-7

GETTING READY

Stop and pray. Take a moment to really talk *with* God—not just talk *at* Him. God desires a relationship with you; thank Him for that and allow Him to teach you what having a relationship with Him really means.

THE JOURNEY

Do you know anyone who carries (or wears) a certain object, thinking it will bring him luck?

"The Philistines are destroying us!" the Israelite leader panicked. "Run!"

It had been a terrible day of battling for the Nation of Israel. Having been attacked by the Philistines, 4,000 Israelite men now lay on the ground, dead. "What happened?!" many of the survivors asked each other. "Why were we defeated?" "Where was the Lord?" Having fallen to the wicked practices of the nations around them, many of the Israelites didn't realize how far they had strayed from the Lord, nor why God wasn't helping them now.

"I know!" someone shouted in a moment of inspiration. "It's because we don't have the ark of the Lord with us! If we take it into battle, the ark will bring us great victory over the Philistines!" Men were quickly sent to Shiloh to get the ark from the tabernacle, while the rest of the Israelite soldiers prepared for battle again. It wasn't long before Eli's sons, Hophni and Phinehas, brought the ark to where the battle was being fought. When they entered the Israelite camp, a great cheer rang out. "We have the ark!" they shouted excitedly, gaining a sudden sense of confidence.

Mizpah was a central location that was a common place of assembly for Israel.

"What's going on? What's all the shouting about in the Hebrew camp?" the Philistine commander asked his soldiers. "A god has come into their camp!" came the fearful reply. "It's the same god who destroyed the Egyptians with plagues when the Israelites were in the wilderness!"

Looking over into the Hebrew camp and seeing the ark, the Philistine commander grew fearful and ordered his men to fight even harder than before. "If you don't," he warned them, "we'll become the Hebrews' slaves just as they've been ours!" That was all the Philistines needed to hear. The battle was on, and they fought fiercely.

"This isn't working!" some Israelite soldiers shouted in fear. "The Philistines are still too powerful for us and are slaughtering our whole army!" Others shouted, "This shouldn't be happening—we have the ark of the Covenant with us!" One by one the Israelite soldiers fell to the ground, dying, as the Philistines drove hard at them. By the time the battle was over, the Israelites had suffered an even greater loss than the day before. Thirty thousand Israelite men lay dead, and the ark of God had been captured by the Philistines and carried off. A messenger from the tribe of Benjamin ran back to Shiloh to report the terrible news. When Eli the high priest heard the ark had been captured and his two sons had died that day, he fell backward in a state of shock, broke his neck, and died. Without the ark, the Israelites felt God was no longer with them.

Meanwhile, the Philistines were greatly rejoicing over their spoils of war. To them, capturing the ark meant they had captured Israel's god, for pagan gods could easily be captured and taken into exile. In a moment of celebration, the Philistines took the ark and placed it in their temple at the feet of their god, Dagon. Thus, it would be known that Dagon was the victor and the Lord his prisoner. Little did they know!

The next day, the Philistines were surprised to see the figure of Dagon lying facedown in front of the ark! Quickly they set it back up on its pedestal. The next day, however, they found it lying facedown again. This time the statue had lost its head and hands, which lay shattered in front of the ark. The Philistines felt embarrassed for their god. They knew something was definitely wrong. They were right.

When a plague broke out against the people of the town, the Philistines sent the ark on to the next town. When a plague broke out there as well, they knew they were in trouble. "The Israelite god is angry," they cried out. "We must send him back to his people!" Taking a cart and hitching two cows to it, the ark of God was sent back to the Israelites, and a great rejoicing went up among the people. When some of the Israelites casually lifted the lid of the ark in order to see if the Law of Moses was still inside, seventy were struck down by the Lord and died. The ark was then sent to the Israelite city of Kiriath-Jearim for safekeeping, since Shiloh had been destroyed. There, Abinadab's son Eleazar was ordained as priest in Eli's place to be in charge of the ark, and there it remained for twenty years. All of Israel mourned, for it seemed the Lord had still abandoned them.

The Philistines believed the ark was a box in which the Israelites' God lived, while the Israelites treated the ark almost as a god. Both were wrong.

By now, Samuel had grown into a young man. He was not only a judge and a priest, but also a prophet. "If you're really sorry and want to experience God's hand of blessing, get rid of your idols and return to Him," Samuel challenged. The people did just that. Gathering at Mizpah to confess their sins, they had Samuel pray for them. Hearing the Israelites were in one place, the Philistines attacked, but the Lord intervened and protected them. God showed His presence among the Israelites—ark or no ark.

exploring deeper

Turn in your Bible to 1 Samuel 4:3 and read it. What does it say? Read it again. What mistake were the Israelites making?

DANGER AHEAD

Many people today use symbols of God as their "good-luck charm." They believe that by having these, they will experience God's blessing. Their religion is based on an object instead of a living relationship with God. Once this happens, they are open to false teachings and ideas of many kinds—including the "New Age" religions which promise much, but deliver nothing. Don't substitute a copy for the real thing.

THAT WAS THEN; THIS IS NOW. . . .

TAKEN FROM 1 SAMUEL 13-15

GETTING READY

Take a moment to ready your heart. If you don't feel like praying, that means you really need to! Ask God to forgive you for those things you have done that seem to push Him away, or keep Him at a distance.

THE JOURNEY

Have you ever felt closer to God in the past than you do now?

Samuel sighed as he looked into the eyes of Saul. *How different Saul seems now from when he first started out,* Samuel thought to himself. Samuel remembered first meeting Saul and installing him as king. He was a young man, full of promise, who stood head and shoulders above the rest of the Israelites. "Here is your king!" Samuel had proclaimed as a great cheer rose from the Israelites. Now they would have a king of their own—and now they would be just like the other nations!

Even though most of the Israelites were pleased with Saul, some wicked men refused to honor him as king. When Saul won his first battle, his supporters rose up and said, "Now where are those who said Saul shouldn't rule us? Bring them here so we can kill them!" But Saul humbly stopped them saying, "No one will be executed, for today the Lord was the One who rescued Israel!" Saul had rightly given credit to God. Killing those who didn't value him as king would only be a waste and a sin. God was the King, and Saul was His servant. Saul had started out well, but . . .

How things have changed, Samuel breathed to himself, seeing that Saul had grown not only in power but pride as well. Saul was not only king over Israel, but also king in his own eyes, and he had little regard for things of the Lord. One time Saul disregarded Samuel's specific instructions for dedicating the troops to God before they went to battle the Philistines. Upon seeing his men begin to lose their nerve, Saul went ahead without Samuel and sacrificed a burnt offering—a job God specifically said only a priest could do.

The Israelites gave three reasons why they wanted a king: 1) Samuel's sons (priests) were unfit to rule them. 2) A king would unify all the tribes of Israel. 3) A king would make them just like all the other nations.

"You didn't arrive when you said you would," Saul had given as his excuse. Saul's foolish disobedience to God would cost him his crown. "Your dynasty will end," Samuel charged, "for the Lord has sought out a man after His own heart." The words hit Saul like a cold slap in the face. Ever since that time, Saul did things his way, fiercely guarding himself and not letting anything stand as a threat to his being king. He even once ran his troops hard while pursuing an enemy—forbidding his soldiers to eat any food for nourishment. When his son, Jonathan, ate mistakenly (for he hadn't heard Saul's decree), Saul was ready to put his own son to death!

Samuel cleared his thoughts of Saul's past and began to speak. God had sent him to deliver a message. "I anointed you king over Israel because the Lord told me to do so," he reminded. "Now then, listen to

174

what the Lord tells you to do," he said, eyeing Saul doubtfully. "Because the Amalekites attacked the Israelites when they came up out of Egypt, you are now to accomplish God's judgment upon them. Go therefore and attack them—only be sure not to leave a single thing alive."

Saul heard God's instructions and slaughtered the Amalekites. However, instead of killing everything as God commanded, Saul took Agag, king of the Amalekites as prisoner. He also spared the lives of the best sheep, cattle, calves, and lambs—everything that seemed of value to him. He then set up a monument to himself in honor of his victory. Actually, it would be a monument to his loss.

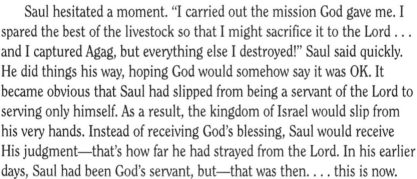

Why did God want the Amalekites destroyed? You can read about it in Exodus 17:8-16 and Deuteronomy 25:17-19. Saul's refusal to obey God's instructions was a bigger deal than Saul thought.

"Why didn't you obey the Lord?" Samuel later challenged.

"But I did!" came Saul's surprised reaction. At that moment, Samuel heard the bleating of the Amalekites' sheep.

"Then what is that noise I hear?"

Saul hesitated a moment. "I carried out the mission God gave me. I spared the best of the livestock so that I might sacrifice it to the Lord . . . and I captured Agag, but everything else I destroyed!" Saul said quickly. He did things his way, hoping God would somehow say it was OK. It became obvious that Saul had slipped from being a servant of the Lord to serving only himself. As a result, the kingdom of Israel would slip from his very hands. Instead of receiving God's blessing, Saul would receive His judgment—that's how far he had strayed from the Lord. In his earlier days, Saul had been God's servant, but—that was then. . . . this is now.

exploring deeper

Open your Bible to 1 Samuel 15 and read verses 22-23. What does Samuel say to Saul? In Saul's perspective, he was doing something for God that he thought was a good thing (even though he disobeyed God by doing it). How does God view this? (See the last part of verse 22.)

Skill Time

Little by little, Saul slipped away from his relationship with God. Each act of disobedience took him a step further away from the Lord. It wasn't long before Saul began operating on "automatic pilot" and leaving God completely out of the "cockpit" of his life! Saul started well, but he didn't end that way.

Take this brief moment to think about your life. Where are you now in your walk with the Lord? If you feel further away from God, then something you have done has created a barrier between you and God. Talk to Him about it right now, and don't think that just because you've messed up you've ruined everything. If you confess your sin, it's in the past. Don't dwell on it, but rather learn from it. In the New Testament (1 John 1:9) we are told that if we confess our sins, God is faithful and just to forgive our sins and cleanse us from all unrighteousness. This is only made possible because of what Jesus provided for you. If you would like to know more about this, then turn to the back of this book. There's a special message just for you.

PAY NO ATTENTION TO HIM

TAKEN FROM 1 SAMUEL 16-17

GETTING READY

Stop and pray. Commit this time to the Lord, allowing God to speak to your heart. Tell Him your desire to become all He wants you to be—even if that might mean stepping out of your comfort zone.

THE JOURNEY

Do you sometimes rate other people's worth based on the way they look?

"No."
"Hmmmm. OK, then what about that one?"
"He won't do either."
"Alright then, how about him?"
"Nope."
"How's this one?"
"Sorry."

"This is the last one—surely . . ."

Samuel didn't know what to think. God sent him to the household of Jesse to anoint one of Jesse's sons as the future king over Israel. Upon arriving, Samuel saw the oldest son, named Eliab, who was tall and handsome in appearance. *His name even means "God is Father"* Samuel smiled to himself. *Surely he is to be the next king!* Samuel was surprised Eliab was not the man of God's choosing.

Goliath was over 9 feet tall (most common ceilings are 10 feet tall). He carried armor that weighed 125 pounds, and the iron point on his spear weighed about 15 pounds! He was a trained warrior—and a large one!

One by one, seven of Jesse's eight sons were brought out before Samuel. One by one, God rejected them. *Each of these men would make a fine leader*, Samuel thought to himself. *They are handsome, tall, strong—some even standing head and shoulders above the rest! Surely God's chosen king to replace Saul has to be one of these!* Samuel grew quiet in thought as he looked upon the hopeful young men, then into the surprised eyes of Jesse. "Are you sure I've seen all of your sons? You don't have any others?" Samuel asked.

Jesse shifted his weight uncomfortably, almost embarrassed by the question. "I do have one more son, but he's a young lad and out tending my sheep . . . ," Jesse's voice trailed off.

"Could you please send for him?" Samuel requested, wondering what God was up to. It didn't take long for David to appear in front of Samuel.

"Rise and anoint him," the Lord spoke to Samuel. "He is the one who shall be king in place of Saul."

Samuel looked at David's size, but did as he was told. He questioned in his heart why God chose to select David above the others. "I am not looking for the same qualities you are," God answered Samuel. "Man looks at the outward appearance, but I look at the heart." So, in front of his father and brothers, David was recognized as Israel's next king.

During this time, Saul began experiencing difficulties. No longer did he experience God's presence with him. Instead, Saul felt tormented and troubled in his spirit, unable to find relief. His attendants noticed this and convinced Saul that perhaps some soothing music would help ease his mind and emotions. "We know of just the musician!" they suggested. "It's one of Jesse's sons who not only knows how to play the harp, but also is a brave man and a warrior as well! He is a fine-looking man, and the Lord is with him!" Saul grunted and waved his attendants off to fetch the one they were talking about. Cautiously, David entered the king's presence, took out his harp, and began playing. Comforted, Saul asked if David could remain in his service. Little did Saul know that one day David would be his rival for the throne! David, the promising "king to be" was serving Saul, the "king who should have been."

One day, David's father sent him to the battle lines to bring back word on how his brothers were doing. Like other valiant soldiers, they had joined Saul's troops to help fight the Philistines. When David arrived at their camp, he was surprised at what he saw. Silently and fearfully, the Israelite soldiers were standing on their side of the battle line—unable to answer the challenge of the huge Philistine soldier who dared someone to fight him. David knew it was a common practice to select one champion soldier to fight the enemy's champion soldier. The results of that fight would then determine which side won the battle. Since it was thought that the soldiers' gods controlled the outcome, David grew especially concerned. God's honor was at stake.

"Who is this man who stands against the Lord's army?" David asked the Israelite soldiers. "Why doesn't someone fight him? Pay no attention to him or his size, God will give the victory!" Many looked away in fear— even Saul had lost his confidence. Goliath looked like a strong and successful warrior. Seeing this, David himself went out to fight Goliath. "This is so the whole world may know there is a God in Israel!" he said. With God's help, David miraculously struck down Goliath with a stone from his sling, then killed him. David had known there were certain things in life you just don't pay attention to.

exploring deeper

Open your Bible and look up 1 Samuel 16:7—especially the last half of that verse. (Go on—look it up!) This is a classic verse that goes against the way we think. What does it say?

It's interesting to note that David was chosen in spite of his size (God did the choosing), and Goliath was feared on account of his size (man did the evaluating).

Skill Time

Too often we evaluate people's worth based on their appearance. How they look, dress, and who they hang around influences what we think of them. Even though we are easily fooled, God isn't. We look at the outward stuff, but God looks at the heart. What do you pay attention to most? On the line below write down the name of one person you know you could reach out to (one you wouldn't normally befriend because of the way he or she looks). Pray for that person this week, then step out and get to know him or her.

_____

(person's name)

THINK NOTHING OF IT

TAKEN FROM 1 SAMUEL 18-19

GETTING READY

As you begin your time with the Lord today, take a few moments to stop and pray. Recognize that all you need is found in Him alone.

THE JOURNEY

Do you sometimes struggle when others get special recognition?

David had slain Goliath, and everyone was celebrating! Because of his brave deed, David was made a commander in Saul's army to the delight of the Israelite soldiers and officers. They knew David had acted bravely and spared them a great embarrassment. Even the bravest of the Israelite soldiers had melted in fear, and the Israelites were held hopelessly captive by one huge Philistine warrior—that is, until David came along. David recognized Goliath's taunting to be against the Lord God Almighty, and knew he must be silenced. With his sling in hand

and his faith in the Lord, David put a quick end to Goliath's boasts, and turned everyone's eyes back to God's greatness. David's bravery brought the praise of many, and won him a spot of favor in Saul's eyes—but that favor would soon fade.

"Saul has killed thousands!" the people sang and danced for joy. "But David has killed his ten thousands!" The street was filled with dancing and singing. Over and over Saul heard this message, and it began to sound like a broken record. Each time he heard it, he became a bit more angry.

"What is this?!" Saul finally said in disgust. "The people credit David with ten thousands and me with only thousands? I suppose next they'll want him to be king!" From that point on, Saul would keep a close eye on David.

The next day, an evil spirit from God came upon Saul, and David began to play the harp as he had been doing to calm Saul down. Taking a spear in his hand, however, Saul suddenly hurled it at David with the intent of pinning David to the wall! Jumping aside, David managed to escape—not just once, but twice! Saul was afraid of David and jealous because the Lord was with David and no longer with him. As a result, he banned David from his presence and stripped him of being commander of such a large army. Now David would be in charge of only a thousand men. Much to Saul's dismay, David faithfully led his troops into battle and succeeded in everything he did. This made Saul panic all the more.

I've got to think of a way to get rid of David! Saul plotted to himself. *Ah! I'll offer him my oldest daughter, Merab, for a wife, but first require him to prove himself a real warrior by fighting the Lord's battles!* Saul secretly hoped David would be killed in battle. His plan seemed

"Evil spirit from God"?! How could God, who is not evil, send an evil spirit? In the book of Job, we learn that Satan must first ask God's permission before harming anyone who belongs to Him. This is also in the New Testament. In Luke 22:31-32 Jesus tells Peter that Satan has asked permission to sift Peter like wheat, then He adds: "But I have prayed for you . . . that your faith may not fail."

perfect. When David humbly declined the opportunity to marry Saul's daughter, stating he wasn't worthy of the honor of being called the king's son-in-law, Saul's plans were destroyed. It wasn't until his younger daughter, Michal, fell in love with David that Saul tried again.

"The king really likes you, and so do we," Saul's men falsely told David. "Why don't you accept the king's offer and become his son-in-law?" they urged. "I can't, for I am poor and come from a humble family," David replied. "How could I afford the bride-price?" When this word got back to Saul, he instructed his men to tell David that all he desired for a bride-price was revenge on 200 Philistines. Saul once again planned for David to be killed by the Philistines and was greatly surprised when David brought back the evidence that he had killed 200 Philistines as required. Reluctantly, Michal was given to David as his wife.

"David," Michal whispered in a panicked voice, "I heard my father is planning to send his men to kill you in the morning! You must escape tonight, or you will be dead in the morning!" Hearing these words, David thanked his wife as she helped him climb out of the window and escape into the night. The next morning, Saul's men came to capture David, but Michal lied and said her husband was sick in bed. When the men left and reported this to Saul, he became very angry.

"Then bring him to me in his bed!" he shouted, sending his men back to Michal. The men returned and demanded to see David. When they went into the back room, they saw him lying in the bed—or so they thought. Michal had placed an idol in the bed, placing goat's hair on top to trick them. She was thankful David had escaped safely.

Night and day Saul was consumed with fear and jealousy toward David. Because David's name had become famous in the land, Saul determined in his heart to spend the rest of his life hunting David down. Jealousy had so taken over Saul, he could think of nothing else.

exploring deeper

Open your Bible and take a quick look at 1 Samuel 18, verse 28. According to this verse, what two things did Saul realize? Now look at verse 29. What was Saul's response? (Note his feelings, which led to his actions.) It's a sad commentary on jealousy and fear.

DANGER AHEAD

Jealousy is a silent killer—often taking victims before they realize they are under its control. The first step of jealousy is comparison of ourselves to others. Through this comparison, we either feel better about ourselves (which leads to pride), or worse (which leads to jealousy that someone else has it better than we do). Both are deadly and lead to self-destruction. Don't imitate Saul's actions. When someone else is praised, rejoice with him, then think nothing more of it.

IT'S MY DUTY

TAKEN FROM 1 SAMUEL 20

GETTING READY

Don't read on until you've taken time to pray first! Commit today's lesson into God's hands, then ask Him to use it in your life.

THE JOURNEY

Have you ever been hurt by a friend who turned against you?

Jonathan couldn't help but think of his friendship with David. Ever since David had been invited to live with them in the palace, Jonathan and David had been friends—and it wasn't long until they had grown closer than brothers.

"Here's my robe, David," Jonathan said, "as a token of my commitment to be your friend at all costs, I want you to have this. I also give you my tunic, sword, bow, and belt." David looked into the eyes of Jonathan and stood speechless. The two of them had a kinship that went beyond words. At the moment, David couldn't think of anything that could express his deep gratitude for their friendship. They had made an agreement to be friends for life—a covenant between them—and it was a covenant David would be sure to honor as long as he lived.

"Jonathan," David said, looking over his shoulder to make sure no one had spotted him, "Why is your father trying to kill me? What offense have I done to deserve this?" Jonathan remained silent for a moment, shocked at the words he heard.

When David became king, he kept a promise he made to Jonathan—almost twenty years earlier! You can read all about it in 2 Samuel 9.

"It's not true, David," he replied, trying to recall anything his father might have said or done to make David feel this way. "You aren't going to die, for my father doesn't do anything without confiding in me. Why would he hide this from me?" Jonathan met the concerned gaze in David's eyes, and they both stood silently together, searching for answers.

"As surely as I stand here today, I know I am only one step away from death," David said quietly. He glanced over his shoulder again, aware of the fact he was being hunted. Already Saul had sent his men to David's house to kill him, but David had escaped. Fleeing to Samuel in Ramah, David was soon hunted down there as well. Through God's help, David had escaped and come back to speak with Jonathan. "Your father knows very well we're best friends, and perhaps he is trying to keep you from being hurt by not telling you of his plans to have me killed," David suggested. Jonathan felt sick in his heart. He knew David was perhaps correct, but he also knew he needed to be sure. If his father were trying to kill David, Jonathan would do all he could to help David escape. But, if his father had no such intentions, David's running would be pointless and unnecessary.

David interrupted the silence with an idea. "Tomorrow is a festival and I am supposed to dine with your father, the king. Instead of going, I'll hide in the field. If your father misses me, tell him I begged your permission to hurry to Bethlehem because a sacrifice was to be made for my whole clan." Jonathan nodded, following David's plan. "If your father says, 'Very well,' and seems unconcerned, then all is well. But if he loses his temper, you can be sure he is determined to harm me." Jonathan saw the wisdom in David's plan. "But how will I know," David suddenly asked, "if your father answers you harshly?" This time Jonathan had an idea.

"The day after tomorrow, go to the place where you hid when this trouble began and wait by the large stone there. Toward evening I'll come and shoot three arrows to the side of the stone as if I were shooting at a target. Then, I will send a boy to fetch them for me. As he is running to get them, I will shout directions to him which will really be my secret message to you. If you hear me say, 'Run farther, for it is beyond you', you will know you need to run for your life. If you hear me shout, 'The arrows are on this side, bring them here,' you will know all is safe, and that your life is not in danger." David agreed, and he and Jonathan sealed their commitment to each other with a pledge. "May the Lord be with you, David, as He had once had been with my father. May He cut off your enemies from before you—but please remember me and treat my descendants kindly," Jonathan requested. David promised he would. He would consider it his duty as a friend.

"What?!" Saul hissed when he heard the answer to why David was missing from the feast. "You are a worthless son! As long as David lives on this earth, neither you nor your kingdom will be established," Saul raged. "Now send for David and bring him to me, for he must die!" Saul demanded. Jonathan looked at his father in horror. He had gotten his answer, and he knew he had a duty to perform.

The next day, Jonathan went out to the field. One, two, . . . three arrows went into the sky toward the large rock in the field. "Run! Run farther, for it is beyond you!" Jonathan shouted. *Please, David, run for your life and never forget our friendship. May God be with you as our next king,* he whispered to himself.

exploring deeper

This is not the last we hear of Jonathan helping David! Turn over to 1 Samuel 23 and read verses 15-16. Saul had been pursuing David and giving him no rest, yet Jonathan appears! What does he do for David (verse 16)? Is this something you would do?

Skill Time

Too often, we think having a friend is having someone to hang around with or talk to. Jonathan and David show us that true friendship means. It's making a commitment to respect, serve, and help the other person. True friendship doesn't look for what it can gain; it looks for what it can give to another. Evaluate your friendships. Are they just "surface acquaintances," or are they a commitment? It's OK to be friendly with as many people as you can, but don't confuse that with true friendship. Being a true friend is a rare skill. What type of friend are you? Could you be called a Jonathan? Use the acrostic below to test yourself!

A true FRIEND:

F- Forgets about trying to meet his own needs.
R- Relies on God's love, not his own.
I - Isn't one to give conditions, saying, "If you do this, then..."
E- Encourages you to grow in the Lord.
N- Never gives up on you—and stays committed, even when you don't deserve it.
D- Doesn't mind being a servant.

YOU'LL GET WHAT YOU DESERVE!

TAKEN FROM 1 SAMUEL 21-24

GETTING READY

Begin your journey today with prayer and use this time to allow God to speak to your heart through His Word. His ways are just, and His timing is perfect. Ask Him to help you learn to trust Him all the more with the circumstances in your life.

THE JOURNEY

Do you have a hard time respecting those in authority—especially when you don't think they deserve it?

"Why are you alone? Why isn't anyone else with you?" Ahimelech the priest asked David fearfully.

"The king sent me on a special mission," David lied, "and told me not to tell anyone why I'm here. I've told my men where they can meet me later." David looked around; he had gone with no food and was extremely hungry. "Do you have five loaves of bread you could spare me?" he asked Ahimelech.

"All I have is the holy bread of presence that has just been replaced with fresh bread," came the answer. "Although it is normally only to be eaten by the priests, you are welcome to it—as long as you or your men aren't ceremonially unclean," Ahimelech added with caution. David eagerly took the bread, assuring the priest they weren't.

After the ark was captured (and returned) by the Philistines, the tabernacle was placed at Nob. Nob means "city of the priests."

"Do you also have a sword or spear?" David asked. "The king's business was so urgent, I didn't even have time to grab my weapon!"

"The only sword here is the one you took from Goliath the day you killed him," Ahimelech said. "You are welcome to it—it's all I have."

"There is none like it! Give it to me!" David said enthusiastically. As Ahimelech went to get the sword, David noticed one of Saul's servants there. Their eyes met briefly, and David recognized the man to be Doeg, Saul's head shepherd. David quickly gathered his supplies and left, trying to put as much distance as he could between Saul's servant and himself.

Saul will never think to look for me among the hated Philistines! David thought to himself. He knew he would be safe from Saul in the city of Gath—the city Goliath had come from. David's plan worked—but only for a brief time.

"Hey! Isn't that David, the king of the land?" one of the Philistines said, pointing his finger at David. Knowing he had been discovered, David began drooling and scratching at the doors, pretending to be insane. "Let him alone! He's harmless!" came the response.

Knowing he couldn't stay in Gath, David left to live in a cave. There his brothers and some relatives came to join him. Soon others began coming who had debts they couldn't pay, or who were simply discontent with Saul as king. It wasn't long before David found himself leader of nearly 400 men! These men would eventually become his mightiest warriors.

"Doesn't anyone care about me?" Saul whined as he rested under a tree with his men. He was informed that David was back in the area and this didn't please him one bit. "Has David promised you things I haven't? Has he promised to make you commanders in his army or promised to give you fields or vineyards?!" Saul demanded. "Is that why you have all conspired against me? Whose side are you on, anyway?!" Saul's servants became quiet.

Doeg, Saul's head shepherd, cleared his throat and began to speak. "I saw David not long ago in Nob. Ahimelech the priest gave him food—and even a sword!" Saul's anger boiled. *So,* he thought to himself, *even the priests are working against me! We'll just see about that!* In a fit of anger, Saul ordered all the priests to be killed, and eighty-five lost their lives that day. Only Abiathar, one of Ahimelech's sons, was able to escape alive and went to David to report the tragic loss.

Saul continued to pursue David. Day after day he hunted him, and day after day David ran. Saul became so consumed he only let up once when an emergency called him away. Upon returning, he found out where David and his men were staying and went straight there. *I'll get you yet, David!* Saul sneered. Needing to relieve himself, Saul went into a cave, which happened to be the cave David and his men were hiding in!

> **David ran from Saul for about ten years, learning many lessons in the process and pouring his heart out to God. David wrote Psalm 52 after learning that Doeg turned in the high priest for helping him. He wrote Psalm 57 when he was living in the cave, hiding from Saul.**

"Now's your chance!" David's men whispered. "God has delivered Saul into your hands this very day!" Listening to his men's words, David slowly lifted his sword. With a quick flip of his wrist, he silently cut off a corner of Saul's robe. "You should have killed him and given him what he deserves!" David's men challenged once Saul had left the cave.

"He is the Lord's anointed—the one God selected to be leader at this time," David replied. "I cannot kill the king—and I did give him what he deserves: respect." Taking the piece of robe, David ran outside and held it high in his hand. "My lord, the king!" David called after him, bowing low. At the sound of David's voice, Saul turned around.

"David?!" Before Saul could think twice, David held up the corner of Saul's robe for him to see. It was then Saul realized—not how close he had been to finally killing David—but how close David had been to killing him, yet didn't.

exploring deeper

Find 1 Samuel 24:17 in your Bible and read it. What does it say? Do you think David's actions made an impression on anyone? Who? Is that all?

Skill Time

Showing honor to a leader who doesn't deserve it takes real character. It is far too easy to make jokes about that person or help spread dishonor about him. Even when it seems that the "opportunity is right" for attacking him, God calls us to a higher level. Take a moment now to think about those in leadership over you—parents, teachers, city officials, congressmen—even the president. How is your heart attitude toward them? Pray for them right now, and ask God to help them in their positions of responsibility.

LET ME AT 'EM!

TAKEN FROM 1 SAMUEL 25-26

GETTING READY

As you come to the end of 1 Samuel, come with an open heart to continue to learn from God's Word. Ask Him to help you apply what He shows you, that you might make wise choices in your life.

THE JOURNEY

Have you ever wanted to get revenge?

Nabal smiled to himself as he considered all his wealth and the festive atmosphere surrounding him. It was sheep-shearing time and a time of celebration! There would be plenty of food for all, and meat would be provided for those busy at the task of shearing his many sheep. This particular season had been good, and not many of his sheep or goats had died or been stolen. *Perhaps it's because my shepherds have finally learned to keep better watch over them,* Nabal reasoned in his heart. Whatever the case, this sheep-shearing time was the best it had ever been.

As Nabal watched the shearers go about their duty, he saw ten men approaching who had come from the desert on the outskirts of Carmel. "Greetings from David, the son of Jesse! May you, your household, and all you own enjoy continued good health!" they said respectfully. "We heard you were shearing your sheep and goats and that this is a festive time for you. Please, do you have anything you could spare to give us? When your shepherds were out in the desert watching your livestock, we didn't harm them. In fact, we protected them so that none of your sheep or goats was stolen or killed. Ask your servants themselves, and they'll tell you the same!" Nabal looked up skeptically. He eyed the ten men standing before him, then chose to ignore their request.

Nabal was a wealthy man who owned 1,000 goats and 3,000 sheep! Jewish custom required sharing of food with travelers, regardless of how many there were— something Nabal could have easily done! His refusal to do so was a huge insult.

"Who is this David? Who is this son of Jesse?" he said in a mocking tone of voice. "Many servants are breaking away from their masters these days. . . ." Nabal let his voice trail off so David's men would feel the sting of his words. Nabal enjoyed the feeling of denying people something they wanted. He was a man of means and a man of power. "Why should I take my bread and water and the meat I've provided for my workers and give it to men coming from . . . who knows *where!*" Nabal added for emphasis. Having said all he pleased, Nabal simply returned to his work and left David's men full of insults, yet empty handed.

"Abigail!" one of Nabal's servants said in a concerned voice. "David sent ten of his men to request supplies from your husband, Nabal, but I heard Nabal refuse them! These men have taken good care of us while we were in the desert with Nabal's sheep. I'm afraid . . ." Abigail heard the servant's words and knew she must go into immediate action. Her husband not only foolishly broke the custom of providing for travelers, but also insulted men who had shown only kindness to him! Without telling her husband, Abigail loaded up 200 loaves of bread, wine, meat, grain, raisins, and figs and had the servant lead her to David. Abigail hoped it wasn't too late. . . .

194

When the men came back empty handed, David was surprised. "Nabal did what?!" David responded angrily upon hearing about Nabal's refusal and his insults. "It's been useless! All my watching over his property in the desert has been taken advantage of! After all the good I've done for him, he pays me back with evil?! Just who does Nabal think he is?! Let me at him!" David threatened, picking up his sword. "We'll pay Nabal another visit. By morning, not even one male who belongs to him will be left alive!"

Abigail looked up and panicked at the sight of David and his men coming in her direction. Her greatest fears were confirmed. Nabal had acted foolishly and brought harm upon them. She hoped her gifts would smooth over the matter. Dismounting from her donkey, Abigail bowed before David and spoke humbly and sincerely.

"Please, pay no attention to my husband's words, for he is a foolish man. Just as his name, *Nabal*, means 'foolish,' he often acts in folly. As for me, I didn't see the men you sent," she said. "Please don't plan on taking revenge." David listened to Abigail's words and heard the truth of what she was saying. Even when he had the opportunity to take revenge on Saul and kill him, he didn't. Needless bloodshed would only be a blot on David's conscience. Abigail went on, "These provisions I have are for you and your men. Please accept them and turn from your anger," she requested. David agreed and returned home. Seeking revenge would not be worth it.

That night, Abigail went to tell Nabal what she had done, but he had been celebrating too hard and was drunk. Waiting for the next day, Abigail told him of David's intent to kill him for the cruel insults he had cast. Hearing this, and being shocked at the thought of losing all he had, Nabal had a heart attack. A few days later, he died. When David heard this, he knew God had honored his decision not to take revenge into his own hands. God had taken care of the matter Himself.

Quickly turn to 1 Samuel 25:39 and read it—go on! What three things does David recognize God did for him when he chose not to take his own revenge?

Revenge is something that promises much but delivers very little. As a matter of fact, it even "steals" from the person getting revenge! It steals part of his or her character, robs peace of mind, and takes away the opportunity to see God working. God says, "Vengeance is Mine!" He can do a far better job than we can! The next time someone insults you, will you take your own revenge, or turn the situation over to God?

GETTING YOUR BEARINGS:
THE BOOK OF 2 SAMUEL

Second Samuel mainly focuses on David's life as a king—the good, the bad, and the ugly! Within its pages you will explore the tragic results of hiding behind lies and the blessings of following through on your word. You will encounter great victory and also see defeat. Even though David was considered a godly man, he wasn't perfect—as you will soon see!

Take your time exploring this book. Spend time looking around, observing the obvious—and the not so obvious! When you finish, you will understand more deeply why God called David a man after His own heart. Enjoy the journey.

YOU, YOU'RE THE ONE!

TAKEN FROM 2 SAMUEL 5-7

GETTING READY

As you prepare your heart, spend a few moments in prayer. Tell God how much you love Him; thank Him for what He has done and what He promises to do for you. Thank Him for who He is.

THE JOURNEY

Are you tempted to take credit for your successes?

David glanced around him. With one sweeping look, his heart flooded with thankfulness. How different this was from the years spent in the wilderness, hiding in caves to escape being hunted by Saul! No longer would David live as an outlaw—now he was king, something he had waited patiently for ever since he had been anointed by Samuel as a youth almost twenty years ago! God fulfilled His promise, and now, at the age of thirty-seven, David would fulfill his. He would be a man after God's own heart and would remember God is the true King.

Already David had experienced great success and admiration from the people. His first mission was to capture the city of Jerusalem from the Jebusites and make it the capital for all of Israel. Then, he sent for the ark and had it brought to Jerusalem, once again establishing a place of national worship. David made wise choices and grew in power. It was clear to all that God was with David. Even a king from the distant land of Tyre sent messengers with cedar logs, carpenters, and stonemasons to build a palace for David! This was the palace David now sat in; he was overwhelmed at God's goodness.

"Nathan," David finally spoke, glancing over at the prophet, "here I am, living in this palace of cedar, but the ark of God remains in a tent!" Nathan looked at the beauty of the palace and then over at David. "Go ahead and do whatever you have in mind to do, for the Lord is with you," he replied. That night, however, God spoke to Nathan. "Go and tell David, 'This is what the Lord says: Are you the one to build a house of cedar for Me? All these years I have moved with the Israelites from place to place with just a tent as My covering. Remember, David, how I brought you from the pastures to be ruler over My people Israel. I've been with you wherever you have gone and have cut off all your enemies from before you.'" Nathan listened carefully as the Lord described how He would establish the Israelites and plant them, so they might live without wicked nations oppressing them. "When your days are over, David, I will raise up your son to succeed you, and he will be the one to build a house for My name. I will be like a Father to him, and he will be like a son to Me. When he does wrong, I will discipline him, but My love will never be taken away from him as I took it away from Saul. Your throne, David, will be established forever, for you are a man after My own heart."

The next morning, Nathan reported to David all that God had spoken to him, and upon hearing this, David went in and sat before the Lord. "Who am I, O Sovereign Lord, that You have brought me this far?" David

Jebusites were warriors who lived in the hill country in the land of Canaan. The city of Jerusalem was their fortress built on an uneven, rocky plateau. It was strategically located where three different valleys came together.

whispered from the depths of his heart. He knew his successes didn't come from his own hand but rather from God. "And if all this weren't enough, You've even spoken about favor upon my offspring! What more can I say to You?" David spoke in awe. "How great You are, God. There is no one like You." David paused a moment in quiet gratitude. "Out of all the nations on the earth, You chose the Israelites to be Your people—that through us the whole world might know You are the one true God. You are the One who has performed the great and awesome wonders of driving out nations before us. It is You who delivered us from troubles and brought us to this point. You are the One, Lord. . . ."

This is the first time the prophet Nathan is mentioned—but not his last! It's interesting to note that God had a prophet living during the reign of each of the kings of Israel.

David's voice trailed off as he recognized all that God had done for him personally, and all that God promised yet to do. Just as God had been with the nation, so He would be with David. To David, there would be no confusing just who was King.

exploring deeper

Although David wanted to be the one to build a Temple for the Lord, God said no. Turn ahead in your Bible and look up 1 Chronicles 28:3 (after 2 Samuel comes 1 and 2 Kings, then 1 and 2 Chronicles). Why wasn't David allowed to build the Temple? (It *wasn't* because he had disobeyed God or turned from Him, and it *wasn't* because he was being punished, either!)

Skill Time

David recognized that his success had everything to do with God fulfilling His plan in and through David's life. God was the One who deserved the credit, and David made sure in his heart to always remember that fact. God was the One who would be King. Take a moment and think about your own life. How often do you recognize God as King? When you have a plan and God says no to it, do you accept that? When others praise you for a success you've had, do you offer that praise up to God as a gift? This week, ponder these questions and see how well you put them into practice.

PAID IN FULL

TAKEN FROM 2 SAMUEL 8-9

GETTING READY

Begin your time today with prayer. Tell God about your struggles when it comes to keeping your word and ask Him to help you in this area. Then, take a moment to praise Him, for He is a faithful God you can count on. He always keeps His word.

THE JOURNEY

Do you have a hard time following through on your promises?

Mephibosheth (me-FIB o-sheth) froze in fear. Messengers from the king stood at his front door, wanting to take him with them. *What have I done wrong? Why have they come after me to take me away?* Mephibosheth panicked. His thoughts began to race, and his heart pounded wildly in his chest. *Why can't they just leave me alone?*

Over and over, Mephibosheth relived that terrible day in his memory—the day word came from Jezreel that both his grandfather and father had been killed in battle. "King Saul and his son Jonathan are dead!" came the shocking news. What would happen next? Who would take the throne? Would the new king kill off the remainder of Saul's descendants in order to guarantee loyalty to himself? Fearing the answers to these questions, Mephibosheth's nurse picked him up and fled. Unfortunately, she stumbled, and Mephibosheth was thrown from her shoulders and became crippled in both feet. He was only five years old at the time. Now grown, Mephibosheth had a young son of his own named Mica. *What will happen to me?* he wondered. *Hasn't there been enough hate between my grandfather and David?* Mephibosheth had no idea of King David's real intentions.

Mephibo-who? Believe it or not, there were two Mephibosheths! One was Saul's son by a concubine. The other was Jonathan's son. Second Samuel 21:7-9 lists them both, and tells what happened to them!

"Is there anyone still left of Saul's household?" David asked one day. "I made a promise to my friend Jonathan when we were younger, saying I would show kindness to his family. I plan to keep that vow, but I don't know if anyone remains alive!" David's servants heard his request and knew that a man named Ziba served as a servant under Saul. They summoned Ziba and brought him before King David. "Is there no one left in Saul's household to whom I can show God's kindness?" David asked. Ziba answered, telling about Jonathan's son who had been crippled. "He lives in Lo Debar, in the household of a man named Makir," Ziba informed. David was delighted to hear such news and sent his messengers to get Mephibosheth.

"Mephibosheth!" David half-said and half-whispered with emotion. Mephibosheth couldn't see David's face, for he had bowed down to pay David honor. "I am your servant—," Mephibosheth said, trying to choke back the rising sense of anxiety in his heart. His words already sounded weak, and he wished he could just disappear. Standing before the king was a terrifying experience. Mephibosheth swallowed hard, then slowly raised his eyes to meet the gaze of David. Their eyes locked for a moment. *Oh, that this day had never come!* Mephibosheth thought. *I am having to pay the punishment for being born in the household of Saul!*

"Don't be afraid," David said gently, noticing Mephibosheth's trembling, "for I plan to show you kindness. This is something I promised your father, Jonathan, that I would do for all his descendants—for he was my friend. . . ." Mephibosheth looked up uncertainly. David continued, "I will restore to you all the land that once belonged to your grandfather, Saul, and you may live with me here at the palace."

Upon hearing those words, Mephibosheth's heart grew light and full of gratitude. *Instead of harm, I am being shown favor?!* he wondered in amazement. *After all these years, he has hunted me down—not to harm me, but in order to fulfill a vow he made to my father—A vow no one would have known if he fulfilled or not?!* Mephibosheth knew that years ago his father had seen this loyalty in David and chosen him as a friend.

Saul's former servant, Ziba, was summoned to come before David. "I have given Mephibosheth everything that belonged to your master and his family. You and your sons and servants are to farm the land and bring in the crops so that Mephibosheth may be provided for," David said. "Mephibosheth will always eat at my table," he then added.

Ziba heard David's words and bowed before him. "I will do whatever you command me to," he said willingly. David's heart was pleased, for he could now consider his debt to Jonathan finally paid in full. . . .

exploring deeper

Keeping a vow is important. Turn to 2 Samuel 21:1 and read it. What happened here? Long before, a covenant had been made by Joshua with the Gibeonites (Joshua 9) that they would never be destroyed by the Israelites. When Saul was king, he didn't keep that vow. How different Saul was from David! Skip down and read verses 2 Samuel 21:3-7. Even though punishment had to occur, David kept his vow to Jonathan (verse 7). What does this tell you of David's character?

DANGER AHEAD

It is very easy to make a promise or vow and not fulfill it. Sometimes we falsely believe that if a great deal of time passes since we first made our promise, it automatically "erases" our commitment! "Out of sight, out of mind!" we say in our hearts. This is a very dangerous and deadly action that quickly grows to be a lifelong habit. Don't let it. Take your cue from David, and fulfill your commitments. The blessing for doing so is unbelievable—for both you and others.

THIS ISN'T LOOKIN' SO GOOD

TAKEN FROM 2 SAMUEL 11-12

GETTING READY

Use this as an opportunity to be honest with God. Ask His forgiveness for the times you "mess up" in your relationship with Him or with others. Take a moment to thank God for His mercy and forgiveness that He extends to you.

THE JOURNEY

Have you ever hidden behind a lie before?

David stretched as he got up from his bed. Normally he would be out leading Joab and the army into battle, but he had decided against going this time. While the Israelites were off to destroy the Ammonites in Rabbah, David remained at home. It was a quiet, uneventful day. Feeling restless and unable to continue with his nap, David decided to take a stroll out onto the roof. It didn't take long for his eyes to find something of interest. There, on the rooftop of a nearby home, was a beautiful woman taking a bath. David glanced at her, then looked away. Then he looked back again. . . .

I must find out who this woman is, for she is very pleasing to look at, David thought to himself. Upon discovering she was Bathsheba, the wife of Uriah, David was pleased. *This is looking really good,* he thought to himself. Uriah was off fighting the Ammonites with most of the other men. Being king, David knew he could command a person to come into his presence, and no one would think twice about it. *I'll send for Bathsheba, that I might enjoy her beauty for myself,* David schemed in his heart. He then did just that—without thinking of the consequences.

Later, David received a message from Bathsheba with alarming news. She was expecting a baby, and everything pointed to David as the father! David knew he needed to do something about the situation—and fast! "Send me Uriah the Hittite," he wrote on a message addressed to Joab, the commander of his army. It wasn't long before Uriah was removed from the battleground and brought to stand before David. *After Uriah gives me his report,* David schemed, *I'll send him home to be with his wife for the evening. Then, Uriah will believe (as will everyone else) that he is the father of Bathsheba's baby!* David felt pleased with his plan. *This is lookin' good!* he thought to himself, relieved that matters could be taken care of so quickly and painlessly.

Unfortunately, David hadn't counted on Uriah being such a man of honor. Instead of sleeping at home in the comfort of his bed with his beautiful wife, Uriah stayed that night at the palace entrance with some of the king's other servants. When David heard this, he was angered. "What's the matter with you? Why didn't you go home to your wife?" David asked, trying to hide his panic.

"How could I go home to the luxury and beauty of my wife when my comrades are sleeping in tents and camping in the open fields?! I will never be guilty of doing such a thing!" Uriah stated.

"Very well," David replied, "stay here tonight, and tomorrow you may

Why did Bathsheba's baby have to die? In Old Testament times, the birth of a son was recognized as a sign of God's approval and blessing. God could not allow this. David was forgiven, and later Bathsheba gave birth to another son—Solomon.

return to the army." *Perhaps if I invite Uriah to dinner and get him drunk—then he will go home to be with Bathsheba,* David plotted in his heart. In spite of this, Uriah showed his dedication and slept at the palace entrance that night. David had been defeated, and he was now afraid of being discovered. In one last effort to cover up his sin, David sent Uriah back to the battlefield with a message for Joab. "Place Uriah on the front lines where the battle is the fiercest," he ordered, "then pull back so that Uriah will be killed." Joab did as instructed, and innocent Uriah, a man of honorable actions, was killed to cover up another man's dishonorable deeds.

> The prophet Nathan told of consequences to David's sin. All came to pass: the baby would die (2 Sam.12:18); murder would follow his family (2 Sam. 13:28-32, 1Kings 2:23-25); and his household would rebel against him (2 Sam. 15:13).

After the time of mourning was over, David married Bathsheba, and she gave birth to a son, but God was displeased with what David had done. It wasn't long before the Lord sent the prophet Nathan to David. Nathan's message wouldn't be one of encouragement for the king—but rather a rebuke. Nathan eyed David carefully, and prayed for the best way to deliver his message. Knowing David was a passionate man, Nathan told a story he knew would stir up David's anger.

"Once there was a poor man who owned just one lamb which he tenderly cared for and nurtured in his arms. There was also a rich man owning hundreds of lambs who lived nearby. One day, a guest came to the rich man's house for dinner. Instead of killing one of his own lambs, the rich man took the poor man's lamb and killed it." Nathan paused to let his words sink in, and David cut him off.

"As surely as the Lord lives," David burst forth, "the man who did this deserves to die! He must pay for that lamb four times over, because he committed such a terrible crime!" Even though David was now king, he hadn't forgotten his years as a shepherd. Stealing from another was inexcusable! Nathan's story was understood by David—and was about to be understood in a deeper way. Nathan looked directly into David's eyes and replied, "You are that man!"

exploring deeper

What was David's response to Nathan? Turn quickly to 2 Samuel 12:13 and read it. Notice David's words— what does he say? Now, turn to Psalm 51:10-13 and read it. David wrote this psalm after Nathan confronted him. What does this tell you about David's heart?

THINKING on your FEET

David had gotten himself into a deep mess and looked for ways of blaming others to get out of it. It didn't work, and it never does. When his sin was pointed out to him, David then publicly admitted it and asked God's forgiveness. Although David's relationship with the Lord was restored, he still suffered the consequences of his actions. His first child by Bathsheba died, murder would be a constant threat in his family, and his household would rebel against him. What once looked like a pleasurable moment suddenly wasn't looking so good. What is it in your life that doesn't look so good?

NA-NA NA-NA NA-NA

TAKEN FROM 2 SAMUEL 15-19

GETTING READY

Begin your time today with a moment of prayer. Prayer is simply talking with God and allowing Him to speak to your heart. Commit your day into His hands that you might live it in a way which honors Him.

THE JOURNEY

Do people ever annoy you? "Hey King! Heh heh. Nobody wants you anymore! Go on, run! Run like a baby! Heh heh." Those words pounded in David's ears, grating at his nerves and causing him to grit his teeth. David looked up at the man standing on the hillside and recognized him to be Shimei, from the same clan as Saul's family. Shimei bent down and picked up stones, then began pelting David and his officials with them. "Get out! Get out, you scoundrel! Heh heh. The Lord is repaying you for taking the throne from Saul! Now He has handed the kingdom over to your son Absalom!" Shimei kept following David from on top of the ridge, kicking dirt down and pelting him with stones and insults!

David continued on silently. He knew Shimei's words were untrue. Never once did he raise his hand against Saul, but waited patiently for God to give him the throne. Now, David was stunned that his son Absalom plotted a revolt against him! For four years Absalom had secretly worked on the people, sowing discontent among them while promoting his own cause. Taking 200 men with him, Absalom left for Hebron saying he was going to pay a vow. In reality, Absalom left to set himself up as king there. When word reached David, the rebellion was widespread. Not wanting to see Jerusalem destroyed, David decided to flee with those who were loyal to him rather than face off with his son. His heart was torn and he grieved deeply. He knew there was a time to fight, and a time to back down.

"Hey, King-o, I'm *talking* to yoooouuuu!" Shimei mocked, pointing at the king and spitting on the ground.

David's men had had enough. "Why do you let this worthless man curse you?" Abishai finally asked. "Let me go over and cut off his head! That'll put an end to his taunting!" But David simply looked at Abishai and said no. He knew there were things of greater concern, such as his son Absalom trying to kill him and take the throne. Shimei was just a small nuisance along the way.

Even though Shimei's life had been spared, David had suspicions about his sincerity and warned Solomon about him. You can read about Shimei's tragic end in 1 Kings 2:8-9 and verses 36-46.

"Let him alone," David continued. "Perhaps God will see my distress and how I am being wronged and bless me because of it." David and his men continued down the road, and Shimei continued following them along the hillside, cursing and pelting them with stones and a shower of dirt. Finally, David and his followers reached their destination—exhausted.

War broke loose, and it wasn't long before word came that Absalom had been killed. Once again David's heart was sorrowful, for although Absalom was treacherous, he was still his son. *Now I have one less son,* David lamented to himself, *and a kingdom that has been torn apart by strife.* David started journeying back to Jerusalem with those who remained loyal to him. He had a big task at hand trying to set the nation back in order. *Oh, Absalom! Absalom!* David grieved, wishing the whole event had never taken place.

When David arrived at the Jordan River, he noticed a large group rushing down to help them across. "We're here to help you cross and to do whatever you wish!" the large mass of people said to David. David looked up and saw a man running to greet him. He recognized him to be Shimei!

"Please, please O King," Shimei begged, falling facedown to the ground in sudden respect, "don't hold me guilty. Please forget the wrong I said and did to you when you were leaving Jerusalem!" he whimpered, fearing for his own life now that David was king again. "I know I've sinned and done wrong, but see? I was among the first down here to greet you and welcome you back!" Shimei groveled at David's feet. His voice, once arrogant and full of insults, now carried an entirely different tone as he begged for David's mercy. Abishai, one of David's men, saw what Shimei was doing and approached David in disgust.

"Shouldn't Shimei be put to death for cursing you, the Lord's anointed?" he asked, eyeing Shimei with contempt. David looked at Shimei and knew Abishai spoke the truth. Death was the normal punishment for those who slandered a king. Yet David would not take that course of action.

"This is not a day of execution, but a day of celebration," he said, "for I am once again the king of Israel!" Looking directly at Shimei, David said, "Your life will be spared." Abishai was stunned, and Shimei was greatly relieved. Shimei didn't get what he deserved—instead, he had been shown mercy.

exploring deeper

Open your copy of the Scriptures to 2 Samuel 17 and read verses 27-29. (Don't get stuck on the names in verse 27, but read through it to see what happened in the verses following it.) It is interesting to note that one of the men was Makir—the same man who had taken care of Mephibosheth when Saul was killed. (See 2 Samuel 9.) Mephibosheth was still living in Makir's household when David sent for him to live in the palace. What did Makir and these other men do for David according to these verses? What impact do you think that had on David?

CROSS ROADS

Shimei's conduct was obnoxious. His taunting and insults weren't occasional, but rather constant attacks on David's character. David, however, refused to enter into the hatred of the moment and retaliate in order to build himself back up. It was then that God sent Makir and the others to meet David's needs—both physical and emotional. Think about it. God's timing is perfect. The next time someone insults you and tries to "cut you down," will you return his or her insults and be pulled into that person's hatred, or will you remain above it and move onward, knowing God will be faithful to provide what you need emotionally—and physically?

YOU, I CAN TRUST!

TAKEN FROM 2 SAMUEL 24

GETTING READY

As you begin your time exploring today, ask God to give you a teachable heart. Come expectantly to His Word, eager to learn more about Him. He is a God who can be fully trusted.

THE JOURNEY

Have you ever felt afraid of God? *It's been many years*, David thought to himself, *years full of both blessing and trials*. David looked out his palace window at the city of Jerusalem, "The City of David" it had been called by many. How well he remembered conquering the city and establishing it as the capital for the entire nation. With great shouts of joy David brought the ark of God to Jerusalem so the Israelites would once again have a central place of worship. Those had been glorious days—ones to look back upon and smile about. Yet, those accomplishments now seemed to slip into the background when compared with everything else David had experienced.

How I remember being anointed as king by the prophet Samuel,

David recalled quietly in his heart. *How long it seemed until I actually got to sit upon the throne!* One by one, memories flooded David's mind killing Goliath, being invited to live in Saul's palace and befriending Jonathan—then finding himself fleeing for his life and living secretly among the Philistines. *But the Lord brought me through it all and preserved my life! Even when I sinned against Him by taking Bathsheba and murdering her husband, God forgave me when I repented.* A cloud of sorrow suddenly rolled over David's emotions as he remembered the heartache he experienced in his family. One son had killed another, then Absalom had rebelled and tried to take the throne from him. . . . quickly David put these thoughts behind him. *But all is peaceful now, and we're no longer at war,* he prided himself. *I would have to say I've done quite well. . . .*

David stepped away from the window and called for Joab, the commander of his army. He had a mission for Joab to accomplish—a mission David wanted done for personal reasons. "Joab," he said when the commander appeared, "I would like for you to go throughout all of Israel and count how many people are in my kingdom." Joab hesitated, not knowing how to respond. Even he knew it was a sin against God to do such a thing, for a census was taken only when God ordered it to be done. David noticed Joab's silence. "Well?" he asked.

"May the Lord let you live until you see a hundred times as many people as there are now, but . . . may I ask why you want to do this?" Joab said, alarmed. King David only dismissed Joab's concerns and insisted Joab do as commanded.

The last time God ordered a census was when Joshua brought the Israelites into the land in order to know how to divide the land appropriately!

Reluctantly, Joab left to accomplish what David ordered and traveled throughout the entire land. It took him nine months and twenty days before he returned to Jerusalem with his report.

"There are 800,000 men of military age in Israel," he stated, "and 500,000 in Judah." Although the numbers pleased David, his taking of a census displeased the Lord. This weighed heavily upon David's conscience. "Please forgive me, Lord, for doing such a foolish thing," David admitted before God. "I have sinned greatly and shouldn't have done this."

A threshing floor is a flat or level place where the kernel of the grain is separated from the stalk. This is done by either beating the grain on a rock or using oxen to walk over it. Araunah's threshing floor became the place where Solomon later built his temple!

The next morning, Gad the prophet came to David with a message the Lord had given him. "Because the Lord is displeased with the Israelites, and because of your sin as well, He has given you three choices. You may choose one of these punishments, and He will do it." Gad informed. "Your choices are: three years of famine, three months of fleeing from your enemies, or three days of severe plague throughout your land. Think upon these and let me know what answer to give the Lord." David looked at Gad, then down at the ground. To him there was no question of choice. He would choose the one that came most directly from God's hand.

"Let us fall into the hands of the Lord, for His mercy is great; but do not let me fall into the hands of men," David replied. He would wisely choose the three days of plague.

That morning, the Lord sent the plague on Israel for a three-day period, and 70,000 people from the northernmost parts of Israel down to Beersheba died. When the angel stretched out his hand to destroy Jerusalem, the Lord said, "Enough! Withdraw your hand!" The destruction stopped at the threshing floor of a man named Araunah.

That same day, Gad came to David and told him to go and build an altar at the sight where the plague stopped. Going to Araunah, David offered to buy his threshing floor, but Araunah would have no part of it. He had seen the angel of death stop there, and desired that David have it as a gift. "Take whatever pleases you and offer it up—here are my oxen, and you may use their yokes for the wood!" he said generously. David understood his kindness but refused to accept it. He knew he must pay for the land in order to show his honor and love to the Lord. "I will not sacrifice to my Lord burnt offerings that cost me nothing," he explained. David then paid Araunah, built the altar, and sacrificed to the Lord. He had trusted God, and God did not disappoint him.

exploring deeper

Look up 2 Samuel 24:14 and read it. What does it say? What was David's reasoning behind this? Would you have done the same?

Skill Time

David had great confidence in God because of his relationship with Him. He knew God was holy and had to punish sin, but he also knew God was just and faithful. The Scriptures say that David had a heart for the Lord. This doesn't mean David was perfect; it just means he confessed his wrongdoing and asked God's forgiveness for the times he made unwise choices. David's first desire was to know God more and be in fellowship with Him. It was this foundation that gave him the courage to trust God all the more. Do you know God in this manner? If you don't, would you like to? Turn to the back of this book and find out how you can!

THE KINGS OF ISRAEL

(dates are approximate)

UNITED KINGSHIP

Saul—1050 BC
David—1010
Solomon—970

DIVIDED KINGSHIP

ISRAEL		JUDAH
	930	
1. Jeroboam I		1. Rehoboam
2. Nadab		2. Abijah
3. Baasha		
4. Elah	**900**	3. Asa
5. Zimri		
6. Tibni/Omri		4. Jehoshaphat
7. Ahab		
8. Ahaziah		5. Jehoram
9. Joram	**850**	6. Ahaziah (Queen Athaliah)
		7. Joash
10. Jehu		
11. Jehoahaz		
12. Jehoash	**800**	8. Amaziah
13. Jeroboam II		9. Uzziah
14. Zechariah		
15. Shallum		
16. Menahem	**750**	10. Jotham
17. Pekahiah		11. Ahaz
18. Pekah		12. Hezekiah
19. Hoshea		
	700	
		13. Manasseh
	650	14. Amon
		15. Josiah
		16. Jehoahaz
		17. Jehoiakim
	600	18. Jeoiachin
		19. Zedekiah

GETTING YOUR BEARINGS:
THE BOOK OF 1 KINGS

The Book of 1 Kings is full of tunnels that lead to more tunnels—each one branching off and providing its own areas to explore. As you enter 1 Kings, you'll stand in a great cavern of glory as you read about Solomon. Soon, however, the room will narrow and lead to a dark passageway. What happened?! See if you can find out!

While you explore this book, you'll also come to a major fork in the road where two tunnels split off in opposite directions. One tunnel will lead to the northern ten tribes, who call themselves Israel. The other will lead to the remaining two tribes, who call themselves Judah. Why did the nation split and what happens next? That's something you'll get to explore as well!

In 1 Kings, you'll come face to face with honor and dishonor, the power of influence, the lure of distractions, and the emotional high of victory and the low of depression. Most of all, you'll see choices being made and the consequences of them. This is what 1 Kings is all about. Carefully observe around you and notice how rough the terrain gets—but also take note of the few smooth places as well. Where 1 Kings leaves you hanging, 2 Kings picks right up—but let's not get ahead of ourselves! Enjoy the journey in 1 Kings and keep your eyes peeled. You never know what treasure is there waiting for you to discover. . . .

Did you know? The Book of Kings was originally written on one scroll in the Hebrew language. When it was translated from Hebrew (a language first written with no vowels) into Greek (a language requiring vowels), it became too long and was divided into two books—1 Kings and 2 Kings.

OOPS...

TAKEN FROM 1 KINGS 1-2

GETTING READY

Start your time today by telling God five things you are thankful for. Use it as a time to praise Him for blessings He's brought into your life. If you have a hard time coming up with five things to praise God for, then tell Him that, too. Be honest before Him. Let the Lord examine your heart and show you areas in your life that need to be dealt with.

THE JOURNEY

Have you ever schemed and pushed in order to get what you want—only to have it backfire on you?

Hmmm, Adonijah mused to himself, *King David is now at the end of his years. According to custom, his oldest son should inherit the throne. Since I am his son and my two older brothers are dead—that means I automatically get to be king!* The thought of power and honor excited Adonijah greatly. *The only problem is what to do with my half brother,*

Solomon. . . . he thought. Feeling worried about not getting his way, Adonijah came up with a scheme. He would influence others to help him get what he wanted and what he thought he deserved.

I will be king! Adonijah declared to himself and even to others. To help convince them, Adonijah got chariots and horses ready with fifty men to run ahead of him. It would be a spectacular display of his power, splendor, and worthiness for all of Israel to see. *In order to be the king, I've got to start acting like a king,* he reasoned. He gave no honor to his father who was still king, and he didn't care. He cared even less that King David hadn't yet named his successor to the throne!

Perhaps if I get my father's commander, Joab, and Abiathar the priest to support me, it'll be better for my cause. These men hold author-ity and positions of power. Others will see their approval of me and want to go along with it. Things couldn't be better! At least, this is what Adonijah thought. Zadok the priest, Nathan the prophet, and two members of David's special guard, including Benaiah, did not give their support to Adonijah.

Adonijah felt pleased with the support he did have, however. He was a handsome man and easily won favor with the people. King David was old and dying; Adonijah was young and exciting. *I am the only logical choice for king!* he thought. Quickly, Adonijah gathered supplies to make sacrifices—sheep, cattle, and fattened calves. He also made arrangements to be crowned. *I'll go to the large rocky plateau by the spring at En Rogel and invite all my brothers—except Solomon—and all the king's royal officials to join me. Since Nathan, Benaiah, and two of the king's guard didn't show me their support, they won't be invited. Today I shall become king, and I want everything to go well!*

Abishag had been King David's personal nurse and companion. To marry a king's companion was considered the same as publicly claiming the rights of the king. It was trying to lay a claim to the throne.

It wasn't long before the prophet Nathan heard of Adonijah's plans to crown himself king that day. But God had already established the fact that David's son Solomon, would be the next to sit on the throne. Nathan knew this and realized something must be done quickly about the situation at hand. . . .

"Call in Zadok the priest, Nathan the prophet, and Benaiah," King David demanded upon hearing Adonijah's plans. "Set my son Solomon on a mule and take him down to Gihon. There, have Zadok the priest and the prophet Nathan anoint him king over Israel. You are to blow the trumpets loudly and shout, 'Long live King Solomon!' Then, bring Solomon back here to sit on my throne. I have appointed him king over Israel and Judah." King David's words were carried out as requested, and Solomon was crowned king that very day.

"What's that noise?" Adonijah asked upon hearing the shouts and celebration. When it was discovered Solomon had just been crowned king, Adonijah's party quickly ended, and the people went home. Adonijah feared for his life. *What if Solomon plans to kill me as I had planned to kill him?* he feared. Panicking, Adonijah ran to the altar, grabbed the horns and wouldn't let go. He begged for mercy from Solomon and was granted it—as long as he showed himself to be a worthy man. Relieved, Adonijah went home. Unfortunately, his heart wasn't content with what he did have—his life—and he soon began to push for more. This time, it would prove to be a deadly move.

exploring deeper

To know what Adonijah did next, you'll have to open your Bible to 1 Kings 2 and read verses 13-25. Notice Adonijah's struggling attitude in verses 15 and 16? He still couldn't let things go! What was his request? (Why do you think he didn't ask Solomon himself?) What was the response? Do you think Solomon overreacted? Before you answer this last question, be sure to look back at 1 Kings 1:52 and see Solomon's warning to Adonijah.

DANGER AHEAD

There are many people in this world who push to get what they want. To them, "no" doesn't mean no; it simply means: my-original-plan-didn't-work-so-I-need-to-approach-it-from-a-different-angle-in-order-to-get-what-I-want. As a result, they push, nag, manipulate, and scheme in order to get their heart's desire—unable to rest until they've accomplished their goal. Thinking they've won a great victory, they often suffer defeat and fall victim to their own selfishness, just like Adonijah. Don't go down that path. Once you start pushing to get what you want, it's hard to stop. Learn to be content with what you have (or don't have).

... AND THAT, TOO? WOW!

TAKEN FROM 1 KINGS 3-4

GETTING READY

Take time to prepare your heart before you begin. Having your heart in the right place will make your time with the Lord more meaningful. Spend a few minutes just praising God for who He is. Thank Him for His faithfulness, His love, His holiness and mercy, His unending power, and the fact that He knows the deepest secrets of your heart and still loves you nonetheless.

THE JOURNEY

Do you sometimes have a problem with wanting the best only for yourself?

Solomon was now king, and it was a great time of peace. Israel was no longer at war with each other or even with surrounding nations. All signs of internal strife had been dealt with, and Solomon's kingdom was firmly established. Yet, at the age of twenty, Solomon knew he needed help—God's help—in order to govern the nation. . . .

"What do you want? Ask, and I will give it to you," God spoke to Solomon one night in a dream. Such an offer was overwhelming! The very same God who miraculously parted the Red Sea for the Israelites and sent plagues upon their enemies now promised to give Solomon whatever he asked! Solomon thought quietly. His options were many.

If I ask for success, I won't have to worry about the threat of my kingdom being taken from me as my father experienced, he thought to himself. *On the other hand, if I ask for honor or wealth, I could live securely and have all that I need.* Solomon knew all of these were tempting choices, but not the one he would choose. "O Lord, You were wonderfully kind to my father because he had been honest, true, and faithful to You. You have continued this great kindness to him by allowing his son to sit on the throne." Solomon paused a moment before continuing. "I am Your servant, Lord," Solomon whispered.

Matthew 6:33 in the New Testament urges us to seek God's kingdom and His righteousness first—above our own desires. God then promises that He will take care of our needs (and not always, but sometimes, our "wants").

"Now I sit as king among Your people, but I am like a child who doesn't know my way around! The nation you have given me to govern is so vast! There are too many people to even begin to count!" Solomon added, feeling the weight of his responsibilities. "Please give me an understanding mind that I might know the difference between right and wrong and be able to govern Your people well," Solomon asked. *Yes, this is my request of You,* he said in his heart. *I need wisdom.*

It wasn't long before Solomon was faced with an opportunity to display the wisdom God had given him. Two women of little honor had come to Solomon to settle a dispute. "We live together in the same house. No one else lives with us. I had a baby—a son," one woman began, "and three days later she had a son as well." Solomon glanced at the other woman, then back again to the one who was speaking. "During the night, her baby died, so she switched her son with mine while I slept! I know this because when I woke up, the baby cradled in my arms was not mine!"

"Liar!" the other woman snapped. "She's making this up because her son is dead, and she's jealous that my son lives!" Solomon took a deep breath and looked closely at each woman. He knew on his own he could never determine who was telling the truth and who was lying. It was at that moment the Lord gave him wisdom, as promised.

"You each stand before me, arguing that the child is yours," Solomon simply stated. "Each person's claim is as strong as the other's. Because of this, I order that the baby be cut in two, and you each can have half! Bring me a sword!" he ordered. Solomon did this as a test, for he knew the real mother would want to save the life of her son at all costs—even at the risk of another keeping him.

"Stop!" the first woman shouted. "Don't kill the child! Please spare his life and let her have him."

"No!" the other shouted, "neither of us shall have him! Cut him in two!" Solomon then knew immediately who the real mother was and returned the baby to her, unharmed. As a result of this, word about Solomon's great wisdom began to spread throughout all the kingdom.

God answered Solomon's prayer for wisdom, and then went a step further. "Because you didn't ask for riches, long life for yourself, or the death of your enemies, but unselfishly asked for wisdom," the Lord told Solomon, "I am greatly pleased. Because of this, I have given you what you asked for—a wise and discerning mind!" God stated. "Moreover, I will also give you riches and honor—something you chose not to ask for. In your lifetime, Solomon, there will be no king equal to you."

Solomon was rewarded for seeking what was best for the nation, not what he wanted for himself. God allowed him to enjoy both.

exploring deeper

Open your Bible to 1 Kings 3:13. What does it say? How sweet these words must have sounded to Solomon! Is the first half of this verse something God could ever say to you?

Skill Time

Asking God for things that benefit you personally is very common, but it's not the most rewarding! Stop to think about your prayer life. What is it like? Do you mainly ask God for things for yourself, or do you look beyond your own wants and desires? If God looked over your prayer "wish list," what would He see—the desires of a selfish person, or a servant-heart attitude? Take a few moments to compare your requests to Solomon's, then make any necessary changes today.

IT'S NOT EASY...BEING KING

TAKEN FROM 1 KINGS 8-11

GETTING READY

Spend a moment to pray for those who hold a leadership position over you (parents, teacher, coach, boss). Ask God to protect them from the temptations they face in their roles. Ask God to help you handle power appropriately whenever it falls your way as well.

THE JOURNEY

Have you ever tried to bend the rules a little?

Solomon was pleased with all that surrounded him. *It's been seven years,* he sighed to himself, *but now the temple is completed, and the ark of God has a permanent resting place—a place my father, King David, dreamed of building.* The temple stood as a marvel for all to see and a reminder of God's magnificence. This pleased Solomon greatly, and at the dedication ceremony, he led all the Israelites in worshiping and recommitting their hearts to the Lord.

"O Lord, there is no God like You in heaven above or on the earth below," Solomon prayed on behalf of the Israelites. "The highest heavens cannot contain You, much less this temple I have built!" Solomon recognized God's vastness, power, and holiness. "Please show mercy to the foreigners who desire to worship You, that all may know You are the one true God. Forgive us for the times we sin against You, and please never turn Your face from Your people." When Solomon finished, he got up and addressed the Israelites. "May the Lord turn our hearts toward Him and may we always have the desire to do His will in everything—carefully obeying the commands, laws, and regulations God gave our ancestors!" Little did Solomon know that the very charge he gave the Israelites he himself would have trouble keeping.

Solomon was not only the wisest man who ever lived but also a master builder. Besides the temple, Solomon directed the building of three fortresses along the Mediterranean coast, a protective wall around the city of Jerusalem, and a palace for himself (as well as other buildings). Solomon continued to grow in riches and honor, and his kingdom continued to expand. By building fleets of ships, Solomon soon began to trade with foreign countries. Every three years, ships returned loaded with gold, silver, and ivory, adding to Solomon's growing wealth and power. It wasn't long before word of Solomon's kingdom spread to faraway lands.

"Your wealth and wisdom are far greater than I ever imagined!" the Queen of Sheba said to Solomon, having traveled 1,200 miles to see him. She asked Solomon riddles in order to test his power and knowledge, and was amazed at his answers. She gave Solomon the many expensive gifts she had brought along—four-and-a-half tons of gold, large amounts of spices, and precious stones. Being on favorable terms with such a powerful king as Solomon was important.

> The three fortress cities Solomon built were strategically located and offered the best defense against enemies. Hazor protected the northern kingdom, Megiddo protected the central parts and the valley of Jezreel, and Gezer protected the southern portions of the land.

Kings from other lands and lesser kingdoms also came to visit, acknowledging the power of Solomon's kingdom and seeking his favor. Often they would give their daughters to Solomon in marriage in hopes of making stronger political ties. Unfortunately, Solomon readily accepted them, bending God's rules. Solomon knew God had commanded the Israelites not to intermarry with foreigners (because of their false gods) and not to accumulate many wives. Soon finding himself with 700 wives and 300 concubines, Solomon's heart was slowly led astray. He forgot other commands God had given, and that was just the beginning. . . .

Solomon's ships brought back more than gold, silver, and ivory. They also carried apes and peacocks (1 Kings 10:22)!

Solomon's wealth and power continued to increase, but he didn't always continue to make wise choices. Bending God's rules came more naturally as time wore on. Although kings over Israel were forbidden to collect large amounts of gold or silver, Solomon continued to do so. Now controlling the major trade route that connected Egypt to the rest of the world, Solomon began collecting taxes as payment for traders traveling through. This brought him even more gold and riches which he then used to purchase 1,400 chariots and 12,000 horses! *This will greatly improve my kingdom and establish our security against enemies who might attack!* Solomon said to himself. Once again, he had bent God's rules. According to the Law handed down through Moses, Israelite kings were not to acquire great numbers of horses for themselves. This was so that God's people would depend on God for protection, not a false sense of security. Because Solomon was not fully devoted to the Lord and didn't follow Him completely in his later years, the hearts of the Israelites began to turn away from God.

exploring deeper

Open your Bible to 1 Kings 4 and read verses 32-34. What do these verses say? Do you find this odd, in light of the unwise choices Solomon began making? According to 1 Kings 9:4-5, God said He would establish Solomon's throne if Solomon was careful to do three things: 1) Walk before God in integrity of heart and uprightness 2) Do everything God commanded, and 3) Observe and obey God's rules. Quickly turn ahead a few chapters and read 1 Kings 11:9-12. This is God's "report card" on Solomon's leadership. What does God say?

DANGER AHEAD

With power and leadership comes temptation—temptation to stretch the rules just a little here and there. No matter how wise leaders may seem, if they bend the rules, they will soon find themselves way off course, and in some cases, ruined. If God allows you to be in a leadership position—be careful! It's not easy being "king." Learn from Solomon's example.

THAT'LL DO IT

TAKEN FROM 1 KINGS 11-12

GETTING READY

Don't forget to pray as you begin your time with the Lord today. Quiet your thoughts before Him, then come expectantly, ready to hear what He has to show you in His Word.

THE JOURNEY

Are you easily distracted?

Jeroboam met Ahijah's gaze and held tightly to the ten pieces of fabric the prophet handed him. "Take these ten pieces for yourself, for God has spoken and said He is going to tear the kingdom out of Solomon's hands and give you ten tribes," Ahijah said. With those words, the prophet had taken off his new cloak. He tore it into twelve pieces (each representing one of the twelve tribes of the Israelites) and then handed ten to Jeroboam. Jeroboam looked behind him just to be sure Ahijah hadn't made a mistake. No one else was in sight. There he stood, on the deserted road out in the country—just he and the prophet.

"For the sake of David, God won't take the whole kingdom out of Solomon's hands, but will allow him one tribe, that there might always be a descendant of David to reign in Jerusalem," Ahijah said. Jeroboam listened carefully. He knew that the "one" tribe referred to Judah and included the smaller tribe of Benjamin. They were represented by the two pieces of cloth remaining in Ahijah's hands. According to the prophet's words, God was sending His judgment upon the nation of Israel and Solomon because they hadn't obeyed God's laws and statutes. Instead, the Israelites had begun worshiping the false gods of the Sidonians, Moabites, and Ammonites. Even King Solomon had been led astray by his many wives and begun embracing the false gods. Ahijah continued, "I

The Sidonians worshiped Ashtoreth. This goddess required gross immoral deeds and the worship of stars. The worship of Molech and Chemosh by the Ammonites and Moabites involved the sacrificing of children.

will not tear the kingdom from Solomon's hands until after he dies because of the promise I made to David. Rather, I will take the kingdom from his son's hands and give the northern ten tribes to you. Just as this cloak has been split, so will the kingdom be split. Solomon's son, Rehoboam, shall have Judah. You, Jeroboam, shall have the northern tribes of Israel." The words left Jeroboam speechless.

When Solomon died, his son went to Shechem to be crowned king by all the Israelites. Hearing about this, Jeroboam went to speak with the new king. "Please, Rehoboam, your father made the people work hard and taxed them harshly. Lighten the load, and we will serve you," he offered. Jeroboam knew what he was talking about, for he had served as an officer in charge of King Solomon's workers. King Rehoboam thought about it for three days but rejected the advice. As a result, the ten tribes of Israel rebelled against Solomon's son and followed Jeroboam instead. Only the tribes of Judah and Benjamin remained loyal to Rehoboam—just as God had said. From that day on, Rehoboam ruled in Jerusalem over those in Judah who remained loyal to the house of David, and Jeroboam ruled in Israel—with Shechem as his capital. The nation of Israel had been torn apart.

If those in my kingdom go to Jerusalem to offer their sacrifices, Jeroboam later thought in his heart, *they might give their allegiance back to the house of David!* Knowing all Jewish men were commanded by God to travel to the temple three times each year to offer sacrifices, Jeroboam became nervous. *By traveling into Rehoboam's kingdom, they might be influenced to join back up with him, then turn around and kill me! I must do something to keep them from going and offering their sacrifices in Jerusalem!* Jeroboam schemed. It didn't take long to form a plan.

There, that'll do it! Jeroboam thought, as he looked at the high places and shrines he had set up. Having made two golden calves, he placed one in the northern city of Dan and one in the southern city of Bethel. The high place (altar) in Bethel was strategically located on the main road, just thirty miles before a traveler would reach Jerusalem. He knew this would distract worshipers from continuing their journey. "Why go all the way to Jerusalem, when we can offer our sacrifices here?" they would say to themselves. The high place in Dan would be more convenient for those living in the north.

> A remarkable prophecy! God sent a prophet to Jeroboam naming a king (Josiah from the house of David) who would rise up and destroy Jeroboam's high places—a king who would not appear for 290 years! The prophecy was fulfilled. You can read about it in 2 Kings 23:15-20.

Jeroboam called the northern tribes together and made his proclamation. "It is too much for you to make the journey to Jerusalem," he announced. "Here are your gods, O Israel, who brought you up out of Egypt!" Jeroboam introduced the golden calves and led the hearts of the people away from their obedience to God. Then he appointed priests from among the people, even though none was Levitea, and came up with his own version of the sacred festival held once a year in Jerusalem. Picking a time of his own choosing, Jeroboam cleverly instituted a new festival to be held exactly one month later than Judah's. He knew this would keep the Israelites from longing for their former ways of worship. . . . *That'll do it!* he said in his heart, pleased with himself. "That'll do it," God would respond—in judgment.

exploring deeper

Quickly turn to 1 Kings 14:8. What did God remind Jeroboam of? Drop down and read verses 9-10. What would happen to Jeroboam? Now, look at the effects of Jeroboam's sin (verse 16).

THINKING on your FEET

Jeroboam set up "convenient" places of worship as a distraction to the Israelites. There, they worshiped idols in high places instead of worshiping the one true God at the altar. What "high places" or distractions have you set up in your life?

FOR BETTER OR FOR WORSE

TAKEN FROM 1 KINGS 13

GETTING READY

Stop and pray. God desires to share from His Word important things that will make your life much easier (and sin-resistant). But you won't hear unless you have a listening and teachable heart. Spend a moment to tell God what's on your mind, so you can better learn what is on His.

THE JOURNEY

Do you ever struggle with being influenced by the behavior of those around you?

The prophet stepped out from the crowd and leveled his message from God—not just against King Jeroboam's wickedness, but against the altar Jeroboam was now making a sacrifice upon. The altar featured a golden calf and had been built as a substitute to keep the Israelites from journeying into Jerusalem and worshiping there. "As a sign that my message of judgment is true," the prophet declared, "this very altar will split apart, and the ashes on it will fall to the ground."

"Enough!" Jeroboam snapped. He stretched out his hand from the altar and shouted, "Seize him!" but the hand Jeroboam stretched out withered and became paralyzed! God was displaying His power and authority over Jeroboam's authority. The altar split apart while Jeroboam helplessly watched. "Please," Jeroboam asked the prophet in a panicked voice, "pray to your God that my hand will be restored." Once he regained the use of his hand, the king extended a generous offer to the prophet to come back to the palace to feast. He was trying to influence the prophet, but the young man refused. "Even though you give me half of your possessions, I would not go with you to eat bread or drink water, for I was commanded by the Lord that I must not eat bread or drink water in Bethel, nor return by the way I came." With that, the young man obeyed the Lord and took a different road out of town.

Meanwhile, word of the young prophet reached the ears of an older prophet who lifted his eyes with interest. *So,* he said under his breath, *this young man believes he has a ministry from God? Hah! We'll just see about that!* In his years of living in Bethel—the very center of Jeroboam's system of false worship—the old prophet had gotten lazy and complacent. His heart had hardened by the influence of his surroundings, and he no longer valued obedience to God. *Talking with this young man of God will be of great interest!* he said to himself.

"Palace prophets" were commonly kept by kings and used for telling the king only what he wanted to hear. Perhaps this was Jeroboam's offer to the young man of God.

Mounting up a donkey, the old prophet rode after the young prophet and found him sitting under an oak tree. "Are you the man of God from Judah?" he asked.

"I am," came the reply.

"Come home to Bethel and eat with me," the old prophet invited. When the young man declined, explaining that God had forbidden him to eat or drink in the city of Bethel, the old prophet tried to influence him. "I too am a prophet of God—just like you," he reassured, "and an angel said to me by the word of the Lord, 'Bring him back to your house that he might eat and drink with you.'" The old prophet made this up, for he wanted to persuade the man of God to return home with him. It didn't matter to him that God had forbidden it.

I know my original orders from God were not to partake of any food or drink in Bethel—the city of idolatry, the young prophet thought to himself. *Yet, this older man is a prophet himself and claims God has given him other directions for me to follow.* After briefly weighing his options, the man of God was persuaded by the influence of the older prophet. As a result, he returned to Bethel to eat and drink at the prophet's home—directly against God's command.

Midway through the meal, God delivered a message through the lips of the older, disobedient prophet. It was a message of judgment for the man of God. "You have defied the word of the Lord and have not kept the command He gave you. Rather, you came back to the place where He told you not to eat or drink. Because of this, your body will not be buried in the tomb of your fathers." When the young prophet left the house, he was attacked on the road by a lion and killed. The older prophet heard of this and felt guilty. He took the young prophet's body and buried it in his own tomb and mourned over him. Because he had allowed himself to fall under Jeroboam's sinful influence and brazen disobedience, the old prophet had influenced another to do the same.

exploring deeper

Open your Bible to 1 Kings, and come along on a quick "tour" of the power of Jeroboam's influence. First stop is 1 Kings 15:25-26. What does it say? Now, turn ahead to verses 33-34 in the same chapter and read them, as well as 1 Kings 16:25-26. Finally, read verse 31 of chapter 16. From these verses, what do you learn about the power of influence?

Skill Time

Influence is a powerful thing—it can be used for either good or evil. It can make others either stronger spiritually, or weaker. What kind of influence does your life have on others? Take a moment to think about the people you influence. Now think about the lives of those you choose to be influenced by. Ask God to forgive you for choices or actions that tend to lead you (or others) away from Him. Then, remember to practice three simple steps to help keep you on the right path:

1) EVALUATE everything according to God's standards. (To do this you need to be in His Word so you know what His standards are!)
2) PRAY before you act (or react).
3) RENEW your commitment to serve God—daily!

PROMISE?

TAKEN FROM 1 KINGS 17-18

GETTING READY

Begin your time today with prayer. Start by thanking the Lord for the lessons you have been learning as you get to know Him better through His Word. Thank Him for His faithfulness and for being a God who cares deeply for your needs.

THE JOURNEY

Do you sometimes worry about how your needs will be met?

It had been forty years since King Jeroboam died. From that time until now, Israel (the ten northern tribes) had experienced five different kings—each following in the wickedness Jeroboam had established; each leading Israel further away from the Lord. Now, a man named Ahab ruled the Northern Kingdom. King Ahab had little concern for God and considered the sins of Jeroboam to be trivial. As a result, God sent a prophet—the prophet Elijah—as His spokesman to challenge the idolatry of the nation.

"As the Lord lives," Elijah proclaimed to King Ahab, "there will not be any dew or rain in the next few years except at my word!"

Elijah obediently delivered God's message of warning to the king of Israel, then followed the Lord's next command. God instructed Elijah, "Leave here, turn eastward, and hide in the Kerith Ravine—east of the Jordan. There, you will drink water from the brook, and I have ordered the ravens to feed you." Elijah did as God said, and God did as He promised. The ravens brought Elijah bread and meat both morning and evening, and Elijah drank from the brook. Some time later, the brook dried up because there hadn't been any rain in the land. "Go at once to the village of Zarephath and stay there," God said. "I've commanded a widow there to supply you with food."

Zarephath was a town on the Mediterranean coast in Phoenicia and the homeland of Ahab's wife, Queen Jezebel!

Arriving at the town gate of Zarephath, Elijah saw a widow gathering sticks. It was obvious the woman was poor and had very little. Her face looked hollow and drawn from hunger. "Would you please bring me a little water in a jar that I might have a drink?" Elijah kindly requested. As the widow went to get it, Elijah added, "And please, can you also bring me a piece of bread?" The widow turned around and looked into Elijah's eyes. She knew it was the custom to take care of visiting prophets, but she also knew she had no bread to offer him. Her sad, tired eyes communicated the situation without spoken words.

"As surely as the Lord your God lives," she sighed, "I don't have any bread—only a handful of flour and a little oil in the bottom of a jug. I was just gathering a few sticks in order to cook this last meal. Then my son and I will die." Elijah looked at the woman who seemed to have so little. His thoughts continually recalled how God had been faithful to provide for his own needs, feeding him from the mouths of ravens!

"Don't be afraid," he replied kindly. "But go home and do as you have said—only first make a small cake of bread from what you have and bring it to me. Then, make something for yourself and your son," he instructed. "For this is what the Lord, the God of Israel, says: 'The jar of flour will not be used up, and the jug of oil will not run dry until the day the Lord gives rain on the land.'" The widow acted in faith and did as Elijah told her. She put her trust in the Lord God to meet her needs and wasn't disappointed. The jar of flour was not used up, and the jug of oil didn't run dry, just as God had promised! Elijah stayed with her and the Lord continued to provide for the needs of the widow—as well as Elijah.

It was now the third year of the famine, and the word of the Lord came to Elijah telling him to present himself before King Ahab. Meanwhile, King Ahab went searching for grass to keep his horses and mules alive. "Obadiah, you go in one direction, searching all the springs and valleys," the king commanded his servant, "and I'll go in another direction." Obadiah obeyed and set out immediately, but instead of coming across grass, he came across something more remarkable. *That's Elijah the prophet!* he thought, recognizing Elijah from a distance. Obadiah knew Elijah was a wanted man. King Ahab blamed the prophet for the terrible drought.

The Obadiah mentioned here was in charge of King Ahab's palace. He also secretly hid a hundred of the Lord's prophets so Queen Jezebel wouldn't kill them. This Obadiah is not the same Obadiah for whom an Old Testament book is named.

Even though Obadiah served under King Ahab, he was a believer in the Lord.

"Go and tell King Ahab I want to meet with him," Elijah instructed Obadiah.

Obadiah hesitated. "I have worshiped the Lord since my youth," he said. "Why do you send me to tell Ahab I have seen you? Have I done something wrong? There's not a nation or kingdom where Ahab hasn't sent someone looking for you! Now you ask me to go and say: 'Elijah is here'? If I tell Ahab and he doesn't find you, he'll kill me!"

Elijah reassured Obadiah, "As the Lord Almighty lives, I will surely present myself to Ahab today." Elijah was confident in God's ability to handle the situation and meet his needs; it was a lesson he had learned first-hand from his experiences during the drought.

exploring deeper

Look in your copy of the Scriptures at 1 Kings 17:22-24. Through the hands of Elijah, another miracle was given to the widow. Notice her response. What does she say?

Skill Time

Trusting God to meet our needs frees us up to act boldly and confidently in obedience to Him. As a result, God is able to use us in dynamic ways. On a small piece of paper, write down one or two needs in your life that you are concerned about. These could be needs for physical or even emotional things. Commit your list to God, then take the next step: trust Him and step out in faith. God promises to be there for you. He won't let you down.

ATTENTION, PLEASE!

TAKEN FROM 1 KINGS 18

GETTING READY

Take a moment to pray and really talk to God. Don't just give a list of things you desire Him to do for you, but spend time praising Him. Thank Him for His power and that He alone is the one true God. Nothing and no one else can compare to Him.

THE JOURNEY

Have you ever been afraid to stand up for the Lord when others attack the honor of His name?

"More water."

"More?"

"Yes—until it overflows into the trenches. . . ."

Silence fell upon the crowd. Some stood curiously wondering; others stood mocking a crazy man. King Ahab stood impatiently tapping his foot. He remembered when Elijah first came to him. . . .

"As the Lord, the God of Israel, lives," Elijah had said, reminding the king of the one true God Israel should have been worshiping, "the One whom I serve . . ." King Ahab flinched at those words and grew restless. Anger started to mount in his heart. *Does he not know to whom he is speaking?* Ahab muttered to himself. Everyone knew that Ahab's wife, Queen Jezebel, had plans to make Baal worship the national religion of the Israelites. Already she had killed off many of God's priests and replaced them with 450 prophets of Baal and 400 prophets of Asherah. Jezebel had also destroyed the altars dedicated to the worship of the Lord. *Baal is the god of this land, and soon will be the god of these people as well,* King Ahab confirmed in his heart. He was not prepared for the challenge that would come from the lips of Elijah.

"There will be no rain in the next few years except at my word," Elijah boldly stated. *Foolish man,* Ahab laughed silently, *doesn't he know that the god in control of rain and the richness of the soil isn't the God of the Israelites; it's Baal—the god of the land! It is Baal who brings forth crops and green grass. Yahweh is a god of the desert—this is the land of Canaan, and the richness of this land is due to the Canaanite gods.* Ahab had scoffed at Elijah's words and found them quite amusing—but he didn't laugh long. Now, three years later, the smile had all but disappeared from King Ahab's mouth. The once fertile soil lay dry and cracked due to drought.

Mount Carmel means "God's vineyard" and is aptly named. Standing 1,000 feet high, it is the most heavily forested area in all of Israel. Today, its slopes are covered with olive groves and vineyards.

"Summon the people and meet me on Mount Carmel," Elijah had requested before the throne of King Ahab. "Have all your prophets of Baal and Asherah join you as well. If the Lord is God, follow Him, but if Baal is God, follow him." *That troublemaker Elijah has challenged the power of Baal!* Ahab raged in his heart. *Now he will see the power of our gods!*

Gathering the prophets of Baal and the people of Israel, King Ahab met Elijah on Mount Carmel. "Take your bull and arrange it on your altar, but don't light the wood," Elijah commanded. "I will do the same. Then, call on the name of your god, and I will call upon the name of mine. The god who answers by fire—he is God." The Baal worshipers smiled to themselves. They knew Baal was the god of weather and was often portrayed carrying a thunderbolt. *Hah!* King Ahab reasoned, *this time Elijah will be proven wrong!*

Elijah means "*Yahweh is God.*" Just saying Elijah's name must have been detestable to King Ahab!

All morning the prophets cried out to Baal, asking him to answer, but there was no response. They then shouted louder and danced about the altar—still no answer. Around noon, Elijah began to taunt them. "Perhaps your god Baal is deep in thought, or busy, or traveling! Maybe he is sleeping and must be awakened!" Elijah of course knew the reason they were not having success; it was because Baal was not God. The 450 prophets of Baal shouted all the louder, slashing themselves with swords and spears, continually calling out—but there was no response. No one answered; no one paid attention. The 450 prophets of Baal and 400 prophets of Asherah had their turn. Now it was Elijah's. . . .

Calling all the people to himself, Elijah repaired an altar of the Lord that had been torn down. He then cut up his bull and arranged the pieces on the altar over the wood. Next, Elijah did something that surprised everyone—he called for water to be poured over the sacrifice, making it all the more difficult to light.

"More water?"

"Yes, still more," Elijah commanded. King Ahab watched impatiently. Others stood by silently as twelve large jars of water drenched the sacrifice and filled the trench below. Then Elijah stepped forward and prayed a simple prayer to the Lord. No sooner had Elijah finished than a lightning bolt ripped down from heaven and consumed the sacrifice—burning up not only the bull, but also the wood, stones, soil, and all the water that was in the trench.

The people instantly fell down, crying out: "The Lord—He is God! The Lord—He is God!" Their attention and their allegiance were now back with the Lord. Moving swiftly, Elijah had all the prophets of Baal seized and then put to death in the Kishon Valley below.

exploring deeper

Open your Bible and turn to 1 Kings 18:36-37. This was Elijah's prayer. What two statements does Elijah first declare (verse 36)? What was his driving goal, according to verse 37?

Skill Time

Elijah had a lot of guts! He wasn't afraid to stand up against the culture and protect the honor of God's name. Because of his courage to do so, others' hearts were turned back to the Lord. Take a moment to evaluate your life. Do you turn a deaf ear and remain silent when God's honor is challenged, or do you allow yourself to be used by God to make a difference? What plan of action could you make to be more like Elijah? (Example: not remaining silent when a friend takes God's name in vain) Think of a few things you can do and make it a point to do one of them this week.

WOE IS ME

TAKEN FROM 1 KINGS 19

GETTING READY

Spend some time in prayer before you begin today's reading. Tell God about some of the disappointments you've been feeling lately. Ask Him to renew your heart and give you a fresh perspective on your circumstances—and on who He is.

THE JOURNEY

Have you ever felt like the whole world is against you?

"Elijah did *what?!*" Queen Jezebel screeched, unable to contain her anger. With a hostile heart, Jezebel impatiently listened to the details as King Ahab explained what had happened.

"There was a contest between Baal and Israel's god on Mount Carmel today," Ahab began. "A sacrifice was prepared on each altar, but no fire was lit. It was left to the gods to light the fire and prove who was stronger. All morning our prophets called out to Baal, begging him to hear . . ." Ahab stated. ". . . All morning and even until the afternoon they tried—but to no avail."

Jezebel narrowed her eyes and gave Ahab her full attention. "And?" she demanded. Ahab looked away uncomfortably. He knew the next words he had to say would anger the queen all the more.

"And then it was Elijah's turn. He rebuilt the altar of the Lord, then said a simple prayer which his God answered. Fire immediately came down from heaven and burnt up not only the sacrifice, but also the wood, stones, and dirt surrounding it." Ahab thought it best not to rub in the defeat by telling Jezebel how Elijah drenched his altar with water, making the task all the harder.

> The broom tree offered Elijah very little protection or comfort from the sun's rays. It was actually a large, leafless shrub the roots of which were used as a source of fuel and charcoal.

"And?!" Jezebel asked, raising her voice to a fevered pitch.

Ahab swallowed hard and finished, "All the people fell to their faces when they saw this and began saying, "The Lord—He is God! The Lord—He is—"

"Enough!" snapped Jezebel. Ahab was not finished.

"Then Elijah had all the prophets of Baal taken to the valley of Kishon and slaughtered."

Silence filled the room. *No one—absolutely no one—is going to make a fool of me!* Jezebel thought. She would have Elijah's head, if it was the last thing she did.

Meanwhile, Elijah received word of Jezebel's threats that very day and became afraid. Although he had called down fire from heaven, stood up to the prophets of Baal, and prayed for God to send rain, Elijah still lost his courage. *Lord! What have I done wrong?* he asked. *I did as You commanded and saw You act mightily and victoriously against Your enemies! There is now no doubt among Israel that You alone are God!* Elijah sighed. Everything within him was drained, and he felt empty— and alone. *Why, why then, am I suffering so? My very life is in danger, for Queen Jezebel will not stop hunting me until I have been killed—just*

as her prophets were slain. . . . Elijah sat in silence, his fists drawn up tightly against his body, and his teeth clenched. He had gone from a very high point to a very low one all in a matter of hours. Elijah felt there was nothing left to do but run for his life. And run he did—not stopping until he reached the southernmost town in the land of Judah.

Leaving his servant in Beersheba, Elijah then went a day's journey into the desert and came to a broom tree where he sat down and prayed that he might die. "O Lord," he sighed heavily, "I've had enough. Take my life, for I am no better than my ancestors." Full of discouragement, Elijah lay down under the tree and fell asleep! . . .

"Get up and eat," the angel of the Lord said, touching Elijah. Elijah looked around. Near his head were a cake of bread baked over hot coals and a jug of water. Elijah ate, drank, and lay down again. The angel came back a second time, encouraging him to eat once more. "Get up and eat, for the journey is too much for you," the angel said. Elijah did as instructed and felt strengthened from the meal. He then traveled forty days and forty nights to reach Mount Horeb—the mountain of God. There he went into a cave and spent the night.

Mount Horeb was part of Mount Sinai—the place where God showed His awesome power to Moses and the Israelites centuries before. Since no one can look upon God's glory and live, Elijah put his cloak over his face before meeting with God.

"What are you doing here, Elijah?" the Lord asked him.

"I have been very zealous to serve You, Lord. But the people of Israel have broken their covenant with You, torn down Your altars, and killed every one of Your prophets!" Elijah answered. He sighed heavily and continued, "They killed every one of Your prophets, and I'm the only one left! Now they are trying to kill me as well!" Elijah moaned, full of distress.

God listened patiently to Elijah's woes, then redirected his attention. He gave instructions for Elijah to stand at the entrance of the cave, for He would pass by. Elijah did as he was told. Just then, a great and powerful wind ripped through the mountains, sending shattered rocks and fragments everywhere—but the Lord was not in the wind. God then sent a powerful earthquake followed by a fire—but He chose not to reveal Himself in those spectacular things either. Then came a gentle whisper. Elijah put his cloak over his face and went out to meet with God. There, he received comfort, encouragement, and marching orders for what to do next. Elijah had found God's care—not just in the spectacular "highs" of life, but in the low and quiet points as well.

exploring deeper

Turn to 1 Kings 19 and read verse 14. Take note of the last part of this verse, then drop down and read God's response to this in verse 18. Was Elijah's perspective on his problems accurate?

DANGER AHEAD

It's very easy to get caught up in the "woe is me" syndrome (sin-drome), which only causes us to focus on ourselves instead of the Lord. Elijah fell into this trap. It is a very easy thing to get so caught up with the spectacular that we feel let down and can't see God's hand in the ordinary. The greatest danger of this happening is usually after an important victory or seeing God work mightily in and through your life. Be careful!

GETTING YOUR BEARINGS:
THE BOOK OF 2 KINGS

Second Kings begins where 1 Kings leaves off—and the tunnels continue to twist and turn with great adventure—and terrible mishaps. Powerful nations are surrounding Israel and Judah—nations God would use to accomplish His purposes and carry out His judgment.

For the most part, reading through this section of Scripture can get confusing, for it often switches between the kings of Judah and the kings of Israel. When reading this for yourself in your own Bible, you might want to take two different colored pencils and highlight the appropriate kings. For example: You could use red for kings of Israel—since God would put a stop to their kingdom first. Use green for kings of Judah, since God would preserve Judah as the nation that would give birth to the Messiah.

As you explore 2 Kings, you'll notice examples of obedience and disobedience to God—sometimes from the same person! You'll see faith in action and faith in need of repair, good actions and chain reactions, brief moments of victory and years of defeat, but most of all, you will see God's hand always there, preventing total disaster. As you go through these passages, keep your head up so you don't lose your way—or your perspective—and keep your eyes on the Lord. That's something Israel and Judah didn't do. Enjoy the journey. I'll meet you on the other side.. . .

SAYS WHO?!

TAKEN FROM 2 KINGS 1

GETTING READY

Before you begin today, make sure your heart is prepared. This is done by simply taking the time to talk with God before you get into His Word. Ask Him to quiet your heart and thoughts so you might be able to learn what He wants to show you.

THE JOURNEY

Have you ever met people who think they own the world and can boss everyone else around?

"What are you doing back so soon?" King Ahaziah asked. "Surely you couldn't have gone to Ekron and back in such a short time!" The king groaned in pain as he repositioned his body. The messengers hesitated before giving their report. Ever since falling through the lattice of his upper room window, the king had been suffering from pain, and the fear of dying.

"Go to Ekron in the land of the Philistines," he had ordered his messengers, "and inquire of Baal-Zebub if I will recover from my injury." The messengers left to seek an answer from the false god of the Philistines but never made it to Ekron. Instead, they received an answer from an unexpected source—the prophet Elijah—who met them on the road.

"Is it because there is no God in Israel that you go to consult Baal-Zebub, the god of Ekron?" Elijah asked. The messengers looked at one another, not sure how to respond. All they knew was their need to return with an answer for the king. "Since Ahaziah has done this, go back and give him this message from the Lord: 'You will not leave the bed you are lying on but will certainly die!'" With those words Elijah left the men standing in the middle of the road, looking at one another and wondering what to do next. After a slight hesitation, they decided to return to the king and deliver Elijah's message.

Baal-Zebub, "Lord of the flies" was a pagan idol specifically worshiped in Ekron. Thought to have healing powers, Baal-Zebub was not the same as Baal.

"We met a man on the road who stopped us," the messengers finally said, in answer to the king's surprise at their quick return.

"What kind of man was he—what did he look like?" the king quickly asked. When the messengers described the clothes made of hair and the leather belt the man wore, the king immediately recognized who it was. "Elijah!" he hissed under his breath. "That man was Elijah the prophet!" King Ahaziah quickly dismissed his messengers and summoned one of his captains. "Take your company of fifty men and bring Elijah here at once!" he ordered. The captain left to arrest Elijah and found him sitting on a hill.

"Man of God," the captain shouted at Elijah, "the king says, 'Come down.' You have been ordered to come along with us." Elijah knew the king hated him and the God he represented. The king had even sent a band of soldiers to arrest Elijah and drag him before the throne like an outlaw. Elijah knew God's honor was being challenged, and he would have no part of it.

"If I am a man of God as you say," he responded, "then may fire come down from heaven and destroy you and your fifty men!" No sooner had Elijah spoken these words than fire fell from heaven and consumed them all.

Instead of learning from this, the king impatiently sent another captain with his fifty men, making the same demands of Elijah. "Man of God," the captain called out with great authority, "the king says, 'Come down now!' You are to come with us right this moment, and *that* is an order from the king *himself!*" The captain believed his message would cause Elijah to come with him immediately *After all,* the soldier mistakenly thought to himself, *Ahaziah is king of Israel, and there is no greater authority than him in all the land. What King Ahaziah wants, King Ahaziah shall get!* The soldier was not ready for the response he received.

Once again Elijah responded, "If I am a man of God who takes my directions and orders from the Lord God, then may fire from heaven come down and destroy you and your fifty men!" In

There were two King Ahaziahs who ruled ten years apart from each other. The Ahaziah mentioned here is the son of King Ahab. He ruled in Israel (the northern tribes) for two years, beginning 853 B.C. The other Ahaziah ruled over the southern tribes of Judah nearly twelve years later. Both Ahaziahs were evil and didn't seek after God.

that instant, fire fell from heaven and consumed the captain and his band of soldiers. King Ahaziah, still not understanding that he couldn't control God, sent yet another captain with his soldiers to Elijah. This time, however, the captain who came had respect for both the Lord and the Lord's servants. He called Elijah a "man of God" not with contempt, but with sincerity. He then made his request of Elijah humbly and didn't command as if he were giving orders to a dog. The Lord saw this and encouraged Elijah to go with the captain—and Elijah did, obediently.

exploring deeper

Open up your Bible and turn to the first chapter in the Book of 2 Kings. Now, look at verses 16-17. According to these verses, what happened when Elijah met with King Ahaziah?

DANGER AHEAD

King Ahaziah knew it was wrong to seek the gods of other nations, yet he chose to do so anyway. Doing evil in God's eyes was of little concern to him, for King Ahaziah had set himself up as his own authority. This move made him an arrogant person who had only contempt for God and those who followed Him.

Life today is no different. It is almost guaranteed you will meet up with arrogant people who think they own the world and can command anything of anyone. Follow Elijah's example and don't blindly and fearfully march at their command. Such people only feed on the sense of power they get from ordering around timid people. Instead, stand your ground and ask yourself, "Says who?!" Then, let power fall where it rightly belongs—into God's hands.

MAY I HAVE THAT... AND MORE?

TAKEN FROM 2 KINGS 2

GETTING READY

Before going any further, stop and pray. Ask God to give you a renewed passion to live for Him in such a way that others would see your life and desire to know God all the more.

THE JOURNEY

Have you ever wanted what someone else has—for nonselfish reasons?

"No," Elisha replied respectfully, "I choose not to stay behind but to go with you." *This is now the third time Elijah has tried to keep me from coming with him. Doesn't he know I am committed to stay with him— even to the very end?* Elisha wondered to himself. Elijah seemed satisfied with Elisha's response and invited him to continue on with him. A school of prophets from Jericho followed from a distance. They knew Elijah would soon be taken from them and watched as the older and younger prophets walked together toward the Jordan River.

Elisha couldn't help but think back to the first time he met Elijah. He was busy plowing with twelve oxen when Elijah approached him in the field and threw his cloak upon him. "Allow me to say goodbye to my father and mother," Elisha said. "Then I'll come with you." Elijah nodded his head in agreement. Taking his oxen, Elisha slaughtered them and burned his plowing equipment to cook the meat. He then offered it to the people and set out to follow Elijah.

Elisha means "My God is salvation." Through Elisha's life, God would work miracles that would point others to Him. You can read about these in 2 Kings, chapters 2—6.

When the two men reached the Jordan River, they stopped, for they could go no farther. Elijah removed his cloak, rolled it up, and struck the water. The water parted, and both men crossed to the other side. *The same God who did those miracles long ago is still choosing to show His power in and through those who are His servants,* Elisha realized. He remembered hearing how God had parted the Red Sea for Moses and the Jordan River for Joshua.

"Tell me, what can I do for you?" Elijah asked the younger prophet who would fill his shoes.

"Please, let me become your successor and inherit a double portion of your spirit!" Elisha responded. Elijah understood what the young prophet desired but knew it wasn't his to give.

"You've asked a difficult thing. But, if you see me when I am taken, it will be a sign that God has given you what you asked," he answered.

As the two were walking and talking together, a chariot of fire suddenly appeared from out of the heavens and swooped down between them—separating Elisha from Elijah. Then, a whirlwind came and swept Elijah off the face of the earth and into God's presence. As Elijah was caught up into the whirlwind, his cloak fell to the ground near Elisha's feet. Carefully, Elisha bent over and picked it up, looking heavenward. He tore his robe in mourning and carried the cloak

A prophet throwing his cloak upon someone represented the passing on of his authority to that person.

with him to the river's edge. There, Elisha stopped. *I know what I have asked of You, Lord, that I might be able to carry on the ministry of Elijah and do even greater things for Your glory. I also remember Elijah's words that if I saw him being taken up, I would know You have granted me my desires,* Elisha prayed silently. He looked at the cloak in his hands and knew what it meant. God was desiring to use Elisha as His next prophet to bring others to Him. Rolling up the cloak, Elisha—full of faith—called out, "Where is the Lord, the God of Elijah?" and struck the Jordan River. Just as God had done for Elijah, He parted the Jordan River, so Elisha could cross back over.

> **Elisha asked for a double portion of what Elijah had. Interestingly, the Bible records he did almost twice as many miracles!**

When the school of prophets who had been watching from a distance saw what Elisha had done, they immediately knew Elisha was operating under God's power—taking over where Elijah left off. The prophet Elisha would be God's next great prophet who would do mighty works in the name of the Lord. Little did Elisha know how God would use him and how greatly the prayer of his heart would be answered.

exploring deeper

Not long after this event, Elisha encountered a difficulty. Open your Bible to 2 Kings 2:23-25 and read about it. What happened? How did Elisha respond? Do you think he overreacted?

It is important to know that the youths were really a gang of young men—possibly young false prophets of Baal. When they shouted, "Go on up!" they were saying that if Elisha was as great a prophet as Elijah had been, he should just follow Elijah and disappear into heaven! Elisha saw the contempt for God in their eyes. His curse was not to protect his own pride but was in response to their disrespect for the Lord.

Skill Time

Although you and I will probably never do any "miraculous" things for God, we are equally called to be the Lord's servants. God desires to work in and through our lives in such a way that the world might know He is God. Elisha's heart was in the right place; he wanted what God had to offer, so he could use it for God's glory.

Lord, there are so many times I fail You. Please forgive me. I want to live my life under Your power so that You can do great things in and through me. However You choose to use me, I give my time, abilities, desires, and all that I am to You. Help me to seek Your best and not settle for anything less than that which will bring glory to You. Amen.

BY THE WAY...

TAKEN FROM 2 KINGS 5

GETTING READY

Before you begin today's lesson, spend time thanking God for who He is. Ask Him to help you better reflect faithfulness, truthfulness, and integrity in your thoughts, motives, and actions.

THE JOURNEY

Do you secretly try to manipulate others for your own personal benefit?

"If only my master Naaman would see the prophet who lives in Israel—his leprosy would be healed," the Israelite girl said to her mistress, Naaman's wife. Naaman was a commander of the Aramean army and very valuable to the king of Aram. Unfortunately, he had leprosy—a disease that would eventually take his life. The king of Aram was most fearful of losing his best commander, so when he heard about the possibility of Naaman being healed, he wrote a letter of introduction for Naaman to carry with him and hand to the king of Israel. The letter simply stated: "With this message I present my servant Naaman to you to be healed."

"What?!" the king of Israel said with disbelief to his attendants. "This king sends me a leper to heal! Am I God that I can kill and bring back to life?!" he shouted. *Does the king of Aram use this leper to pick a fight with me? I can't heal him any more than I could heal myself! Why does this king insist on stirring up trouble and putting me in such a position?!* he thought to himself. The king of Israel tore his robes, expressing both grief and deep concern over the situation at hand. The thought of calling on the Lord, or even God's prophet, Elisha, never once crossed his mind.

Elisha heard about the king's distress over Naaman and came saying, "Why have you torn your robes? Send the man to me and he will know there is a true prophet of God in Israel."

Aram was a pagan nation that frequently made war upon Israel. The Arameans often swooped down in a raid and took captives back with them. The Israelite servant girl in Naaman's household was one such captive.

It wasn't long before Naaman came to Elisha's door with all his horses and chariots. Instead of speaking to him directly, Elisha sent his servant to the door with instructions for Naaman. "Go and wash yourself seven times in the Jordan River, and your leprosy will go away." Naaman stood stunned. He was a proud man and didn't like being treated like an ordinary person.

No healing ceremony?! The prophet won't even speak to me himself? he muttered under his breath. *What kind of joke is this?!* Naaman went away angry. "Wash myself seven times in the Jordan River?!" he repeated to himself. "Never!! Are not the rivers in Damascus better than the Jordan River?" Naaman's servants could see that their master's pride had been wounded, but they believed he had nothing to lose and encouraged Naaman to obey Elisha's instructions.

"If he told you to do something great, would you have done it?" they gently coaxed. "Surely then, if he tells you to do something simple, why not do it and be cured?" Naaman looked at his servants and saw their concern. Slowly, his anger faded and he journeyed to the

Jordan River to do as Elisha had instructed. When Naaman came out of the water, everyone stood amazed—his leprosy was gone! Not only that, Naaman's skin was restored to what it looked like in his boyhood! Quickly, Naaman returned to Elisha to thank him and offer gifts as payment for this great deed.

"Now I know the God in Israel is the one true God!" Naaman exclaimed. With that, he offered Elisha the gifts he had brought with him—750 pounds of silver, 150 pounds of gold and ten sets of clothing. Elisha looked at the generous gifts but refused them. Unfortunately, Gehazi, Elisha's servant, looked at them with desire, seeing nothing wrong with receiving them. Secretly, Gehazi planned how he could manipulate Naaman in order to get some of the "goods" Elisha turned down. *As surely as the Lord lives, I will run after Naaman and get something from him,* Gehazi thought to himself, *for he was more than willing to give those gifts!*

> In Elisha's day, there were many false prophets who made a habit of "lining their pockets" by accepting gifts for their services. Elisha wanted to show Naaman that God's gift of healing couldn't be bought.

If Elisha won't take them from Naaman, then I will! Gehazi's thoughts faded as he caught up with Naaman's caravan.

"Is everything all right?" Naaman asked, concerned.

"Yes," Gehazi replied, "everything is fine, except that my master, Elisha, sent me with word that two prophets came to visit him unexpectedly, and . . . by the way . . . could you please give him 75 pounds of silver and two sets of clothing?"

"By all means!" Naaman responded generously, believing Gehazi's lie. Gehazi's eyes gleamed, and he secretly delighted at his gain. When he saw Naaman didn't give just one bag of silver, but two, Gehazi delighted all the more! *I've got it all!* he breathed to himself, pleased with his actions. Upon returning home, Gehazi quickly stashed the silver and clothes in his house and returned to Elisha. . . .

exploring deeper

Quickly turn in your Bible to 2 Kings 5:25-27 and read it. (Go on!) What did Elisha ask of Gehazi? What was Gehazi's response (verse 25)? Gehazi's motive was to gain something for himself. What did God allow Gehazi to gain (verse 27)?

CROSS ROADS

Gehazi fell into the temptation of looking out for his own personal gain instead of serving the Lord. He readily manipulated Naaman in order to get what he wanted. Gehazi ended up getting more than he bargained for!

By the way . . . the next time an opportunity comes your way, will you try to get all you can for yourself, or will you be satisfied with letting God get the glory?

OH.

TAKEN FROM 2 KINGS 6-7

GETTING READY

Before beginning your time of exploring today, stop and pray. Commit this time to the Lord. Ask God to help you see that with Him, nothing is impossible.

THE JOURNEY

Do you find it hard to believe God's promise of victory when you're surrounded by defeat?

"I think I will set up my camp right . . . there!" The king of Aram pointed to a spot that would make capturing the Israelites easier. Unfortunately, the king's plans so far had all been spoiled by Elisha. For each plan the king of Aram made, the prophet Elisha informed the king of Israel—who then checked on those places.

"Which one of you men is on the king of Israel's side?!" the king of Aram demanded. He was furious because not just once, but several times, his plans had failed.

"None of us!" came the loyal response. "It is Elisha the prophet who lives in Israel! He informs the Israelite king of even the words spoken by you in the privacy of your own bedroom!" This angered the king of Aram.

The chariots and horses Elisha's servant saw were part of God's heavenly army. There is an entire world out there our human eyes can't see.

"Go and find out where this Elisha lives," he snapped, "so I can send men and have him captured!"

When word came back that Elisha was in Dothan, the king of Aram sent a great army with horses and chariots to surround the city during the night. The next morning Elisha's servant looked over the city walls in fear. "Elisha, what shall we do?!" he asked anxiously. The situation looked hopeless. There was no escape!

Elisha looked at his servant and replied, "Don't be afraid. Those who are with us are more than those who are with them." His servant looked up and met Elisha's gaze, confused. To him Elisha was clearly outnumbered, and defeat was soon in coming. "O Lord," Elisha prayed, "open my servant's eyes so he may see!" Suddenly the young servant gasped in surprise, for God had opened his eyes. Now he could see the Lord's horses and chariots of fire on the surrounding hills!

Elisha prayed once more and asked the Lord to strike the Aramean army with blindness. He then went out to the blind soldiers and said, "This isn't the road or the city you want. Follow me, and I'll lead you to the man you're looking for!" Elisha led them away, then prayed for their sight to be restored once they arrived where he had taken them. When their eyes were opened, the soldiers found themselves in the capital city of Samaria standing before the king of Israel!

Sharing a meal with someone symbolized friendship. Because the soldiers ate with the king, they were now obligated under a treaty of friendship and could no longer raid Israel.

They were terrified. Elisha instructed the king not to harm the soldiers, but rather to feed them and send them back to their country. The soldiers left—and stopped their raids on Israel's territory.

Time passed, however, and the king of Aram marched against Samaria and laid siege to it. No supplies could go in or out. Food and resources eventually became so scarce, even a donkey's head was selling for 40 ounces of silver! The Aramean king knew it would only be a short time before the Israelites died of starvation or surrendered.

Elisha lived in the city of Dothan, which was twelve miles north of Samaria—the capital of Israel.

People inside the city gates grew desperate, and the king of Israel grew frustrated and angry. He was totally helpless. *That Elisha is responsible for this—surely he can do something about it!* the king grumbled under his breath. *Where is that God of his now?* Going to Elisha, the king demanded, "It is the Lord who brought this trouble upon us! Why should I wait on Him any longer?!"

Elisha could hear the hostility in the king's voice, yet he addressed the issue at hand. "This is what the Lord says: 'By this time tomorrow there will be food enough for all.'"

The king's servant heard these words and laughed. "Yeah, right. Even if the Lord opened the floodgates of heaven, it could never happen," he spat with disbelief.

Elisha directed his gaze toward the servant. "Tomorrow," he said firmly, "you will see it with your own eyes. But *you* won't be able to eat any of it because of your disbelief." The servant glared back and then turned to leave with the king.

That same day four Israelite men with leprosy said to each other, "If we stay here outside the city gate, we'll starve. If we go inside the city, we'll starve there too. Let's go to the enemy and turn ourselves in. If they kill us, it will only mean we die sooner." At dusk they made their way to the Aramean camp and found it completely stocked with food—yet abandoned! Supplies were strewn all along the road, for God had caused the Arameans to hear the sound of approaching horses and chariots, and they quickly fled in fear. The starving men grabbed supplies for themselves and took all they desired. Then they went to the city gate and shouted the good news to the Israelites. At first the king thought it was a trick, but when he sent five soldiers to investigate, their reports came back the same. That morning, there was food for all—just as God had promised through Elisha. God had brought victory in the midst of defeat.

exploring deeper

What was the response of the king's servant when he heard there was food that morning? We can only imagine! However, open your Bible to 2 Kings 7:19-20 and find out the facts. What happened to the king's servant (verse 20)? Note: "Man of God" refers to Elisha.

THINKING on your FEET

The king's servant only saw defeat. The last thing he saw ahead was victory. Unfortunately, he wasn't able to stick around and enjoy it.

When defeat is all around you—yet God promises you victory—what will your response be?

CHARRRGE!

TAKEN FROM 2 KINGS 9-10

GETTING READY

As you begin today, ask God to examine your heart and show you where you run on automatic pilot—fueled by your own emotions and enthusiasm. Ask Him to help you bring your heart under His control, so it won't have mastery over you.

THE JOURNEY

Have you ever gotten caught up in your own enthusiasm for a certain cause, only to later discover you left God out of the picture?

"Are you Jehu?" the young man from the school of prophets asked.

The commander of King Joram's army looked up and said, "Yes, I am he."

"I have a message for you," the prophet said. Jehu got up from where he had been sitting with his fellow officers at Ramoth Gilead and followed the young prophet into the house. When the door closed, the prophet pulled out a flask of oil and anointed Jehu's head, declaring, "This is what the Lord, the God of Israel, says: 'I anoint you king over the Lord's people. You are also to destroy those in King Ahab's family, for I am bringing about justice for the innocent blood of My prophets and servants shed by Jezebel.'"

Ramoth Gilead was an important fortress city on the east side of the Jordan River. King Joram was injured in battle while trying to take it back from the Arameans.

The young prophet gave his proclamation, anointed Jehu, then fled from the house as instructed by Elisha. Jehu was left standing there, surprised, yet excited at the message he had been given. Trying to push aside his own thoughts and mounting zeal, Jehu left the room to rejoin the others outside.

"What did that madman want?" the others asked curiously. They had seen the young prophet open the door and run out. "Oh, nothing. You know how strange he can be sometimes," Jehu said, trying to brush off the encounter. The men looked at each other, not believing Jehu's words. They could tell by the look on Jehu's face that something strange and important had happened.

"That's not true!" they responded in unison. "Tell us!" In hushed tones, Jehu excitedly told them what the prophet had done. "Jehu is king!" they shouted, and quickly spread their cloaks underneath him. They then blew their trumpets, announcing a new king had been anointed and shouted again, "Jehu is king!"

Jehu looked at the men and could tell he had their support. This gave him all the more drive to get on with the task at hand. "If this is how you feel, don't let anyone in this city leave to tell those in Jezreel," he urged. Jehu wanted to catch King Joram off guard. He knew the king was at his palace in Jezreel, trying to recover from an injury. After his fellow officers nodded in agreement, Jehu set off with his troops. *This is a job I can really get into!* he whispered to himself. . . .

"I see some troops coming!" one of the lookouts in Jezreel shouted.

"Send a horseman to ride out and ask if they come in peace!" King Joram commanded. When the horseman reached the troops led by Jehu,

Jehu assured him all was fine and told the messenger to fall in behind and ride the rest of the way in with them. When the horseman didn't immediately return to the palace, King Joram sent out another. The same thing happened.

"The messenger has reached them but isn't coming back!" the lookout reported. He then strained to see who was driving the chariot. "The driving of the chariot is like that of Jehu—he drives like a madman!" Upon hearing it was the commander of his troops, King Joram and visiting King Ahaziah got into their chariots and rode out to meet him. Although King Joram was recovering from an injury, he was concerned something might have happened at Ramoth Gilead he needed to know about. He was right.

"Jehu," King Joram said upon reaching him, "do you come with news of peace?" The king couldn't help but notice the unusual look in Jehu's eyes.

"How can there be peace," Jehu replied, "as long as the idolatry and witchcraft of your mother, Jezebel, are all around us?!"

King Joram, realizing the intent of Jehu's words, turned about and fled, shouting, "Treason! Treason!" but Jehu drew his bow, aimed at the king, and killed him. When King Ahaziah of Judah saw this, he fled up the road but was chased down and killed as well. Jehu then went into Jezreel.

Hearing that Jehu had killed her son, King Joram, Queen Jezebel waited at her window, still feeling secure in the power she held.

Because of an unwise treaty, King Jehoshaphat of Judah gave his son in marriage to the daughter of Ahab and Jezebel! Her name was Athaliah, and she became the mother of King Ahaziah. (Read more about them in the devotions "Friend or Foe?" and "Excuse Me, Is This Yours?" on pages 297 and 301.)

"Who is on my side? Who?" Jehu shouted, looking up at the window where Jezebel stood. Two or three servants looked down at him. "Throw her down!" Jehu commanded—and they did. Queen Jezebel was no more. Jehu then set about destroying the rest of the family of Ahab, just as God commanded.

exploring deeper

Jehu killed the family of Ahab as God commanded, but open your Bible to 2 Kings 10:11 and read it. This verse tells us some things Jehu did that God *didn't* command. What does it say? (Hint: Look for the words "as well as" and read what follows.) Now, turn to 10:28-31 and read that. Although Jehu did what God asked, he also got carried away. Jehu did too much of his own thing (what God did *not* command) and not enough of what God *did* command.

CROSS ROADS

It's an easy thing to follow the lead of your own enthusiasm—and a dangerous one as well. Be careful not to charge ahead of God, letting your passions and zeal dictate the actions you take. They will only take you in one direction, and that is off the mark from where God wants you to be. The next time your passions scream, "Charrrge!" will you plow ahead full speed with your zeal at the wheel, or will you put the brakes on and allow God to do the driving?

NO OFFENSE?

TAKEN FROM 2 KINGS 16

GETTING READY

Spend a moment praying and getting your heart settled before the Lord. Ask Him to give you the desire and passion to live for Him—no matter what others may think.

THE JOURNEY

Do you know people who are more concerned about offending others than they are about offending God?

King Ahaz of Judah sighed as he thought about his difficulties. Unlike his father and grandfather (King Jotham and King Uzziah), he didn't seek after God. Instead, Ahaz chose to make cast idols of Baal and worship them in the high places. He even set up altars for burning incense on the hilltops and under every spreading tree, leading the people into idolatry. Because of the wickedness in Judah, God would judge the kingdom and use the powerful nations of Aram and Assyria against it.

Perhaps their god is stronger than ours, Ahaz thought when he suffered defeat at the hands of the Arameans. *From now on, we will worship the god of the Arameans in addition to our God, and hopefully be able to stand stronger against our enemies!* Although King Ahaz was pleased with his own reasoning, God was not. Instead of success, King Ahaz continued to suffer defeat. Even the king of the northern tribes of Israel came against Judah, raiding and taking captives back with him. In one day, Ahaz lost 120,000 soldiers, while 200,000 wives, sons, and daughters were carried off from Judah with the rest of the plunder.

King Ahaz's grandfather, King Azariah (also called Uzziah), ruled for fifty years and did great things for Judah (built up the army, strengthened agriculture, and improved water supplies). However, he neglected to tear down the high places, which became Judah's undoing.

King Ahaz grew both frustrated and fearful. However, instead of turning to the Lord, Ahaz turned to the Assyrians for help. King Ahaz knew the Assyrians were a powerful nation greatly feared by many. So, without further thought, the king of Judah gathered the silver and gold from the temple of the Lord as well as from the treasuries of the royal palace. He sent all this wealth with messengers to the Assyrian king, saying, "I am your servant and willing to live under your control. Please accept my gifts and come save me from the hand of the Arameans and from Israel!"

King Tiglath-Pileser readily accepted the gifts, attacked the Aramean capital of Damascus, and deported its people to Kir. He then killed the Aramean king and claimed Damascus for himself. King Ahaz felt relief and freedom—not realizing he had opened his doors to the power-hungry nation of Assyria.

In an effort to express his thanks to the Assyrian king, King Ahaz personally traveled to Damascus. Upon arriving, King Ahaz was impressed by a large altar he saw there. *This is what I need!* he said to himself, and he drew a sketch of detailed plans of the altar. Sending his sketch to Uriah the priest, King Ahaz instructed one to be built just like it. Uriah did accordingly, and King Ahaz was pleased when he returned home.

The large altar was impressive and looked just like the one in Damascus. "From now on, sacrifices will be made upon this altar," Ahaz proclaimed with delight, pointing to the new altar. "The bronze altar will be used only occasionally when I am seeking guidance, but for nothing more than that," he added, moving it out of the way. Sadly, King Ahaz would seek little guidance from the Lord.

"Now, let's strip away the side panels and remove the basins from the portable water carts," Ahaz suggested. He then took the large basin in which the priests were to wash and removed it from the backs of the twelve bronze oxen. It was placed on a stone base instead. King Ahaz "remodeled" and removed several of the furnishings of the temple of the Lord—even taking down the Sabbath canopy that had been built at the temple.

"There!" Ahaz remarked as he removed the royal entryway outside the temple. He did it out of courtesy and respect for the Assyrian king. "That will show him honor and cause no offense," Ahaz said triumphantly. That's what Ahaz thought! Sadly, he hadn't given any consideration to what *God* considered offensive. . . .

exploring deeper

Open your Bible and turn past the Book of 2 Kings until you get to 2 Chronicles 28:24-25. (Chapter 28 of 2 Chronicles is the "companion" passage to 2 Kings 16 and gives additional information about King Ahaz and his actions.) According to verses 24 and 25, what else did King Ahaz do?

Skill Time

Whether he realized it or not, King Ahaz was getting rid of the "signs" that connected him to the Lord and worship of the one true God—all in the name of trying not to be offensive! We often do the same, only in subtle ways, such as not bowing to give God thanks for a meal we're eating in public, or remaining silent when we should speak up for the Lord. In an effort not to cause offense, we hide the truth of who we really are and all God means to us. In so doing, we bring the greatest offense against God. Take a moment to examine your heart. If the prayer below expresses how you feel, pray it, then sign and date it. Refer back to this as a reminder when your courage wanes.

Lord, please forgive me for the times I've been ashamed or afraid to call You my own. I really want to live for You, and I want others to see a difference in my life. Please help me to be more courageous. I desire to please You above all.

_____

(signed)   (today's date)

NEVER!

TAKEN FROM 2 KINGS 18-19

GETTING READY

Stop to pray, so your heart will be properly ready and teachable before the Lord. (It doesn't help to get into God's Word if God's Word doesn't get in you!) Ask God what He wants you to learn, then act on it!

THE JOURNEY

Have you ever known a team who thought they couldn't be beat?

Although my father, King Ahaz, did what was evil in Your sight, I will strive to serve You with my whole heart, Lord, King Hezekiah silently prayed. He was only twenty-five years old when he became ruler over Judah, yet he had seen enough to know what paths to avoid. Instead of doing evil, King Hezekiah sought to do what was right in the eyes of the Lord. Immediately, he set about removing the high places, smashing the sacred stones, and cutting down the Asherah poles. He even broke into pieces the bronze snake Moses had made, for he saw the people worship it as an idol. In all the king did he followed the Lord and held fast to Him, keeping the commands the Lord had given to Moses. God rewarded him by giving him success and boldness in everything. King Hezekiah even rebelled against Assyria—the powerful nation to the north that held them in bondage.

I saw King Shalmaneser of Assyria march against Samaria and lay siege to it before destroying Israel and carrying the people off, he thought. It was only Hezekiah's sixth year as king when he saw Israel's downfall. He knew it was because they had violated God's covenant and didn't obey the Lord their God. God had warned it would happen.

King Hezekiah shows us how to say "never!" to being defeated:

N - **Never give in to fear.**

E - **Examine what you have faith in.**

V - **Value going to God in prayer.**

E - **Expect God to help you.**

R - **Rely on Him, no matter what.**

When King Shalmaneser died and King Sennacherib came into power, Hezekiah had hoped his act of not paying tribute would slip by unnoticed. It didn't. Looking at this as rebellion, Sennacherib gathered his army, attacked all the fortified cities of Judah, and captured them.

"I have done wrong. Withdraw from me and I will pay whatever you demand we owe," King Hezekiah pleaded. The Assyrian king demanded—and received—eleven tons of silver and one ton of gold. It was all the silver Hezekiah found in the temple of the Lord and in the treasuries of the royal palace. He even stripped off the gold that had covered the doors and doorposts of the temple and gave it to the king of Assyria. The powerful Assyrian king felt satisfied with the results. He sent his commander in chief, his field commander, and his personal representative with an army to challenge King Ahaziah and the kingdom of Judah.

"What are you trusting in that makes you so confident?" the commanders challenged Hezekiah's leaders. "Don't you know that your rebellious words can't take the place of military skill and power? Who will come to your rescue? Egypt isn't dependable, and none of your other allies have been able to stand against us! We're undefeated!" they boasted loudly.

King Hezekiah's leaders asked the Assyrians to speak in Aramaic, so those listening on the walls wouldn't understand or hear the threats. "What the king of Assyria has to say, he wants everyone in Judah to hear!" the chief commander arrogantly replied. He then shouted in Hebrew to those on the wall. "Don't let King Hezekiah deceive you! He will never be able to deliver you from my power! Don't let him fool you by telling you to trust in the Lord! Have the gods of any other nations ever saved their people from the mighty power of Assyria?!" he challenged. "Never! So, what makes you think the Lord can rescue Jerusalem?!" The commander laughed as Hezekiah's men returned inside the city walls and made their report to the king.

Upon hearing their words, King Hezekiah tore his robes in despair, then went to the temple of the Lord to pray. Sending his leaders to the prophet Isaiah to learn what the Lord would have them do next, Hezekiah was encouraged. "Don't fear, for Jerusalem won't fall to the Assyrian king," the prophet said. "God has heard your prayers and will Himself deal with the king of Assyria and his army. Sennacherib will be called back to his country on urgent business, and there he will be killed with a sword."

Just as Isaiah said, King Sennacherib of Assyria was called back to his land with haste—Ethiopia threatened war. Before leaving to return home, however, Sennacherib sent a message to Hezekiah: "Don't let this God you trust deceive you with promises that Jerusalem won't be captured. You know perfectly well the kings of Assyria have crushed anyone who stands in their way. You will never be able to stand against us—Never!"

exploring deeper

Quickly turn in your Bible to 2 Kings 19:17-19 and read it. What does King Hezekiah do? Now, look over at verses 35-37. What does God do?

DANGER AHEAD

It's easy to feel defeated by the boasting and attacks on our defenses, ourselves, and our God. Our first impulse is to give in, or at least consider whether the claims could be true. Don't. Hezekiah heard the claims of victory against him, yet he took those claims right to the throne of the One who really rules—God. The king of Assyria said he would never be defeated—never. God simply shows that with Him, all things are possible. Never say never.

EVERY LITTLE BIT HELPS

TAKEN FROM 2 KINGS 21-23

GETTING READY

Spend a moment to pray and clear your mind of distractions. Ask God to show you the importance of how just one life lived for Him can make a difference.

THE JOURNEY

Do you ever feel like you want to give up resisting the evil around you?

"You found *what?*" King Josiah said, jumping to his feet.

"The Book of the Law of Moses!" Shaphan eagerly said. "While cleaning out the temple as you commanded, we came across this scroll! Shall I read it?" The king of Judah sank back into his chair in wonder. His mind clouded with all the thoughts of the wickedness that had been done by his father, King Manasseh. *Lord, You know how my father worshiped the sun, moon, and stars, built altars for Baal, and set up an Asherah pole in the temple—Your temple! You saw when he rebuilt the pagan shines my grandfather had torn down, practiced sorcery, and consulted with mediums and psychics,* Josiah prayed silently. He then stopped for a moment, overwhelmed at all the evil his father had done. *Lord, I want to make a difference!* Josiah uttered with passion.

"King Josiah . . . sir?" Shaphan asked once more, "Shall I read from the scroll?" King Josiah's attention returned to Shaphan, and he nodded his head, then listened with both delight and dread to God's words in the Law of Moses. Tears streamed down the king's face, and he tore his robes in distress. Although Josiah strove to bring the kingdom of Judah back to following the Lord, he knew much damage had already been done. *O Lord, our ancestors have not obeyed the words in this scroll,* he sighed with great desperation. *As a result, Your anger is burning against this place, for I know in Your righteousness and holy judgment, You will do as You promised according to Your Law.*

Seeking direction from God, King Josiah sent Hilkiah the priest along with Shaphan and three others to visit the prophetess Huldah. "God has seen how King Josiah was sorry and humbled himself before the Lord when he heard what God said about Jerusalem and its people," she said. "Because he tore his clothes in despair and repentance, God will not bring the disaster He promised on this place until after King Josiah has died and is buried in peace," the prophetess concluded.

King Josiah tore down the altar at Bethel and burned on it the bones of the false prophets who had been buried nearby in order to forever defile that place. This was a direct fulfillment of prophecy (1 Kings 13:2-3)!

The men returned to King Josiah with the message that God intended to destroy Jerusalem, but not until after he was gone. Not content to give up on resisting the evil around him, Josiah summoned all the leaders of Judah and Jerusalem. He then went to the temple of the Lord and stood before the priests, prophets, and people—from the least to the greatest. Opening the scroll, King Josiah began to read aloud and didn't stop until he had read the entire Book of the Covenant. Silence filled the air like a heavy blanket. Some looked down at their feet, ashamed. Others shifted their weight uncomfortably, knowing they had strayed far from the very God who called them by name.

King Josiah finished reading and looked out at the sea of faces before him. He then took the lead and pledged himself to obey the Lord by keeping all God's commands, regulations, and laws with all his heart and soul. The people then followed the king's lead and dedicated themselves as well—renewing the terms of the covenant that were written in the scroll. After that, a great Passover celebration was held—one that carefully followed all the laws of God more carefully than any other Passover celebration since the days of the judges.

> The Mount of Olives, a favorite place to build shrines and high places for idol worship, was often called the "Mount of Corruption" (2 Kings 23:13). Interestingly, in New Testament times, Jesus often chose the Mount of Olives as a place to sit and teach His disciples about serving God only.

Although King Josiah knew God was going to carry out His judgment, he also knew God wanted him to make a difference and resist the evil in the land while he lived. As a result, King Josiah finished having the temple of the Lord cleansed. All the tools and utensils used to worship Baal, Asherah, and the stars were removed and burned in a nearby valley. The Asherah pole from the temple was removed and burned; pagan priests appointed by previous kings of Judah were done away with; and altars, shrines, and idols were all torn down, broken, and crushed. Not one remnant of idolatry was left in the land of Judah because of the difference Josiah made.

exploring deeper

Open your Bible to 2 Kings 22:19-20 and read it. What does it say? What was King Josiah's reaction (2 Kings 23:24)? Do you think you would have done the same?

Skill Time

King Josiah didn't just think about himself. He strove to make a difference and change what he could—even when he was personally guaranteed he wouldn't be around to see God's judgment on the nation. King Josiah cleansed the land in spite of the judgment coming—he didn't give up, and he didn't give in.

Take a moment to evaluate your own life. What difference do you make? What can you do to make more of a difference in the lives of those around you? Think of one thing you can start to do, and begin doing it today!

GREAT. WHAT NEXT?!

TAKEN FROM 2 KINGS 23-25

GETTING READY

Take a moment to pray before you begin this last lesson in 2 Kings. In the quietness of your own heart, think about your life and everything that affects you—both good and bad. Ask God to help you understand and accept the fact that everything happening in your life happens for a reason.

THE JOURNEY

Have you ever felt like your whole world was starting to fall apart before your very eyes?

"King Josiah, turn and go back to Jerusalem," Neco, Pharaoh of Egypt, warned. "The quarrel I have is not with you, but with Babylon." King Josiah refused to listen. He feared Egypt and Assyria might join together to come against Judah in the future, so he engaged the Egyptian king in battle. It was a deadly mistake, and King Josiah was killed. As a result, Judah fell under Egypt's control. All of Judah mourned, and the people buried King Josiah in Jerusalem and chose his middle son, Jehoahaz, to be their next king. When Pharaoh Neco of Egypt saw this, he took Jehoahaz away in chains so he couldn't reign, and then imposed a heavy tax upon the people.

Jehoahaz has far too much leadership strength, and this could be a problem. I will make his older brother, Jehoiakim, ruler instead. He is weak and will make a good "puppet king," the Egyptian ruler said to himself. So, Jehoiakim became king over Judah and readily paid the gold and silver Neco demanded.

During Jehoiakim's reign, there was an unexpected turn of events. Nebuchadnezzar, king of Babylon, defeated Pharaoh Neco in battle. Babylon would be the new world power—gaining control over Egypt and all the kingdoms Egypt controlled—including the kingdom of Judah! Things were not looking good. . . .

To make sure Judah is securely under my control, King Nebuchadnezzar thought to himself, *I'll raid Jerusalem and take captives back to Babylon with me.* When he stormed Judah, it sent a strong message of Babylon's power to King Jehoiakim. Willingly, Jehoiakim submitted to the Babylonian king—but only for three years. Hoping to revolt, he sought help from Egypt but was unsuccessful. No one could stand against the powerful Babylonian empire. As Judah was weakened, it fell victim to other raiding bands from Babylonia, Aramea, Moab, and Ammon. God was removing Judah from the Promised Land and using other nations to accomplish His purposes.

King Jehoiakim died, and his son, Jehoiachin, came to the throne at the age of eighteen. He had ruled for only three months when Nebuchadnezzar came back through on a second raid, eight years after his first one. Readily, Jehoiachin surrendered and was taken prisoner

> When the Babylonians conquered a land, they took the "cream of the crop" as captives—often providing them with food and limited freedom in order to win their allegiance. The poor were left behind to tend the land, for they were no threat. In Nebuchadnezzar's first raid against Judah in 605 B.C., Daniel was taken as one of the captives (Daniel 1:1-3).

along with 10,000 others—all the officers and fighting men, craftsmen, and artisans. Only the poorest in the land were left in Jerusalem. All the treasures from the temple of the Lord and the royal palace were taken away as well. Even the gold articles that Solomon had made for the temple of the Lord were carted off and used in Nebuchadnezzar's temple. Women were also taken captive along with the officials and leading men of the kingdom. Nebuchadnezzar appointed Jehoiachin's uncle, Zedekiah, to be king and rule over the remaining people in Judah.

In 597 B.C. Nebuchadnezzar made his second raid against Jerusalem and looted Solomon's temple, fulfilling the prophecy of 1 Kings 9:6-9. A third and final raid was made in 588 B.C., when Jerusalem's walls were destroyed and the city burned.

Zedekiah did evil in the eyes of the Lord and also revolted against Babylon in his ninth year of ruling by seeking help from Egypt. Once again, Babylon was too powerful. Those who remained in Jerusalem only suffered all the more. "Ram the walls of the city!" the Babylonian soldiers were told, and they did. With the walls of Jerusalem destroyed, Judah would be weak and unable to stand against attackers. Zedekiah tried to escape, but was caught and then blinded so he might not lead any more revolts. His sons were killed so there would be no heirs to the throne. Things were looking hopeless for the remnant in Jerusalem.

Nebuchadnezzar finished tearing the walls down, broke the large bronze pillars of the temple in order to carry them off (as well as other temple furniture), and then ordered the city to be burned. He carried off the majority of poor people, leaving only a few farmers to keep the land from growing completely wild. Jerusalem was left in ruins. The people of Judah were all held captive in Babylon. Yet, through the smoldering ashes, God would raise a spark of hope. . . .

exploring deeper

Open your Bible to 2 Kings 25:27-30 and read it. The Babylonian king who replaced Nebuchadnezzar gave former King Jehoiachin of Judah special favor and released him from being a strict prisoner. Although the people of Judah were in another land, they were together—and being preserved. God was still faithful to them even while they were experiencing God's judgment as a nation.

Skill Time

When our world falls apart and nothing seems to be going right, our first response is to become angry or even rebellious. Instead of seeking what God might want to show us in our circumstances, we only look to escape our difficulties—often missing the whole point of our trials. This week, as you experience difficulties, watch your attitude and reaction. Give your disappointments and difficulties to God. Trust Him to make something great out of them, even the ashes.

GETTING YOUR BEARINGS:
THE BOOK OF 1 CHRONICLES

Just glancing at the first nine chapters of 1 Chronicles seems like enough to put anyone to sleep! It appears to be nothing more than a straight list of names and genealogies—all important historical records, but not necessarily something that's on your list of hot items to read! Don't be discouraged—or fooled! After the genealogies, 1 Chronicles begins giving vital information on the kings of Judah and offers more detail than the Books of Kings. Although these books are similar (Kings and Chronicles), 1 and 2 Chronicles were written after the Books of Kings.

Jewish tradition says that Ezra was the author of this book. He wrote it about 150 years after the events happened. The Israelites had been taken captive by the Babylonians and lived in exile for 70 years. Ezra returned from exile even later, and the Israelites needed to regroup. They needed to be reminded of who they were, where they had been, and where they were going. That is the point of the Chronicles.

Perhaps the best way to view this particular book is to think of it as a flashback in history—remembering the details of some of the nation's highlights (and low times). Since we already covered some of the background history in the Books of Kings, we'll only take a short time to explore 1 Chronicles. But don't zone out! There's more here than you think (that's why we're exploring it!). Keep a sharp eye open, and enjoy the journey.

WATCH YOUR STEP!

TAKEN FROM 1 CHRONICLES 13-15

GETTING READY

As you begin your journey through 1 Chronicles, ask the Lord to guide your heart and thoughts. Ask Him to point out areas in your life that seem more like the world's approach to God, rather than God's guidelines for a relationship with Him.

THE JOURNEY

Have you ever tried to do something good, but only got in trouble for it?

What a great celebration it was! After a hundred years of not having the ark of God in their midst, the Israelites were witnessing its return. Their new king—King David—planned to bring the ark into Jerusalem, so it could have a permanent resting place among the people. Excitement mounted as the Israelites went down to Kiriath Jearim to retrieve it from the house of Abinadab. The ark had been kept there after the Philistines returned it.

The Israelites remembered only too well how the ark of the Lord had been brought down to the battlefield (in King Saul's time) and used as a "good-luck charm" against the Philistines in battle. They remembered with horror how the ark of God—the very symbol of His presence with them—had been captured and carted off by the enemy. Later, they saw the ark returned on a cart pulled by cattle. They remembered and regretted—but today was not a day for regrets! It was a day for celebration!

The priests, Levites, and even King David wore their linens as they went to Abinadab's house to retrieve the ark. It was loaded onto a new cart and began its journey to Jerusalem with Abinadab's sons, Uzzah and Ahio, carefully guiding it. King David and all the Israelites rejoiced. Music from songs, harps, lyres, tambourines, cymbals, and trumpets filled the air. It seemed like nothing could go wrong—well, almost . . .

> **To this day, on the road to Jerusalem (about 1-2 miles from Kiriath Jearim), there is a small village that is named *Khirbet el-Uz*, meaning, "the ruins of Uzzah"!**

"Easy, easy does it!" someone warned, seeing the uneven ground on the threshing floor. "Watch it!" A shout went out as the cart lurched to one side and the ark of God slid across. Looking up in time to see the disaster, Uzzah quickly reached out his hand to steady the ark. Although he meant well, his actions only brought trouble. Uzzah died before the Lord as punishment for touching the holy ark of God.

David felt both angry and fearful at this display of God's wrath. "How can I ever bring the ark of God back into my care?" he asked no one in particular. He decided not to move the ark into Jerusalem, but instead took it to the nearby home of Obed-Edom. There it remained for three months.

David came back after three months to move the ark and complete its journey to Jerusalem. But this time he would do it differently. In preparation, David gathered all the Levites. He then summoned Zadok and Abiathar the priests. "You are the heads of the Levitical families," David said. "Because of this, it is your job to consecrate yourselves and bring up the ark of the Lord to the place I have prepared for it." David solemnly looked at the faces of the men who were gathered before him.

They all clearly remembered what happened to Uzzah and didn't want to see that happen again. "No one but the Levites may carry the ark, and this must be done according to God's commands!" David announced. "It was because you, the Levites, didn't carry the ark that God's anger broke out against us. We didn't ask God how to move the ark—the way He commanded of Moses!"

Silence filled the air for a moment as the importance of the lesson sunk in. Then, with a new determination and much celebration, the Israelites went down to Obed-Edom's house and returned with the ark in triumph. This time, the ark was not placed on a cart and hauled like merchandise. This time it was carried on long poles shouldered by Levites, as it had been carried years ago in the wilderness.

exploring deeper

Turn in your Bible back to Numbers 4 and read verses 4, 5, and 15. According to these verses, how was the ark of God to be treated? The Kohathites were descendants of Kohath, the second oldest son of Levi (from whom the Levites got their name).

DANGER AHEAD

David's first mistake was to move the ark of God on a cart much like the pagan Philistines had used earlier! This showed little respect for the holiness of God. The ark represented God's presence among His people. It was holy and was to be treated with respect, not casually without regard. We can't approach the things of God the way the world does. God deserves—and demands—better treatment than that. Watch your step!

IT'S MINE

TAKEN FROM 1 CHRONICLES 28-29

GETTING READY

As you begin your time today, be still before the Lord and evaluate how you feel about your posses-sions. Think of all the good things you have (not what you don't have or wish you did). Spend a moment to thank the Lord for His provisions in your life. Ask Him to challenge you to realize who really owns them.

THE JOURNEY

Do you have a hard time letting go of what you own?

David paused a moment, scanning the crowd of leaders who listened attentively to his words. *These, Lord, are the leaders who will help my son, Solomon, when he becomes king. These are those who will continue to lead Your people long after I am gone,* he prayed silently. *Help them to do what is right and good in Your eyes. . . .*

Clearing his throat, David continued with his message. "As you know, I brought the ark of the Lord here to Jerusalem that it might be among us in a permanent place. I also made plans to build a temple to house it. Yet, the Lord, the God of Israel, told me I wasn't the one to build Him a temple since I was a warrior and have shed blood," David informed them. "Instead, God has chosen my son Solomon to sit on the throne over all Israel and to be the one to build the Lord's house." All eyes shifted quickly over to Solomon, then back to King David. He explained how Solomon's throne would be established, and gave a challenge to the Israelite leaders to be careful to follow all the Lord's commands. David then turned his gaze to his son. "And you, Solomon," David said with a tender voice, "serve God with wholehearted devotion and with a willing mind. For God searches the heart and understands every motive behind the thoughts. If you seek Him, He will be found by you; but if you forsake Him, He will reject you forever." Solomon looked up into his father's eyes and nodded. He both heard and understood his father's words. King David then handed Solomon the complete plans for the temple—plans that God had given him to draw up, but not to build. "The Lord has chosen you to build a temple as a sanctuary. Be strong and do the work."

> It's not what we have that counts with God, but rather our willingness to give it. It is interesting to note that both the tabernacle and the temple were built with voluntary gifts.

Solomon carefully opened the plans and looked at them. The task seemed enormous! There, written down, was everything Solomon would need—from the plans for each room and their furnishings to job assignments for the priests and Levites once the task was complete. Everything was described, right down to the exact weight of gold that was to be used for decorating the temple. Solomon looked up at King David, who now addressed the rest of the group. He heard his father's words urging the people to support Solomon's efforts—encouraging them to become a personal part of it.

"With all my resources as king," David said, "I have provided for the temple of my God—gold, silver, bronze, iron, wood, onyx, turquoise, and all kinds of fine stone and marble. All of these have been given in large amounts." The leaders looked on approvingly. As king, David had used his resources wisely. David continued, "I now also give my personal treasures of gold and silver for the temple of my God. This is over and above everything else I have already provided." The leaders looked at King David in silence. His example of giving went above and beyond the call of duty and showed David's wholehearted devotion toward the things of the Lord. "Now then, who will follow my example? Who is willing to give offerings to the Lord today?"

It didn't take long for the leaders to step forward. "I will!" "I will too!" they said. Encouraged by David's personal example of integrity, all the leaders gave willingly and wholeheartedly to the Lord. The Israelites rejoiced at the willing response of their leaders, and King David rejoiced greatly, for through their generosity, God's name was being honored.

exploring deeper

Wait! Don't skip this part. Open your Bible to 1 Chronicles 29:16-18 and read these verses. (Go on, look it up! These three verses are rich!) What do they say? Read them again. What is David's perspective on ownership? Now, look at the last half of verse 18. Is this prayer request of David's descriptive of you and your attitude?

CROSS ROADS

Whether you recognize it or not, what you have to offer God is only what He Himself has provided for you! Take a look around at the things you own. Just whose are they—really? Will you hold on to your possessions with a tight fist, or will you open your hand?

GETTING YOUR BEARINGS:
THE BOOK OF 2 CHRONICLES

The purpose of 2 Chronicles is to deliver a "pep talk" to the Israelites who have just been released from captivity. At the close of the Books of Kings, the nation of Israel (northern tribes) had been carried off by the Assyrians. The king of Assyria resettled Samaria with his own people, thus putting an end to the northern tribes. Their identity was lost, and they were no more. The southern tribes of Judah, however, were carried off by the Babylonians and later allowed to return to their homeland in Jerusalem. The Books of Chronicles were written to these refugees. Since seventy years had passed, they would need to be instructed and encouraged in the things of the Lord. God had lived among them in the past—could He do it again?

Second Chronicles focuses mainly on the kings of Judah, since Israel is no more. Israel had only bad kings who brought the nation down quickly—150 years before Judah! Although Judah also had some bad kings, there were a few good ones who helped to preserve the nation and turn it back around—if only temporarily. As you explore this book, you'll get a close-up look at the lives of Jehoshaphat and Joash—two kings of Judah. What did they do right—and what did they do wrong? There's exciting adventure and great lessons to be learned in 2 Chronicles!

FRIEND . . . OR FOE?

TAKEN FROM 2 CHRONICLES 18-22

GETTING READY

Start your time by committing today's events into God's hands. Ask Him to go before you and to help you make wise choices. Thank Him in advance for His guidance that is available to you.

THE JOURNEY

Have you ever seen how someone's choice of friends became a source of trouble for him?

"That sounds acceptable to me," King Jehoshaphat said to King Ahab, "but first, let's inquire of the Lord."

"Who? Oh, yeah, yeah . . . right," Ahab responded as he called his 400 prophets to come before them.

"O King!" the false prophets agreed in unison, "today you will have victory against Ben-Hadad, the king of Aram, and his armies!" Ahab was satisfied with what he heard; Jehoshaphat was uncomfortable.

"Don't you have a prophet of the Lord you can inquire of?"

Jehoshaphat asked. It didn't take long to summon one of the Lord's prophets, but his response was not favorable. It spoke of defeat.

Jehoshaphat made his alliance with King Ahab in hopes of bringing peace between Judah and Israel, but this only brought turmoil in the future.

Instead of listening to the counsel of the Lord, King Ahab became angry and impatient. As a result, the prophet was thrown into prison, and God's counsel was ignored. Ahab turned to Jehoshaphat and declared, "Together we will go and fight against Ben-Hadad. As a seal of our agreement to be friends, I give you my daughter, Athaliah, in marriage."

King Jehoshaphat accepted King Ahab's offer, ignoring the past sins of his new ally. "Agreed. Friends!" Jehoshaphat said foolishly.

It didn't take long for Jehoshaphat to realize that his friendship with King Ahab was not the wisest choice he could have made. On the battlefield against Ben-Hadad, Jehoshaphat's life was put in danger. King Ahab selfishly instructed Jehoshaphat to go to battle in his royal cloak while he himself would be disguised as a regular soldier.

"Only go after Ahab—the king of Israel!" King Ben-Hadad told his warriors. When the warriors saw Jehoshaphat in his royal cloak, they assumed it was King Ahab and pursued him. In the nick of time, Jehoshaphat cried out, and the warriors realized Jehoshaphat wasn't the king they were after. Jehoshaphat's life was needlessly put in danger because of his alliance with wicked King Ahab.

King Jehoshaphat also made an alliance to build a fleet of trading ships with Ahab's wicked son, Ahaziah. Before the ships could sail, Jehoshaphat's plans were sunk— literally (2 Chronicles 20:35-37)!

King Ahab died, and Jehoshaphat asked God's forgiveness for having sought friendship with those who despise God. He then turned his attention to strengthening the spiritual condition of those in his kingdom, just as his father, King Asa, had once done. Jehoshaphat appointed officers to carry out the laws of the land, and Levites and priests to teach God's Law to the people.

When the countries of Moab and Ammon threatened war against Judah, King Jehoshaphat sought God and led his people in prayer and fasting. The Lord fought their battle for them, and they won. Although King Jehoshaphat tried to do what was right in the eyes of the Lord, he made some unwise choices in his friendships, and these would affect his family long after he was gone. . . .

Athaliah was the wicked daughter of Queen Jezebel and King Ahab, given in marriage to Jehoshaphat as a seal of their friendship.

Upon Jehoshaphat's death, his oldest son inherited the throne. Unfortunately, Jehoram was evil and did not follow in the steps of his father. Instead, he was influenced toward wickedness by his mother, Athaliah (daughter of King Ahab and Queen Jezebel). Jehoram immediately killed all his brothers, then built up the high places to Baal that his father had torn down. Jehoram led the nation of Judah into both idolatry and destruction. He made an unwise friendship with the king of Israel (Ahab's son) and ended up losing his life, as well as the lives of his relatives. Seeing that her son Jehoram was dead, Queen Athaliah began to destroy the whole royal family of the house of Judah. She succeeded in killing all—but one.

Being as wicked as her parents, Athaliah had little regard for the things of God. She didn't care that she had turned against her husband and her descendants. "I will rule!" she vowed—and she did just that, since there were no longer any capable heirs left. Queen Athaliah reigned for six years, not realizing her infant grandson, Joash, survived. He had been hidden by Jehoiada the priest and secretly lived in the temple, growing up under Jehoiada's godly instruction.

exploring deeper

Turn to 2 Chronicles 18:1 and read it. Then, quickly turn ahead to chapter 22 and read verse 3. This verse talks about Jehoshaphat's son. What does it say? Lastly look at verse 10 in this same chapter. Athaliah not only introduced Baal worship into Judah, she also nearly destroyed the entire royal line of David!

THINKING on your FEET

Friendships really do matter. Decisions you make in relationships today will affect your future—in one way or another. Jehoshaphat learned this the hard way. "Friends" can have a dynamic effect on your life. Think about it: friend . . . or foe? How wisely do you choose when making friends?

EXCUSE ME, IS THIS YOURS?

TAKEN FROM 2 CHRONICLES 23-24

GETTING READY

Spend a few minutes preparing your heart and quieting your thoughts before the Lord. Ask yourself how well you know Him. If all the props were kicked out from underneath you, would you still stand strong spiritually? Tell God about it, and honestly admit to Him any weaknesses. God wants you to know Him personally—He calls you by name.

THE JOURNEY

Have you ever met someone whose faith relied heavily upon someone else?

"Now is the time," Jehoiada whispered to himself, having endured six years of Queen Athaliah ruling over Judah. Athaliah had single-handedly undone everything her godly husband, King Jehoshaphat, had accomplished during his lifetime. As daughter of King Ahab and Queen Jezebel, Athaliah followed in her parents' wickedness and introduced Baal worship to Judah. She even corrupted her son to follow in her wickedness. Upon his death, Athaliah attempted to kill off the entire royal line of David! Unknown to Athaliah, the Princess Jehosheba had secretly saved one infant heir and hidden him in the temple. There he grew under the priests' instruction. Jehoiada the priest thanked God for keeping the baby safe.

Now that Joash is seven years old, he is old enough to take back the throne of his grandfather, Jehoshaphat, and rule as king over Judah! Jehoiada thought with great pleasure. Because Joash was so young, Jehoiada would be there for him as advisor. *He'll need help to turn Judah around,* the priest thought, and thus made himself available as Joash's trusted friend and counselor. *Young Joash is the rightful heir . . . and it's about time he sits on the throne!*

Jehoiada armed the Levites with weapons and gave them orders to guard the temple, the palace, and the Foundation Gate. An additional group was assigned to stay close to Joash and protect him at all times. Jehoiada and his sons then brought out young Joash and put the crown on him. They presented him with a copy of the covenant—as God required—and pronounced him king. A great celebration rang out from the Israelites. Trumpets were blown and singers with instruments led praises.

"What? What's that noise?!" Athaliah wondered, making her way to the temple to investigate. She stopped cold in her tracks. Before her very eyes people were shouting, "Long live the king!"

Queen Athaliah fumed at the sight. "This is treason! Treason!" she shouted in an angry panic. Trying to make her way quickly back to the palace, Athaliah was captured and put to death on the palace grounds.

Because Joash was only a boy when he became king over Judah, Jehoiada stepped in to help. His first act was to make a covenant with the Lord that he, the people, and the king would live for the Lord. The people rejoiced, and all went to the temple of Baal and tore it down. They smashed the altars and idols and put the priest of Baal to death—ridding the land of its idolatry. Jehoiada then placed the care of the Lord's temple into the hands of the Levite priests who would present burnt offerings as written in the Law of Moses. It was a great time of revival for God's people.

Years went by and Joash was now a young man. Seeing the temple in need of repair, he decided to restore the temple of the Lord and the articles and dishes that had been ruined. He had a chest built and placed it outside the gate of the temple where the people came and generously gave their contributions. Burnt offerings were continuously being offered in the temple of the Lord as long as Jehoiada the priest lived. However, Jehoiada was reaching old age and finally died, leaving King Joash on his own. King Joash was unprepared to stand alone without another to give him strength spiritually.

"King Joash, listen to us!" some of the officials said to him. Joash listened carefully to their poor advice and, unfortunately, followed it. Joash and his people soon stopped worshiping God in the temple. It wasn't long before God was abandoned altogether. Since Jehoiada the priest was no longer around, the people began reverting back to their old ways! Soon Asherah poles and idols took the place of the worship of God. Sadly, Joash went right along, for now that Jehoiada was gone, Joash's source of spiritual strength was gone as well. . . .

exploring deeper

There's an interesting point made in 2 Chronicles 24:2! Look it up and read it. Now, read it again by reading the first half only and stopping. What does it say? Unfortunately that first half of the verse hinges directly on a statement made in the second half, and cannot stand alone—much like Joash. Take a close look at it.

Skill Time

One mistake King Joash made was to rely on others to be spiritually strong for him. He did what was right in God's eyes as long as Jehoiada was priest. The problem King Joash had was that he didn't "own" his own faith; it wasn't his. Do you own your faith, or do you depend on others? It's easy to pretend we're something that we're not. God wants us to depend upon Him. He wants to be the source and the foundation of our faith. Do a quick spiritual inventory by asking yourself these simple questions. Then, close your time in prayer—asking the Lord for His help in your areas of weakness.

1. What is my foundation like?
   - Do I even have a relationship with the Lord to build on? (If you can't answer this one, turn to the back of this book and find out more about what this means!)
2. How do I build on my foundation?
   - Am I dependent upon others?
   - Do I read the Bible for myself, daily?
   - Do I talk to God (prayer) and take my concerns to Him, first?
3. Have I purposed in my heart to follow Him and learn more about what that means, in spite of what others do (or don't do) around me?

GETTING YOUR BEARINGS:

THE BOOK OF EZRA

As you explore Ezra, you will come to know the person for whom this book is named. You will also be set for an adventure down unknown passageways and into unexplored territory. Before you begin your journey, it is important to understand where you currently are and where you're headed.

As you already know, the Israelites had split into two different kingdoms. Those in the north called themselves *Israel*, and the Israelites to the south called themselves *Judah*. Still, both kingdoms were Israelites. Don't let that confuse you! *Israel* had nothing but wicked kings, while *Judah* had a few kings who sought after God. (If you haven't read 1 and 2 Kings and 1 and 2 Chronicles yet, now would be a good time to do so!)

Because of their wickedness, God judged the Israelites and removed them from the land as He promised He would do. The Books of Chronicles leave us with most of the Israelites from *Judah* being carted off to Babylonia as captives. (The kingdom of *Israel* was destroyed much earlier.) The Book of Ezra tells us what happens next and picks up where 2 Kings left off. It is a record of a fresh start and second chances. What will the Israelites make of it? Well, you'll just have to read on to find out!

Did you know? Other books of the Bible fit in with the Book of Ezra! For instance, the events in the Book of Esther happened between the events of chapters 6 and 7 in Ezra! Also, the Books of Haggai and Zechariah are written by prophets who encouraged and challenged the Israelite refugees while they were rebuilding the temple—all in the Book of Ezra!

FIRST THINGS FIRST!

TAKEN FROM EZRA 1-3

GETTING READY

As you begin reading in the Book of Ezra, start your time with prayer. Commit your life to God and ask Him to help you be more consistent in following Him with your whole heart.

THE JOURNEY

Do you struggle with putting God first in your life?

King Nebuchadnezzar had destroyed Jerusalem. The temple had been torn down and stripped of its gold and silver, the walls protecting the city were left as rubble—charred remnants of what was once a glorious city. Jerusalem would not be a pretty sight. However, 49,897 Israelites were willing to make the 900-mile trip back to their homeland—a dangerous journey that would take almost four months!

"This is what Cyrus, King of Persia, decrees," came the announcement to the Jews living in Babylon. No longer was King Nebuchadnezzar king over Babylon, and no longer was Babylon a kingdom of its own!

With the death of Nebuchadnezzar came a weakening in power. Thus, Babylon was quickly conquered by King Cyrus of Persia—a kind ruler who gave even greater freedom to his captives than they already enjoyed. In an effort to set up "buffer zones" around his kingdom for protection and to create loyalty, King Cyrus allowed all captives to return to their homelands to live and worship their own gods. The Persian king knew that in the event of enemies attacking his empire, the released captives would fight loyally in order to protect the freedoms they enjoyed.

"Israelites from Judah may go up to Jerusalem to build a temple for the Lord, and may your God be with you!" King Cyrus said. "Furthermore, those who live in any place where Jewish survivors are found are to provide them with silver and gold, goods and livestock, and also a freewill offering for God's temple in Jerusalem."

After seventy years of captivity, this was good news to many who yearned to return to the land God had given them—and return to worshiping the Lord. Others, however, grew up having never seen Jerusalem. Babylon was the only home they knew. These Israelites chose to remain in Babylon, for now. Everyone whose heart God had moved prepared to go up and build the house of the Lord in Jerusalem. Carefully, they loaded up their supplies as they prepared for the long and dangerous journey ahead. All their neighbors assisted them with articles of silver and gold, goods and livestock—just as King Cyrus had commanded. Then, the king himself brought out the articles that had once belonged to the temple of the Lord. King Nebuchadnezzar had carried them off and put them in the temple of his own god, but they had been preserved for this moment. They would be going back to their rightful place to one day be used again in the service of the only true God—the God of the Israelites.

> **The prophet Isaiah mentioned King Cyrus by name and foretold the decree he would make 150 years before it happened (Isaiah 44:28 and 45:1-13)!**

Eagerly, the first group of Israelites set out under the leadership of Zerubbabel. Many were priests and Levites who wondered what lay ahead in the rubble at Jerusalem. *What will we return to?* they wondered. *After almost seventy years, what will we find?* No one really knew.

When they arrived at the site of the temple in Jerusalem, silence hung over them like a heavy cloud. They were relieved they had made it safely, yet were stunned by the destruction they saw. *If only we and our ancestors had obeyed the Lord, none of this would have happened!* many thought, picking their way through the debris.

Zerubbabel, meaning "begotten" in Babel, was the grandson of King Jehoiachin who reigned only three months before surrendering to Nebuchadnezzar (2 Kings 24:10-12)!

Looking at the task that lay ahead, some of the family leaders unloaded their valuables and gave generously toward the rebuilding of the Lord's temple on its original site. Each of the leaders did the same. Having done this, the refugees settled in the villages around Jerusalem, while others returned to their hometowns in Judah. Once the people were settled, they assembled back at Jerusalem to begin the work of rebuilding.

Under Zerubbabel's direction, repairing the altar of the Lord would be the first and most important priority. Little else mattered. Through the altar the Israelites could once again come to God in worship, approaching Him as He instructed and being obedient to His commands. Yes, Zerubbabel repeated to himself, *the altar will be built before anything else, so that we might put God first . . . and keep Him there.*

exploring deeper

Turn to Ezra 3:3. According to this verse, what did the Israelites fear? Notice what the Israelites did *not* build (walls for protection)? They were putting first things first—God would have a prominent place in their lives, and He would be the center of all their activities, interests, and concerns.

Skill Time

How does God rate in your priorities? Can others tell God is truly first in your life? Perhaps the best way for you to answer that is to ask yourself how much time you spend with Him. Different people call this different things, such as having a "quiet time" (QT for short), "personal devotions," or even doing their "spiritual disciplines." What you call it is not important. The important thing is that you do it—daily. Take a moment now to think about the condition of the "altar" in your life. Do you regularly meet with God? Follow these simple steps of rebuilding what needs repair in your life.

Step 1: Designate a time and place where you can be alone for 5 to 10 minutes. (This could be the first thing in the morning when you wake up, or the last thing at night before you go to sleep.)

Step 2: Begin your time with a simple prayer and really talk things over with God.

Step 3: Open His Word and read it for yourself. A good place to start is reading in the Book of Proverbs—talk about wisdom for the day! Since there are 31 chapters, that allows you to read one chapter a day for a month. (Example: If it is the 7th of the month, you will be reading chapter 7.)

Step 4: Think about what you've read and ask God to use it in your life. Then, close in prayer, thanking Him in advance.

AH- HAH!

TAKEN FROM EZRA 4-6

GETTING READY

Spend a moment in prayer before beginning. Don't just rush through this part and move on with today's devotion. Instead, use this time to honestly check in with God. Tell Him your fears, desires, and frustrations. He has a willing and ready ear to listen. Not only that—He alone has the power to help you.

THE JOURNEY

Have you ever faced roadblocks and people who try to discourage you from doing something God wants you to do?

"God is good! His love for Israel endures forever!" the people shouted when the foundation to the new temple of the Lord had been laid. Priests blew their trumpets, and the Levites who were descendants of Asaph clashed their cymbals—both leading the Israelites in praise and thankful worship. Older priests, Levites, and others, however, wept when they saw the foundation for the new temple. They remembered how glorious

Solomon's temple had been and were saddened at what had been lost. Already they could tell this new temple would be only a shadow of the greatness of the original. A great noise rang out through the land—both of rejoicing and weeping, and it didn't take long for enemies in the land to come investigating.

"Let us build with you," they said to Zerubbabel and the other leaders, "for we worship the same God you do." Zerubbabel knew they weren't telling the whole truth. These people who stood before him may have chosen to worship Yahweh, the God of Israel, but that was only in addition to the many other gods they worshiped. Zerubbabel and the other leaders knew when Assyria conquered Israel, most of the Israelites in the Northern Kingdom were carted off and dispersed among other lands. Foreign people were then brought in to replace the Israelites and inter-marry with those who remained. This was a common strategy of the Assyrians when they conquered a land, and it kept the people they conquered from reorganizing as a strong nation and rebelling. These "neighbors" were a mix of many lands and many religions. Migrating south, they laid claim to the land in Judah during the seventy years the Israelites (from Judah) lived in Babylon as captives.

Zerubbabel and the leaders knew these local people—the Samaritans—had no sincere interest in worshiping only the God of Israel. Rather, they saw the opportunity to build the temple as a way to maintain their sense of ownership over the land. Feeling threatened by the Jewish refugees' return to the land of Judah, they sought to stop it—in any way possible.

"No," Zerubbabel and the leaders replied to their demands. "You cannot help, for we have nothing in common with you. We alone will build the temple to our God, just as King Cyrus gave us permission to do." The local residents became angry and defiant at those words. Their scheme of offering to help with the temple had

The Book of Haggai (the third book from the end of the Old Testament) describes the condition of the Israelites' hearts when they stopped rebuilding the temple. It also sheds light on the events described in Ezra 5:1-2.

failed. Now they wouldn't be able to infiltrate the ranks and destroy the project from the inside out. *If the temple is built, the Israelites will reunite and become a strong kingdom once again. Then, they will drive us away,* the Samaritans thought. *We can't let that happen!* This was a serious threat, for they had no intention of losing control over the land they had enjoyed for the past seventy years.

The hostility between the Israelites in Jerusalem and the Samaritans continued even to the time of Jesus! (Check out Luke 9:52-53.)

Realizing they couldn't pretend to be the Israelites' friends, the locals made it known they would be the Israelites' enemies. Hiring people to come against the Israelites with threats and lies, the Samaritans sought to discourage the Israelites and keep them from their task. Their efforts worked, and the building of the temple was abandoned. . . . until fifteen years later.

"Why are you living in nicely paneled homes while the house of the Lord remains unfinished?" the prophet Haggai challenged. Using two prophets, Haggai and Zechariah, the Lord stirred the hearts of the people to finish rebuilding the temple. This, however, was met with resistance once again.

"Who gave you permission to rebuild this temple and restore this structure?" Tattenai, a regional governor, demanded. Over the fifteen years the Israelites had left the temple project abandoned, the great Persian Empire had undergone some changes. The throne had changed hands twice! Now, King Darius was ruler, and Tattenai made it his duty to report any suspicious activity. "There is a great and mighty work these people are doing in the city of Jerusalem of Judah," he reported to the king. "When I tried to stop them, they refused and said King Cyrus had given them a decree to build it. I think they are lying. You might want to check the historical records and see if their words are true." King Darius did just that, and was surprised at what he found. . . .

exploring deeper

Quickly turn in your Bible to Ezra 6! Read verses 1-5. What did King Darius discover? Now, read verses 6-7. What did the king command? Finally, look at verses 8-9. What did God provide?

DANGER AHEAD

If you are on the right path and striving to serve the Lord, you will undoubtedly run into opposition. Sometimes this will come through those claiming to be your friends, and sometimes through others who might feel threatened or suspicious of you! Don't let it discourage you or cause you to stop doing what is right. Even in the most difficult of circumstances, God can raise up encouragement and support to meet your needs. Just think: He used a paragraph from a forgotten document stashed away in a pagan library to provide what the Israelites needed!

HAVEN'T WE BEEN HERE BEFORE?

TAKEN FROM EZRA 6-7

GETTING READY

Pause for a moment and give your time to the Lord today. Ask Him to help you learn to rely on His power so that you might not be trapped in the cycle of sin.

THE JOURNEY

Do you find yourself repeating the same sins over and over?

Surely, Lord, this is Your hand of blessing upon us! Ezra whispered under his breath. With great excitement Ezra continued to read the letter he held in his hand. It was from King Artaxerxes and addressed directly to him. "Greetings from Artaxerxes, the king of kings, to Ezra the priest, the teacher of the law of the God of heaven," the letter began. "I now decree that any of the Israelites in my kingdom, including priests and Levites, who wish to go to Jerusalem with you, may go." Ezra read on. In the letter, King Artaxerxes explained he was giving them gold and silver to take back with them, with his permission to get more in Babylon. They would be free to offer sacrifices to the Lord on the altar at the temple and make their own decisions on how the gifts were to be used. Ezra read on, eagerly devouring each word written on the page.

"And you, Ezra, are to use the wisdom God has given you to appoint judges who know God's laws and who will govern all the people. For those who aren't familiar with those laws, you are to teach them," the king added. Ezra looked up from the letter and out across the horizon. It had been eighty years since Zerubbabel left Babylon under a decree by King Cyrus to rebuild the temple. *Eighty years!* Ezra whispered to himself. *Now, the temple has been up for fifty-seven years!* He sighed. Ezra couldn't help but wonder how it must feel to celebrate the feasts and sacrifices once again in obedience to what God had commanded. He yearned to travel to Jerusalem and join the others in worship, teaching them to love God's Law, for Ezra had a deep understanding and appreciation of God's Word.

With King Artaxerxes' decree in hand, Ezra gathered together Israelites who desired to return and set off on the long journey toward Jerusalem. His group totaled nearly 4,000, including women and children. It was much smaller than the first group that had left under Zerubbabel, but that didn't bother Ezra. With determination and a love for the Lord, Ezra would bring his group to Jerusalem. It would be a victorious time—or so he thought. Ezra was not prepared for what he faced when he arrived.

"How could the people do this?!" Ezra cried out after hearing the reports from the concerned leaders in Jerusalem. "Don't they know it was because of this very thing that God judged our nation and sent us into exile?" The leaders stood by silently, uncertain how to respond. Although the Israelites were offering sacrifices and celebrating the feasts and cere-

Take action!

A - Anchor yourself in God's Word.

C - Confess your shortcomings daily.

T - Take responsibility.

I - Include God in your day.

O - Organize and set your course under God's control.

N - Never underestimate the power of a habit.

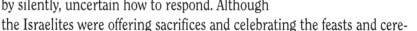

monies in keeping with the Law of Moses, they were not living in obedience to God. Old habits had found their way back into the people's hearts. Several of the Israelites had married foreigners who lived in the land—something God specifically forbade them to do!

Ezra was speechless. He fell on his face in front of God on behalf of the people, asking for God's mercy and forgiveness.

Artaxerxes was Xerxes' son. Xerxes was the king who married Esther!

"O Lord, I am too ashamed and disgraced to lift up my face to You because our sins are piled higher than our heads and our guilt reaches the heavens," Ezra agonized in prayer. Even though Ezra wasn't part of these sins, he identified with the people, for their sin would affect the well-being of the entire nation. "From the days of our forefathers until now, our guilt has been great. Once again, we have disobeyed the commands You gave through Your servants when You told us not to marry or make treaties with the pagans in the land—the land You were bringing us into. . . ." Ezra's prayer continued on behalf of the Israelites who were grieving at what they had done. They realized they were repeating the same mistakes and desired to correct the matter with God's help.

Gathering the Israelites together, a decision was made for those who had taken foreign wives to deal with their situation as prescribed by the Law. Ezra knew this would be a harsh action to take, but he also knew it was a necessary step in breaking the cycle of sin that had begun to take root in the lives of the Israelites. Having traveled down this road before and having experienced the consequences of their sins, the Israelites knew the sin cycle was one they didn't want to repeat again.

exploring deeper

Open your Bible to Ezra 7:10 and read the description of Ezra. What does it say? Notice the word "devoted." What was Ezra devoted to? (See if you can find three things listed in this verse. Hint: The first two lay the foundation for the third.) How does this compare to your life?

THINKING on your FEET

Ezra was a man of prayer and a man of action! He not only prayed for forgiveness and guidance, but he acted as well. This is the only way to break the cycle of repeating the same sins over and over. Ezra set his course, grounded himself in God's Word as his anchor, and acted. Have you?

GETTING YOUR BEARINGS:
THE BOOK OF NEHEMIAH

The Book of Nehemiah is an extension of the Book of Ezra, and continues the story of the Israelites' return to Jerusalem and what they faced. If you have been reading the devotions in order, you'll have a great understanding of the full background and history of the Israelites and what they were doing in Babylon in the first place! If you haven't been going in order and you're curious—good! Put a bookmark in this spot and make a quick detour down the tunnel of 2 Kings. There's great stuff back there waiting for you to explore!

Already, two groups of Israelite refugees have left Babylon and are back in Judea. The first group returned in 538 B.C. led by Zerubbabel, who supervised the rebuilding of the temple. The next group came eighty years later (458 B.C.), led by Ezra, who helped turn the Israelites back to the Lord. Now, the stage is set for the Book of Nehemiah. It is appropriately named for Nehemiah, who led the third group of Israelites back to Judea. Nehemiah sought to rebuild the walls of Jerusalem, and this is his account of what happened.

As you explore this book, you will see the results of prayer and the importance of teamwork. You will also experience crawling up difficult inclines and looking for light at the end of the tunnel—just as Nehemiah did. Watch closely how he reacts and journeys through it, then take your cues from him. There's much you can learn from his life.

... AMEN

TAKEN FROM NEHEMIAH 1-2

GETTING READY

As you begin exploring Nehemiah today, commit your time to the Lord and ask Him to challenge you to desire a greater and more meaningful prayer life. Don't read on until you've done that!

THE JOURNEY

Do you ever struggle with not knowing how to pray (or not wanting to pray)?

Nehemiah stood speechless, stunned at the words he heard. "Those who live in Jerusalem in the province of Judah are in great trouble and disgrace," the men reported to Nehemiah. They had just traveled through that area on their way back to Susa, where Nehemiah lived and served as cupbearer to King Artaxerxes. Upon hearing of their return, Nehemiah eagerly questioned them, excited for any news about how his fellow Israelites were faring. The report wasn't good, for the men had concerns over the state of matters in Jerusalem. "The walls of Jerusalem are broken down, and its many gates have been burned with fire," they sadly reported. Nehemiah's heart felt sick, and he could only wonder about the decree King Artaxerxes had made in the recent past in response to a report by some Samaritan officials concerning Jerusalem. . . .

"You should know, O king, that the Jews who came to Jerusalem are rebuilding that rebellious and wicked city by restoring the walls and repairing the foundations!" the spiteful officials said. "Furthermore, the king should know that if this city is rebuilt and the walls restored, these people will rebel and refuse to pay their taxes, tributes, and duties—and your royal treasury will suffer! Now then," the Samaritans wrote deceitfully, "we are sending this message since we remain loyal to you and don't want to see you dishonored in any way. Search the records, and you will see that this city is a place of rebellion against kings from ancient times. That is why this city was destroyed. If it is rebuilt, you, O king, will be left with nothing."

A king's cupbearer was a position of importance and trust. The cupbearer would taste the wine before serving it to the king, making sure it was not poisoned.

Taking the advice of the wicked Samaritans, King Artaxerxes had the historical records searched and found that powerful kings had once ruled Jerusalem. Responding immediately, he issued a decree to halt the work in Jerusalem. When the regional governors received the king's decree, they enforced it, and all rebuilding stopped dead in its tracks.

So, nothing has been done since then, Nehemiah sadly realized. His heart grew heavy with concern, for once a king gave a decree, no one else could change it, except that king himself. Nehemiah prayed. He acknowledged God's character, power, and attributes. He then asked that he might be granted favor in the eyes of the king. Then, Nehemiah waited.

"Why does your face look so sad?" King Artaxerxes asked Nehemiah one day. Nehemiah, who was the king's cupbearer, grew afraid. He knew that showing any negative emotion was dangerous, for it could be interpreted as dissatisfaction with the king! Humbly, Nehemiah responded and told the king he was sad because the city where his ancestors were buried lay in ruins. "What is it you want?" the king asked. Nehemiah knew God had opened up the door of opportunity for him to lay his request before the king. He also knew it was a dangerous request.

Shooting a quick prayer up to the Lord, Nehemiah answered. "If it pleases you, I would like to go to the city in Judah where my fathers are buried so that I can rebuild it," he said.

"How long will your journey take, and when will you get back?" the king asked, hinting at his approval. Nehemiah gave the king a time, and the king readily agreed.

"If it pleases the king, may I have a letter to the governors in the provinces so they will provide me with safety until I arrive in Judah? And may I have a letter to Asaph, the keeper of the king's forest, that he might provide me with the necessary timber to make beams for the gates and city wall, as well as a house for myself?"

> Ezra 4:7-23 is the companion passage that tells of King Artaxerxes' decree to stop construction in Jerusalem. Because of Nehemiah's request (and prayers!), the king gave a new decree to allow construction to resume.

King Artaxerxes agreed and wrote a royal decree giving Nehemiah permission to rebuild the walls of Jerusalem. God had answered his prayers.

exploring deeper

Turn in your Bible to Nehemiah 1:1-2 and read it. The month of Kislev is around November or December (depending on how the Jewish calendar fell that year). Now, read the last verse in chapter 1 and the first verse in chapter 2. The month of Nisan is in the March-April time frame. How long had Nehemiah been praying and patiently waiting?

Note: A cupbearer could only go before the king when the king requested him.

Skill Time

Perhaps this lesson doesn't seem like a big deal because to Nehemiah, prayer wasn't a big deal. He spent time in extended prayer, pouring his heart out to God (see Nehemiah 1:5-11), as well as shooting up a quick "arrow prayer" while in the middle of a conversation with the king! (See Nehemiah 2:4-5.) Prayer was something Nehemiah did both purposefully and automatically.

Ironically, we try to make prayer more than it is, and it becomes so cumbersome, we often end up skipping it altogether. We lose sight of the fact that it is simply talking to God, much like we would talk to a person standing in front of us.

P - Pour out your heart to God.
R - Remember He is concerned and listening.
A - Avoid the temptation to "put it off" for another time.
Y - Yearn to develop that relationship with Him.
E - Enjoy your time.
R - React to your situations by first talking to God about them.

JOIN THE TEAM

TAKEN FROM NEHEMIAH 2-4

GETTING READY

Stop and pray. Don't go any further until you've dedicated this time to the Lord. Ask God to help you better understand how He uses people working together to accomplish great things.

THE JOURNEY

Do you find it difficult to work with other people?

Carefully Nehemiah picked his way around the ruins of the city walls, closely examining the task that awaited him. Only the moon lit the path before him as he set out on his mule with a few trusted men. *I must see what I'm up against and draft a plan before I tell others why I'm here,* Nehemiah said to himself. During his three days in Jerusalem, he had mentioned to no one the reason he had come. He did this in order to avoid unhealthy gossip and any enemies. Until Nehemiah could see the damage to be repaired, he would keep the purpose of his arrival a secret. The darkness of the night provided him the greatest opportunity to view the walls without suspicion.

Quietly, Nehemiah rode his mule out the Valley Gate, past the Jackal Well, and over to the Dung Gate. By starting at the southwest corner, he made his way around the wall, traveling in a clockwise direction. However, when he got to the Fountain Gate and the King's Pool, there wasn't enough room to pass because of the rubble that blocked his way. Seeing this, Nehemiah turned and went through the valley in order to complete his inspection of the city walls. Upon finishing, he and his trusted companions quietly reentered the city through the original gate they had left from. *The task is enormous,* Nehemiah thought to himself, *but if we work together, it can be accomplished—with God's help.* He had seen what needed to be done; now it was time to get to work. Nehemiah called a meeting.

City gates were more than just doors to keep out the enemy! They were wider portions of the wall housing built-in rooms where official city business was done. The area outside the gate often became a marketplace.

"You see the trouble we are in," Nehemiah declared to the priests, officials, and people living in the city. "Jerusalem lies in ruins, and its gates have been burned with fire." The people nodded their heads at the sorry state Jerusalem was in. Without walls for protection, they knew they were an easy target for attacking enemies. The rubble that lay about them only served as a shameful testimony to all they had lost because of their disobedience to God. "Come," Nehemiah announced, "let us rebuild the walls of Jerusalem so we'll no longer be in disgrace." *This is a time of new beginnings,* Nehemiah said to himself. *We must begin now.*

The people looked up at Nehemiah with hope and concern. *Doesn't Nehemiah know we tried to rebuild in the past—only to have everything halted because of a royal decree?* some wondered in their hearts. *How can we build when the king has forbidden us?* others thought to themselves. Nehemiah could see the fear reflected in their faces. He then told them of his conversation with the king, and all that God had wonderfully provided. When the people heard this, their hearts rejoiced. "Let's rebuild the wall!" they cheered, and listened for further instruction from Nehemiah.

Wisely, Nehemiah got everyone involved and assigned each group a portion of the wall to work on. Many were near their own homes or places of business. On the north wall, Eliashib the high priest and other priests repaired and dedicated the Sheep Gate. They also worked on the towers that lay between that gate and another. Work on the west wall was done in sections by various people. Everyone joined in and worked together. Whether perfume makers, goldsmiths, or officials—all worked wholeheartedly to accomplish the task at hand. The Israelites were a team, and they were accomplishing much.

All around the city, north, south, east, and west, the walls of Jerusalem were being restored. It wasn't long, however, before trouble came from local Samaritans. They were angry about the work being done on the walls and would do all they could to stop it—just as they had successfully done in the past. The leader of this opposition was an official named Sanballat. When he saw the wall restored to half its original height, he became hostile. He and his two companions, Tobiah the Ammonite and Geshem the Arab, stopped their mocking of the Israelites and started seriously threatening. Sanballat would attack the workers when they weren't looking and destroy their team efforts. At least . . . that's what *he* thought!

exploring deeper

What happened to the project? Was Sanballat successful in his attempts? Quickly turn to Nehemiah 4 and read verses 8-9 to find out! Do you think this was the end of their troubles?—*Read on!* Notice what happens in verses 10-18!

DANGER AHEAD

It has been said, "There is no letter I in the word *team*." Getting along with other people and doing work alongside them isn't always an easy thing to do—but it's the best thing. When we cooperate with others, we gain a sense of perspective and see that life doesn't just revolve around ourselves and our own ideas. The Israelites needed each other to do the job God had given them to do. At one point, their very lives depended upon it! It is no different for us. God has a job for each of us to do, and more often than not, it will involve working with others. Watch out for prideful attitudes that whisper, "I don't need anybody else." They are lies.

YOU WIN THE PRIZE!

TAKEN FROM NEHEMIAH 5

GETTING READY

Start your time today by asking God to examine your heart and show you how you can become more of a blessing, rather than a burden, to others.

THE JOURNEY

Have you ever been around people who are only out to help themselves?

"This is enough!" Nehemiah said angrily. It was one thing to have the *Samaritans* attacking the morale of his people, but when the *Israelites* turned on each other, it was more than Nehemiah could stand.

Nehemiah looked into the weary eyes of some Israelite families and listened to their complaints. It was well known that families who returned with the first group of exiles under Zerubbabel almost ninety years ago were able to get well established. Some who had great wealth in Babylon were able to bring it with them, gaining a good start for themselves. But the newer exiles who had journeyed back from Babylon most recently didn't have established fields or businesses—or even great wealth. They had to borrow money to keep the land they did have.

According to Deuteronomy 23:19-20, God clearly commanded the Israelites not to take advantage of one another by charging interest "... so that the Lord your God may bless you in everything you put your hand to in the land you are entering to possess."

Instead of being helped by their fellow Israelites, they were being taken advantage of. The money borrowed wasn't loaned in an effort to help others; instead, it was loaned in order to make a profit—it had to be repaid with an extra fee! Several families had no more resources to draw upon, and soon their children were sold into slavery just to get enough money to live. This angered Nehemiah, so he called a meeting to address the problem.

"Some of us are doing all we can to redeem our fellow Israelites who have had to sell themselves to pagan foreigners. But you are causing them to have to go back into slavery again! How long will you continue this?" Nehemiah accused.

Those who were guilty of trying to benefit themselves remained silent, saying nothing in their own defense. Nehemiah continued, "What you are doing is wrong." He then reminded them of God's Law, which forbade such actions. "This lending of money and grain for an additional fee needs to stop—now. You must give back to these people their fields, vineyards, olive groves, and houses— as well as the extra you charged!" Nehemiah ordered. Those guilty knew they had no choice but to obey, for Nehemiah was governor over Jerusalem. "We will give it back and not demand anything more from them," they answered.

Nehemiah knew talk of trying to benefit others was easier than actually doing it, so he made the people take an oath to do as they had promised. While everyone watched, Nehemiah stood up and shook out the folds of his robe. "Just as I do this, may God shake out and empty every man who doesn't keep his promise."

"Amen," the Israelites agreed in unison.

Ruling as governor, Nehemiah continued to seek to help others, even though he held a position that could get him benefits for himself. Declining these privileges, Nehemiah acted differently than Jerusalem's previous governors, who used the system to their advantage by demanding a daily ration of food and wine, as well as a pound of silver. They placed a heavy burden on the people, but Nehemiah would not—even though he had a legal right to do so. Instead, Nehemiah devoted himself to work on the wall alongside the other Israelites. Although as governor he could make loans and legally take the land from those who could not repay, Nehemiah chose not to. Rather than lay a burden on the people, he fed 150 Jews and officials at his own expense. Nehemiah did this, not to bring glory to himself, but to be a blessing to others. He did this because of his love for God.

exploring deeper

Open your Bible to Nehemiah 5:15-16 and read it. What does it say? Now, look at verse 19. What does this tell you about Nehemiah's priorities? Where did Nehemiah seek his reward?

CROSS ROADS

When we serve other people instead of ourselves, we only give up small benefits to gain a greater prize—a reward in heaven. This week, will you use others to benefit yourself, or will you strive to help others?

HASTA LA VISTA, BABY

TAKEN FROM NEHEMIAH 6

GETTING READY

Pause a moment to pray and commit this time into God's hands. Instead of rushing on, really talk to God and tell Him about a difficulty you've been experiencing lately. Don't worry; God can't be surprised, but you can—when you experience the release that comes from placing your troubles into His care.

THE JOURNEY

Have you ever wanted to run from your problems?

"That Nehemiah is really getting on my nerves!" Sanballat hissed under his breath. Tobiah and Geshem nodded their heads in agreement. The building of the walls of Jerusalem had continued under Nehemiah's leadership and skillful planning in spite of their threats. When the people feared being attacked (one of Sanballat's threats), Nehemiah simply reorganized the builders so some worked while others stood guard. Instead of fear dividing the Israelites and discouraging them from their mission, it only brought them together as a team. This annoyed Sanballat and his companions all the more. Having failed in their earlier attempts at attacking the builders, they would now change their strategy and attack Nehemiah directly. . . .

"Please come and meet with me in one of the villages on the plain of Ono," the message stated. Nehemiah looked out toward the horizon, unsure of the intent behind the message. *Why would Sanballat have such a desire to meet with me at this time, and at the place he selected?* Nehemiah thought to himself. He knew the plain of Ono was about twenty-five miles northwest of Jerusalem—a whole day's journey away! He also knew it bordered Samaria, which was Sanballat's hometown. Nehemiah read the letter over again, carefully reading between the lines. *This message makes it sound as if Sanballat desires to make peace with me,* Nehemiah thought, hopeful in his spirit. And yet . . .

Sanballat was a Samarian official who targeted Nehemiah as an enemy. Sending Nehemiah an unsealed letter enabled its contents (rumors!) to easily be made public.

Nehemiah knew Sanballat's actions in the past had been nothing more than attempts to keep the Israelites from rebuilding the walls in Jerusalem and reclaiming their city. *Perhaps this is just another one of his attempts,* Nehemiah thought, not even considering the possibility that Sanballat was trying to ambush and kill him. "Tell Sanballat that I am carrying on a great project and cannot leave it," Nehemiah wisely replied to the messenger. "Why should the work stop while I leave to go meet with him?" Nehemiah's response was a test for Sanballat to prove his sincerity. *If Sanballat is really interested in seeking peace,* Nehemiah reasoned, *then he can come to Jerusalem and meet with me here.* As Nehemiah soon found out, this was not the case. Four different times Sanballat sent his message to Nehemiah, urging him away from Jerusalem. Four different times Nehemiah refused. It was now clear to Nehemiah that Sanballat only sought to harm him. And his troubles were only beginning.

Soon another message came to Nehemiah—this time in an unsealed letter. It contained lies and rumors that were unfounded and aimed against Nehemiah's character. "It's reported among the nations—and Geshem says it's true—that you and the Jews are plotting a revolt, and that's why you are building the wall. According to his reports, you also plan to be their king, and have hired prophets to say, 'Look! There is a king in Judah!' You can be very sure this report will get back to the king, so I suggest you come so we can talk about it," the message from Sanballat stated. Nehemiah was shocked. *Nothing could be further from the truth!* his heart screamed within him.

According to Numbers 3:10, only the priests were allowed to enter the temple. All others would be put to death.

Collecting himself, Nehemiah sent his response back with the messenger. "These are all lies that have been made up! Nothing of what you've described is happening." The messenger left, and Nehemiah sank to his knees in prayer. His troubles only mounted. *Strengthen my hands, Lord,* he prayed.

One day, the prophet Shemaiah asked to meet with Nehemiah. "Let's go inside the temple and meet behind closed doors where you'll be safe, for there are men coming to kill you!" the prophet whispered, pretending to be concerned for Nehemiah's safety. Nehemiah listened to Shemaiah's words, not knowing the prophet had been hired by Sanballat in order to lure Nehemiah into the temple—a place only priests could go. Nehemiah looked up into the cold, steely gaze of the false prophet's eyes. He realized no true prophet would ask someone to disobey God's laws. This was just another attempt to discredit him and give him a bad name—this time by trying to get him to sin against the Lord!

"Should a person like myself run away from danger?" Nehemiah challenged. "Should I run into the temple and sin in order to save my life? I will not do it!" he said firmly. Nehemiah had better things to do with his time and his problems. . . .

exploring deeper

Turn to Nehemiah 6:8-9 and read it. What was Nehemiah's first course of action? (Hint: Look at the end of verse 9.)

THINKING on your FEET

Nehemiah faced many difficulties at the hands of enemies who tried to oppose him. Yet God gave him the strength and wisdom to handle his conflicts. Instead of running from problems, Nehemiah ran to God—then he stood his ground.

The next time conflict comes your way, which way will you run?

WHAT'S THE EXPIRATION DATE?

TAKEN FROM NEHEMIAH 8-13

GETTING READY

As you close your time of exploring in Nehemiah, reflect on what you've learned. What lessons have hit close to your heart? Tell God about them, and invite Him to use them in your life. His Word (the Scriptures) gives strength and direction.

THE JOURNEY

Have you ever been inspired to want to change—only to find yourself quickly falling back into old patterns?

All eyes directed their attention to Ezra as he stood on a high wooden platform. Having spent the past two months rebuilding the walls of Jerusalem, the Israelites would now rebuild their spiritual lives—making sure their foundation was in the right place. Men, women, and children had gathered in the square to hear the reading of the Scriptures. The people listened expectantly—eagerly—as Ezra cleared his throat and read from the Law of Moses. His voice projected across the crowd, and

God's Word penetrated the people's hearts. Once again, people were reminded of where they had fallen short of God's ways. Many wept. Others resolved in their hearts to make a change, planning to seek God more faithfully. It was a solemn moment for all.

"Don't be sad," Nehemiah said when he saw the people dejected, "for this day is sacred to God! Go and celebrate with a feast and share with others who have nothing prepared. The joy of the Lord is your strength!" The Israelites looked up at Nehemiah and considered his words, then left encouraged in their hearts to go and celebrate with great joy because they heard and understood the Scriptures. The next day, the Israelites gathered once again to hear Ezra read from the Law. Day after day, Ezra read from the Book of the Law during the celebration of the Feast of Tabernacles. He did this in keeping with the Scriptures. Later, toward the end of the month, the people would meet once again for a special assembly where they would confess their shortcomings and worship God.

The Law of Moses includes the first five books of the Old Testament (Genesis through Deuteronomy). We often refer to it as the *Pentateuch—penta* meaning five. According to Deuteronomy 31:10-13, the Law was to be publicly read aloud every seven years.

"You alone are the Lord, who made the heavens and all that is in them," the people acknowledged in worship. "It is You who gives life to everything, and the multitudes of heaven worship You." For three hours, the people took turns asking God's forgiveness and recognizing His power and faithfulness toward them. They remembered how God had called Abraham and made a covenant promise with him. They recalled how God had saved their ancestors from slavery in Egypt and brought them safely through the desert and into the Promised Land. Even when the people turned from God, He did not abandon them because of His loyal love and faithfulness to keeping His covenant—His Word. "In all that has happened to us, Lord, You have been just; You have acted faithfully while we did wrong," the Israelites confessed. "Our kings, leaders, priests, and fathers didn't follow Your laws or pay attention to the warnings You gave them. As a result, they were taken from this land, just as You had warned, for they didn't turn from their evil ways. Now, we are like slaves because another kingdom rules over us and enjoys the goodness of the land. Hear our cry, O Lord, for we are in distress," the Israelites prayed. "We desire to live the way You want us to live. In view of this, we now make a binding agreement and put it in writing. . . ."

> God is never impressed by what we do for Him out of our own efforts. He is only pleased with what we do through Him, and then, with what He does through us.

One by one, promises of change were recorded on the parchment. "We promise not to let our sons or daughters marry the pagan people of the land. When neighboring peoples bring merchandise or grain to sell on the Sabbath, we will refuse to buy it on that day—or any other holy day. We promise to obey the command to pay the temple tax and to bring the first part of every harvest to You. We promise to supply the storerooms of the temple with food, so the priests may be provided for as they go about their jobs—just as You commanded. We will not neglect the house of our God, and we will not neglect You, Lord." Once the Israelites' promises had been recorded, the leaders, Levites, and priests put their seal to them. In the eyes of the people, they had decided to make a change, and they would live by it . . . or so they thought.

His job done, Nehemiah went back to serve under King Artaxerxes as he had promised. Sometime later, however, Nehemiah had the opportunity to return. He was shocked at what he saw. Eliashib, the priest in charge of the storerooms of the temple (which lay empty), allowed a foreigner to move in and live there! That foreigner was Tobiah, who had been an enemy against the rebuilding of the walls! Also, because the people didn't keep the storerooms full, the priests had gone back to their own fields to work and neglected their duties in the temple. Nehemiah kicked Tobiah out of the temple and rebuked the officials who let the storerooms go empty. When he noticed foreigners coming into the city with merchandise on the Sabbath and the Israelites buying from them, Nehemiah drove the vendors out, rebuked the people, and ordered the city gates to be locked until the Sabbath was over. It seemed the promises the Israelites made to change had little value and no lasting effect.

exploring deeper

Open your Bible to Nehemiah 9:38 and read what it says. Do you think the Israelites were sincere about what they were doing? Now, turn over to Nehemiah 8 and read the last sentence in verse 10. What do you think this means? Do you find it a little odd? According to this, where should their focus be?

DANGER AHEAD

The Israelites had a great "revival," and everyone was emotionally charged to live wholeheartedly for God. Unfortunately, they didn't realize that true revival is more than enthusiasm and keeping to a new set of standards or rules. It's a plan of action carried out by dependence upon God for help. "Turning over a new leaf" is never effective when it's our own power that is doing the turning. Yes, we need to be determined, but more importantly, we need to be dependent. If our dependence is upon our own self-effort, our revival will be fruitless. Be careful of "self efforts." They are only a trap to keep you from seeking true strength in a relationship with the living God.

GETTING YOUR BEARINGS:
THE BOOK OF ESTHER

The story of Esther takes place in 483 B.C.—after the first group of exiles led by Zerubbabel had returned to Jerusalem and before Ezra came with the second group. Historically speaking, if we were to plug the Book of Esther into its proper time sequence, it would fall between chapters 6 and 7 of the Book of Ezra.

Apparently, Esther's family chose not to return to Jerusalem under King Cyrus' decree, which granted them permission. Under the Persian empire, many Jews enjoyed freedom and became established in their way of living. Others simply feared the long and dangerous journey back to their homeland. For whatever reasons, Esther's family remained in Babylon; God had a plan for it.

As you explore Esther, you will see the glory of God's timing and the twists and turns of man's pride. Although a short book, Esther is packed with great life lessons! There's more to Esther than meets the eye.

IT'S NO COINCIDENCE

TAKEN FROM ESTHER 1-4

GETTING READY

Start your time today with prayer, and invite God to help you understand and apply what you learn. God has a specific plan and purpose for your life right now. Ask Him to help you see that purpose.

THE JOURNEY

Have you ever secretly wished you could do something great—something that really made a difference?

For my guests, I shall have the best of everything! King Xerxes of Persia thought to himself. It was a six-month celebration he was hosting with important leaders and dignitaries eating at his table. The purpose was to plan a battle strategy for invading Greece, as well as to provide an opportunity for King Xerxes to show off his wealth—proving his power to carry out his plan. In a moment of thoughtless merriment, King Xerxes decided to show off more than his riches. "Summon Queen Vashti to come and show off her beauty to my guests!" he commanded. A satisfied smile curled the edges of his lips as he waited in anticipation for Vashti to come. His smile soon faded, for Queen Vashti would not come. Knowing the king and his cohorts had become drunk, she refused to be a part of it. This angered the king greatly, and the queen was dethroned and sent away from the king's presence. Vashti would easily be replaced by another.

The beauty treatments the women had to undergo required six months of using oil from myrrh and six months with perfumes and cosmetics (Esther 2:12)!

"Let a search be made to find a new queen for King Xerxes!" The announcement soon spread across the land. Officials were appointed to gather young women from every province in the kingdom and bring them to Susa to be placed in the king's harem. After undergoing beauty treatments for twelve months, they would have the opportunity to be presented to King Xerxes. Until that time, or unless the king specifically called for them by name, the young women would remain in the king's harem. A young Jewish woman named Hadassah (also called Esther in the Persian language) was among them.

Mordecai paced, wondering how his cousin was faring. She had been taken to the king's palace for the selection process. Every day Mordecai walked back and forth near the courtyard of the harem to find out what was happening to her. Since Esther's parents had been killed, Mordecai had taken his cousin in and raised her as his own daughter. Now, he had to check on her welfare. "Don't tell anyone your nationality," he advised her before she was taken away, and Esther obeyed. Little did she know how important that simple fact would be!

Esther's turn came to be presented before King Xerxes. She found favor in his eyes. The king was more attracted to Esther than he was to any of the other women, so he set a royal crown on her head and made her queen in place of Vashti. An announcement was made and sent throughout all the provinces declaring a national holiday, and a huge banquet was held in Esther's honor. King Xerxes was greatly pleased.

One day, while Mordecai was sitting at the king's gate awaiting news of how Esther was getting along, he overheard a conversation. Two of the king's officers were talking between themselves in hushed tones. They were angry at King Xerxes and planned to have him killed! *I must inform Esther so she can warn the king!* Mordecai thought quickly. Making contact with Esther, Mordecai revealed the plot against the king. Esther reported the plot to King Xerxes and gave credit to Mordecai for finding it out. When the report was investigated and found to be true, the guilty officers were hung on the gallows, and the whole event was recorded in the king's royal records—along with Mordecai's name.

God had commanded the Israelites not to bow to anyone but Him. But there was another reason Mordecai refused to bow to Haman. Haman was an Amalekite. In Deuteronomy 25:17-19, the Israelites were commanded by God to destroy the Amalekites and wipe their memory from the face of the earth. Bowing to an Amalekite was something Mordecai could not and would not do.

Not long after these events, King Xerxes honored a man named Haman and elevated him to a position higher than all the other nobles. All the royal officials at the king's gate knelt down and paid honor to Haman, for the king commanded it. Mordecai, however, would not bow to Haman. "Why don't you bow to him?" the royal officials at the king's gate asked Mordecai. "Why do you disobey the king's command?"

Every day they asked Mordecai the same question, and each day he refused to bow and remained silent about his reasons. This was reported to Haman, and Haman's anger boiled. When it was discovered that Mordecai was a Jew, Haman came before the king with a request. "There is a certain people in the provinces of your kingdom whose customs are different from ours. They don't obey your laws, and they should not be tolerated," he exaggerated. "If it pleases you, let a decree be issued to destroy them, and I will contribute 375 tons of silver into the king's treasury for the men who carry out this business."

King Xerxes thought Haman's request was reasonable and handed Haman his ring to officially seal the decree. He didn't realize the people

Haman spoke of were Jews—and Queen Esther was one of them! Mordecai grieved when the decree was announced and sent word to Esther. He knew it was no coincidence she had been chosen to be queen. "Perhaps you can present yourself before the king and plead for your people," Mordecai suggested. . . .

exploring deeper

Quickly turn to Esther 4:14 and read it. Especially look at the last part of that verse. What does it say? Now, look at verses 15-17. What was Esther's response? Want to know what happens next? You'll have to read the next lesson or take a sneak peek in your own Bible (Esther 5–8)!

THINKING on your FEET

God places you in situations so He can use you. Sometimes they are places of great honor and position like Esther experienced, and sometimes they are unnoticed places—"outside the gate," such as where Mordecai was. Whether you find yourself on center stage or behind the scenes—God has you there for a reason. It's no coincidence. Both are equally important. How do you value where God has placed you?

I DESERVE IT

TAKEN FROM ESTHER 5-6

GETTING READY

Spend a moment or two preparing your heart before you explore God's Word. Quiet your heart before God and ask Him to help you learn to put pride in its proper place.

THE JOURNEY

Does it ever bother you when others receive special recognition and you don't?

Queen Esther's heart pounded wildly within her. *I know I risk death by coming before the king without being summoned, but the risk of not doing so is even greater!* Esther breathed to herself. The matter at hand was urgent and involved more than just her own life. Already Esther had spent three days praying and fasting in order to seek God's direction— and protection!

The doors opened, and the king looked up. Esther froze, unsure if she would be received by the king or not. She knew her bold actions

could easily cost her life. Her gaze was fixed upon the scepter King
Xerxes held in his hand. If he raised it, she would be pardoned for such
an interruption, and her life would be spared. If
he didn't . . .

**Because Persian kings
were protective of their
wives, it was very
unusual to be invited to
a private banquet with
the queen.**

King Xerxes tightened his grip on the scepter
and pointed it in her direction. He then raised it.
Esther sighed in relief as she knew her life would
be spared, but the burden of her mission still
weighed heavily on her heart. Timidly she went
forward, touched the end of the scepter, and
bowed before the king.

"What is it, Queen Esther? What is your
request?" the king questioned kindly. "If it is even up to half the kingdom, it will be given to you." Queen Esther knew God had opened the
doors for her request, but she also knew such matters had to be handled
correctly. Instead of making her charge against Haman's wicked decree to
kill all her people, Esther would approach things differently. She would
invite the king and Haman to a party in the king's honor, then wait for
God's timing to make her request.

"If you regard me with favor," Queen Esther responded, "please grant
my request to come tomorrow to a banquet I desire to prepare for you
and Haman. Then I will answer your question." The king agreed. He and
Haman would plan to return the next day. . . .

This is too wonderful! Haman said under his breath with both
delight and arrogance. He felt really important to have been invited to
eat at Queen Esther's private banquet. As Haman exited through the
king's gate, something caught his attention. It was Mordecai—the only
one who refused to bow before him. Haman's anger boiled. *You just
wait,* he muttered under his breath. *You'll get what you deserve!* Little
did Haman know . . .

Reaching home, Haman boasted to his wife and friends about all the
ways the king had honored him above other nobles and officials. ". . . Not
only that!" Haman eagerly added. "But I'm the only person Queen Esther
invited to join the king at a banquet!" Everyone was impressed with the

honor Haman had received. Haman, however, received little satisfaction from it. "All this gives me no pleasure as long as I see that . . . that Jew Mordecai sitting at the king's gate!" he stated angrily.

"Why not have a huge gallows of seventy-five feet built and ask the king in the morning to have Mordecai hung on it!" they suggested. "Then go to the dinner with the king and be happy!" A fiendish smirk rose from Haman's lips as he gave orders to have the gallows built.

That night King Xerxes had difficulty sleeping and ordered his book of records to be read to him. The king listened intently as the record of his officials who rebelled against him was read. "The plot was discovered by a man named Mordecai, and through his quick action the king's life had been spared," it stated.

Although the king's records contained twelve years of events, the official "happened" to turn and read from the portion concerning Mordecai—an event that had occurred five years earlier and had gone unrewarded!

King Xerxes looked up and asked his official, "What was the reward given to this Mordecai?"

"None," came the response. Not realizing Mordecai hadn't been properly rewarded, the king resolved in his heart to attend to the matter in the morning.

A sudden noise indicated someone was in the outer court. The official noticed it was Haman and summoned him in. "You're just the person I want to talk to!" the king stated. "Tell me, what should I do to honor a man who truly pleases me?"

Haman's heart pounded with delight, believing the king spoke of him. "Instruct one of the most noble princes to dress that man in the king's robe, place him on the king's own horse, and lead him through the city square proclaiming: 'This is what is done for the man the king delights in!'" Haman eagerly replied.

King Xerxes nodded in agreement, pleased with the suggestion. "Go at once and do just as you have suggested for Mordecai the Jew who sits at the gate. . . ."

exploring deeper

Quickly open your Bible and read Esther 7:1-6 and then verses 9-10. After Haman did what the king commanded (against his will, no doubt!), he was summoned to Esther's banquet. What happens there?

DANGER AHEAD

Haman had a real problem with wanting others to show him honor, and he got what he deserved. In striving to be appreciated, Haman only ended up humiliated. Don't let yourself fall into the same trap of being ruled by your pride and thinking you deserve to be honored, for only God deserves to be honored and worshiped. Often honor comes to those who don't seek it—that's God's blessing. Those who set themselves up in pride only come to ruin. Don't be one of them.

GETTING YOUR BEARINGS:
THE BOOK OF JOB

As you've already seen, the books of the Old Testament aren't necessarily presented in chronological order in our Bible—and Job is no exception! Although the exact time this book was written has been debated, many facts support the idea that Job possibly lived around the time of the patriarchs (Abraham, Isaac, and Jacob). If this is true, then the correct placement of this book would be somewhere in the middle of the Book of Genesis!

The Book of Job is full of surprises—and disappointments. It allows us to see the inside view of suffering and the outward reactions of observers. Many have regarded this book as a great piece of literature. However, caution must be observed! Because Job centers on the sufferings of one man and the bad counsel of his friends, it is important not to pull the Scripture verses out of their context. To do so would be to state examples of bad advice as truth!

As you explore this book, you will gain an inside view into Job's life and wrestle with the age-old question: If God is good, then why do the godly suffer? Enjoy the journey—and watch out for hidden surprises. . . .

READY ... AIM ... FIRE!

TAKEN FROM JOB 1-3

GETTING READY

As you begin your journey through Job, pause a moment to ready your heart. Pray and ask the Lord to show you what He wants you to learn, and allow Him to use it to change your life.

THE JOURNEY

Have you ever felt like a target—with everyone and everything firing upon you?

"The Sabeans did *what*?" Job said with unbelief, turning his full gaze on the man bringing him the bad news.

The messenger repeated his words, trying to calm himself as he spoke. "The oxen were plowing and the donkeys were grazing nearby," he explained once again, "when the Sabeans attacked, killed all your servants, and carried off all your cattle. I'm the only one who escaped to tell you!"

Job was stunned. *All my servants—gone?* he thought to himself. The

Sabeans' attack was totally unprovoked, unexplained, and unexpected. Job knew there was a great loss of life, for he had many servants who helped care for his 1,000 oxen and 500 donkeys. While the messenger was still speaking and giving Job his report, another servant came up with equally bad news.

"Sir," he said, out of breath, "fire from heaven fell from the sky and burned up all 7,000 of your sheep as well as your servants! I am the only one who escaped to report it to you!" Job looked from one messenger to the other, hardly able to believe such events were taking place. Just as the second messenger finished telling Job of the tragedy, another servant approached. He didn't have good news either. Job looked wearily into the messenger's eyes, wondering if it might be another bad report. It was.

"The Chaldeans formed three raiding parties, swept down on your camels, and carried them off—killing all of the servants tending them!" the messenger announced. Job's jaw clenched down tightly as he gritted his teeth in frustration over such unexplained attacks. Job had been a respected man in the city and blessed with great wealth. Now, with the loss of every one of his 3,000 camels—along with all his oxen, donkeys, and sheep, he was reduced to poverty—all in a matter of minutes. Job looked up, thinking he could receive no further bad news. He was wrong. One more messenger approached even while the last servant was still speaking. His news was the worst yet.

> The Sabeans were people from southwest Arabia. The Queen of Sheba, who visited King Solomon (950 B.C.) was a Sabean.

"Sir, a strong wind like none I've seen before came through and ripped apart the house where your sons and daughters were celebrating a feast together. The house collapsed in a rubble and killed them all. I'm the only survivor," he said quietly, observing the effects of his solemn news.

Job stood in shocked silence as great anguish swelled within him. He tore his robe in deep grief, shaved his head, then fell to the ground in worship before the Lord. "I came into this world with nothing and will one day leave it with nothing," he breathed. Although in deep sorrow, Job could not and would not raise his fist against God. Little did he understand the significance of his actions.

Unknown to Job, Satan had presented himself before God in order to accuse God's people. "They only love You for what they can get from You!" Satan hissed, his words full of spite and hatred. "If You remove Your blessings," Satan accused, "people would curse You and not worship You!" Satan's words were an attack not only on humanity, but also on God's character. God allowed Satan's theory to be put to the test and gave permission for Satan to test his theory on Job. God knew Satan's accusations would be quickly silenced and Job's faith greatly strengthened. In a fury of destruction, Satan acted quickly. One on top of another, he fired upon Job, stripping away everything that gave him a sense of security—wealth, a strong family, and his health. Satan's first attack was on Job's wealth, then on his beloved children. The final attack would be on Job's health. . . .

"Are you still holding on to your integrity?" Job's wife spat with disgust. "Curse God and die!" But Job would not. He reached for a piece of broken pottery while sitting among the ashes and scraped his inflamed sores, which seeped with infection and itched. Job had lost his appetite and his strength. His body was racked with pain and his flesh seemed as if it were rotting on his bones as it turned black and peeled. Dark circles caused Job's eyes to have a sunken look, and depression curved his lips downward as he sat stooped over in misery. He was feverish and restless, gasping for his breath. Each effort only intensified his physical pain and added to his emotional agony. Even though he was in a state of hopeless misery, never once did he curse God. Job did, however, curse the day he was born.

"Oh, that my mother never gave me birth!" he moaned in great pain and sorrow. "Why was I given life by God only to be destined to live in distress with no future?"

exploring deeper

Turn in your Bible to Job 3:25-26 and read it. Have you ever felt like saying this?

THINKING on your FEET

Unfortunately, many people seek God and worship Him only to gain something for themselves. They worship God as long as they experience a life without pain and difficulty, or one of great success and happiness. When success and happiness are missing, so is their faith in God! Job, however, was different. His love for God was real—and God knew it. Job knew that no matter what, God was in control of the circumstances of his life, and God deserved his allegiance.

Today, if you were to experience the extreme testing Job experienced, how would your faith hold up?

IF YOU ASK ME...

TAKEN FROM JOB 4-14

GETTING READY

Take a moment to pray and allow God to check your heart, motives, and actions. Ask Him to help you avoid making false assumptions about others—or yourself.

THE JOURNEY

Has anyone ever given you bad advice?

Suffering hung over Job like a heavy blanket that threatened to suffocate him. Words couldn't describe the mental, emotional, and physical pain Job was feeling as he sat on the ash heap. For a week now, Job had sat in silence and mourning. Only the sound of a piece of broken pottery scraping against his infected skin broke the silence in the air. Job's friends sat with him, saying nothing, as was the custom of the day. It was out of respect for those suffering great grief. Although Eliphaz, Bildad, and Zophar had said nothing for the past seven days, they could hardly quiet their own thoughts. They had time to think, and the thoughts and reasons they had for Job's unusual suffering all boiled down to one thing—something they believed was an obvious explanation.

Job groaned, and his three friends looked at him expectantly. Coughing and clearing his throat, Job's weak voice finally shattered the long days of silence. "If only my mother never gave me birth!" he whispered. "Cursed is the day I was born! What I feared has come upon me; what I dreaded has happened to me. I have no peace, no quietness; I have no rest, but only turmoil!" Job moaned. He briefly looked at his friends, then drooped his head to stare at the ground in agony. Eliphaz, one of Job's friends who had sat with him in silence for the past week, took this as his cue to speak. Being the oldest, Eliphaz would be first to speak. Clearing his throat, he began to offer his explanation for the suffering he saw Job experiencing.

"Will you listen to something I have to say?" Eliphaz asked Job—not waiting for Job's reply. "Under such circumstances, who couldn't speak? In the past, you've supported those who were weak. Your words strengthened and encouraged others who had fallen or wavered. But now that trouble strikes you, you are faint and downcast," Eliphaz observed. He paused for a moment before challenging Job. "Has the innocent person ever perished? When has the upright person ever been destroyed?" Eliphaz reasoned. "My own experience tells me that those who plant evil and cultivate trouble only experience the same! God stands beside the upright and punishes those who do evil, therefore, do not despise the discipline of the Almighty."

Job heard Eliphaz's words and the sting of what he was implying. *Eliphaz states that if I confess my sins to You, Lord, my suffering will end! Yet, I have lived uprightly before You. I have done no wrong that I need to confess!* Job silently prayed to God. He knew deep down that Eliphaz was wrong in

In three rounds of different speeches, Job's friends gave their bad advice to Job. At first they questioned if Job had sinned, then they assumed he must have. In their last round, they openly accused Job of sinning! In chapters 38—42, God had the final word and set the record straight!

assuming the godly never suffer. Eliphaz relied on his own experiences and gave advice from those observations. His advice was not helpful.

Bildad was the next to speak. Hearing Job's response to Eliphaz, Bildad became more forceful and spoke not from his own experience, but pulled in examples of past generations and tradition to give his words more authority. "Ask the former generations and find out what their fathers learned!" Bildad challenged. "Surely God doesn't reject a blameless man or strengthen the hands of evildoers!" he added. "When your children sinned against God, He gave them what they deserved. If, however, you are upright, God will remove your suffering. If not . . ."

It was the custom of the day to remain silent until the grieving person spoke first. Putting ashes upon one's head or sitting among the ashes showed grief and mourning.

Job understood the intent of Bildad's words. Like Eliphaz, Bildad believed only the wicked suffered while the godly experienced nothing but success. He wrongly assumed that Job's children were killed because they were unrighteous. It didn't take long for Job's third friend, Zophar, to chime in with his own observations. Zophar pressed his point more forcefully than the others. "God is wiser than you, Job, and He knows deceitful men and brings them to account!" Although Zophar's words were true, Job was not being deceitful or trying to hide his sin from anyone—let alone God. Once again, the advice of his friends did not apply.

As much as they tried to argue, persuade, dominate, and reason with Job, they were doing it in vain, for they assumed they knew God's mind in the matter. Their advice was based on personal experience, the experience of others in the past, and the logical religious thinking of their day. Job knew the advice he received was shallow, and that his friends had quickly jumped to false conclusions. Although Job didn't fully understand the reason for his suffering, he knew what it was *not* from! Job allowed God to be big enough to have other reasons for allowing him to suffer.

exploring deeper

In your Bible, look up Job 5:27 and read it. What does it say? What does the person saying this assume? Notice the words, "we," "examined," "true," "so . . . apply it."

DANGER AHEAD

There is much that goes on behind the scenes in a person's life that we know nothing about. Unlike God, we cannot judge the thoughts and motives of a person's heart. Often, in trying to help someone, we draw wrong conclusions. Sometimes, we even tell ourselves false things! Suffering is NOT always because of sin. Be wary of people who tell you otherwise.

Interestingly, in the New Testament times Jesus was confronted with this very question of why people suffer. In John 9:1-3 Jesus and His disciples came upon a man who was blind from birth and forced to beg on the streets. Immediately, the disciples asked whether the blind man or his parents had sinned to cause such a condition and suffering. Jesus responded, "Neither this man nor his parents sinned. Rather, this happened so that the work of God might be displayed in this man's life." Jesus later healed the blind man. Don't assume all suffering is a result of sin.

GETTING YOUR BEARINGS:
THE BOOK OF PSALMS

The Book of Psalms is the longest book in the Old Testament—but don't let that scare you! It's also one of the most stirring, for it speaks directly to the heart. Although many of the psalms were written by David, he wasn't the only writer. Korah's sons (Korah led a revolt against Moses in the desert) and a man named Asaph wrote some as well. God used each of these men to pull together the message He wanted to communicate to us in His Word.

Although the ancient Hebrews called this book "songs of praise," the word psalms comes from a Greek term designating "music on stringed instruments." These took the form of personal testimonies, songs of praise and thanksgiving, prayers, and even prophecies of the future and the coming Messiah. It is interesting to note that New Testament writers quoted the Book of Psalms more than any other book, and saw how the "Messianic" psalms were fulfilled in Jesus' life!

As you explore this last phase of your journey, keep your eyes peeled—and your heart open. By the time you exit Psalms, you will have gained a better understanding of who God is and how you relate to Him. It's a message that hits the heart.

GET REAL

TAKEN FROM PSALM 13

GETTING READY

As you begin exploring Psalms, don't just read it for head knowledge. Instead, allow God to use today's lesson to transform you from the inside out. Commit your time to Him and come expectantly and openly.

THE JOURNEY

Have you ever been afraid to let God know what's really on your heart—fearing He might be disappointed?

David agonized in his heart. Hurt, pain, frustration, and a feeling that God had abandoned him kept mounting in his emotions. It was a frustrating and uncomfortable place to be. David valued his relationship with God and knew he couldn't sweep his emotions under a rug and pretend they didn't exist. He also realized that God knew his heart and thoughts anyway. Being honest with God was not an option—it was a necessity. David's prayer would be open, honest, and come from the deep corners and darkness of his heart.

"How long, O Lord? How long will You forget me?" David complained. "Will it be forever?! How long will You hide Your face from me—looking the other way?" he questioned. David's heart felt as though it would pound through his chest as he admitted his true emotions. There was no holding back. David knew that God despised liars. It would be far better to express his honest feelings than it would be to try to cover over them for fear he might somehow offend God. David would be honest and not play games. His prayer today would continue to be one of honesty over his own struggles and disappointment. . . .

> Real prayer can be words off the top of your head or a well-thought-out poem. It doesn't matter which as long as you are communicating with God and sharing with Him what's in the bottom of your heart.

"How long must I wrestle with my thoughts and face the sorrow in my heart every day?" he asked impatiently. To David, it was a bitter disappointment that God was allowing his enemy to get the upper hand over him. It was a personal embarrassment and also a threat to David's kingship. Would it also be a threat to his trust in God?

"How long will my enemy triumph over me?" David cried out with his complaint. "Turn and answer me, O Lord my God! Don't let my enemy gloat, saying, 'Hah! I've overcome him!' Don't let my foes rejoice at my downfall!" he added, expressing both the fear and frustration in his heart.

David sat a moment in silence. A feeling of relief began to wash over his soul. The pounding in his heart and frustration on his lips seemed to melt away as his words had spilled forth. Even though God had not delivered David from his situation and seemed to delay in coming to his rescue, David knew God was trustworthy. Nothing he could say or do would shock God, for God already knew it all. This was of great comfort to David, for he knew he could come to God as he was—and be accepted. His relationship with God was based on honesty. It was not an empty religion based on the fear of saying and doing the right thing. David knew he could be real with God and not be rejected, and that encouraged his trust.

> Although we aren't told in the Scriptures what situation David was referring to in this psalm, we do know it was something that brought him great disappointment.

"I trust in Your unfailing love, and my heart rejoices in Your salvation," David was able to admit. "I will sing to You, for You have been good to me," he whispered quietly.

exploring deeper

Although this prayer of David's is from Psalm 13, turn in your Bible to Psalm 34:4 and read it. What does David say here? Take a close look at the first half of the verse. What did David do? Now, look at the second half of the verse. What two things did God do?

Skill Time

God desires that we come to Him with our deep feelings—whether they are good or bad, complaints or praise. That is the whole purpose and point of prayer—communicating with God. God knows us intimately and longs for us to be in relationship with Him. That can't happen if we are hiding behind a lie or kidding ourselves that everything is OK when it's not. We can come to God honestly with our deep feelings and without fear. Give it a try—allow God into the dark corners of your heart and "get real" with Him. Don't hide from God.

In the quietness of your heart, open up those doors and closets where you have conveniently stored your hang-ups, fears, and "unacceptable" emotions. Let them air out in God's presence. Here are some sentences you can complete to help you get started:

Lord, it hurts when _____

I feel frustrated because _____

I don't think it's fair when _____

Now, just as David did, trust God to help you with those emotions. If they keep coming back, keep handing them over to the Lord. God will be there for you—just as He was for David.

359

IT'S MY TREAT

TAKEN FROM PSALM 40

GETTING READY

Pause a moment to prepare your heart. Commit your time to the Lord and ask Him to help you realize all that He is, and all that He desires to do in and through you.

THE JOURNEY

Do you know people who say they don't believe in God?

It was a troubling time in David's life as his enemies seemed to be as many as the hairs on his head! Sins in his own life seemed to cloud the waters even more, making his situation appear all the more desperate. Yet, in the midst of the storm, a quiet hope filled his soul. David knew to whom he could turn, and reflected upon all that God had already done in his life.

"I waited patiently for the Lord to help, and He turned to me and answered my cry," David reminded himself. David knew he had been in helpless situations before—unable to deliver himself and totally dependent upon God. He knew God had been faithful to deliver him—even when he deserved it the least.

David paused a moment before writing down the next few words. His heart filled with awe over God's display of mercy and grace toward him. "The Lord lifted me out of the slimy pit, out of the mud and mire," he wrote. "He set my feet on a rock and gave me a firm place to stand." David looked over the words he had written. There was

> Even atheists who claim not to believe in anything, really do—they believe in themselves as their own god.

such a contrast between the hopelessness of being in a quicksandlike pit and being pulled out and set upon a solid rock. "God put me on a rock and placed a new song in my mouth—a song of praise to Him," David added. "Many will see what God has done in my life and be amazed. As a result, they will put their trust in the Lord."

> It is interesting to note that Psalm 53 and Psalm 14 are the same! Was this a mistake? No. It simply emphasizes the importance of the message. God's grace and salvation are not earned—they are God's treat for those who will accept them.

David's hand skimmed across the parchment as he continued to express his thoughts. "Blessed are those who trust in the Lord and don't place their confidence in the proud or in those who chase after false gods," he wrote. David reflected upon God's character and works. "Many are the wonders that You have done, Lord. The things You planned for us are too many to count! I couldn't possibly describe them all!" he quickly wrote. "It's not empty religious duties that You desire—rather, our hearts and our love."

David thought about that for a moment, then reflected upon his own life and the need to share such a message. "I don't hide the news of Your righteousness in my heart, but I speak of Your faithfulness and salvation to others. I tell them of Your love and truth that they, too, might come to know You. May all who search for You be filled with this same joy and gladness. May they also shout, 'The Lord is awesome!'"

exploring deeper

After David wrote this portion reflecting upon what God had done in his life, he then completed his psalm as a prayer and asked God to deliver him from the enemies who surrounded him. David knew his own limitations and God's abundant power to rescue—not only for eternity, but also for daily living. In your own Bible, turn ahead to Psalm 53 and read verses 1-3. What do they say? This is a good description of people caught in a "slimy pit"—and not even aware of it!

Skill Time

God has chosen us for a relationship with Himself—even when we're in the "slimy pit" and least deserve it!

Unfortunately, many of us don't seek Him. We mistakenly think if we don't believe in God, He doesn't exist. Wrong! God exists whether we're willing to admit it or not. He no only exists, but He's there for us—offering deliverance. Have you let Him pull you out of your slimy pit? Have you taken that step? If this is something you desire, turn to the back of this book and read the special message that's there for you.

If you've already experienced God pulling you from the slimy pit, setting your feet upon a rock, and giving you a new life—have you shared this with anyone else? Begin to follow David's example this week and tell others. Make a point to tell one person (someone you've never told before) what God has done in your life. This is called "sharing your testimony." Here's how it's done:

1. Pray silently that God will guide you and give you wisdom and understanding.
2. Find out where the other person is "coming from" and how your message can help her in her life.
3. Simply tell her where you've been and what God has done for you.
4. God uses His Word, so if appropriate, share a Scripture verse showing God's desire for all to come to know Him. (John 3:16 would be a good one!) Then, let God take care of the rest; that's His job!
5. Realize others will be watching your life to see if what you say is true or not. Continue to live for Him—in His strength and power.

RUB-A-DUB-DUB

TAKEN FROM PSALM 51

GETTING READY

Take a moment to ask God to soften your heart. Thank Him for the forgiveness He gives when we come humbly to Him.

THE JOURNEY

Do you know people who never admit when they've made a mistake or done wrong?

King David was stunned. Ever since the prophet Nathan approached him and pointed out his wrong, David's heart was filled with remorse. He had not only sinned before God, but also tried to cover up his sin by having an innocent person murdered! All of this was done so that David could have his way. David now knew it wasn't worth it, and his conscience tormented him. The prophet Nathan's words had pierced him in his heart, making David realize the wrong he had done. Knowing that no one is above God's laws—not even a king—David came to God for forgiveness.

"Have mercy on me, O God, because of Your unfailing love," David prayed in the anguish of his soul. "Because of Your great compassion, blot out my sin. Please wash away my wrongs and cleanse my heart," he pleaded. "I recognize what I have done, and my disgraceful deeds are ever before me," David admitted.

In a moment of silence, the king humbly considered the bottom line. "Against You—and You alone—I have sinned, and done what is evil in Your sight. You are right in what You say, and Your judgment against me is just," he confessed. David sighed heavily before continuing his prayer. He knew it wasn't a matter of finally being caught—it was a matter of being honest with God and getting back on track. Only God could forgive his wrong and restore the purity of his heart.

> **The full story behind this psalm can be found in 2 Samuel chapters 11–12 (or by reading the corresponding lesson entitled, "This Isn't Lookin' So Good" on page 206).**

"Cleanse me with hyssop, and I will be clean. Wash me, Lord, and I will be whiter than snow. I have been broken. Please restore the joy and gladness that was once in my heart," David humbly asked. He knew only God could do such a miracle. "Create in me a pure heart, O God, and renew a steadfast spirit within me. Don't cast me from Your presence, but restore to my heart the joy of Your salvation," he prayed. David paused, knowing the weakness of his own heart. "Grant me a willing spirit to obey You," he whispered. "Then I will tell others of Your ways so sinners will return to You."

David knew God was not impressed by "bargains" or by religious acts done to make up for wrong deeds. He knew God was only interested in matters of the heart. "O Lord, I know

> **When David mentioned God cleansing him with hyssop, he wasn't referring to a special soap! Hyssop was a plant commonly used in sacrifices. The Israelites used hyssop branches to apply the blood of the lamb to their doorposts during Passover (Exodus 12:22), so God's judgment might "pass over" them.**

You wouldn't be pleased with sacrifices, or I'd bring them. If I brought You a burnt offering, You wouldn't accept it," David acknowledged. "The sacrifice You desire is that of a broken and repentant heart. For a humble and sorrowful heart, O Lord, You will not despise." David knew that for a fact. Forgiveness wasn't granted on the basis of David's goodness—it was based on the fact of God's mercy.

Turn to Psalm 51 in your Bible and read verse 10. What two things did David ask of God? Why do you think he asked specifically for those?

David saw the importance of confessing (admitting) his sin to God. No effort on his own part could ever set his heart straight or remove the blot of his sin. Trying to hide behind his mistakes, hoping no one noticed, and wishing they'd go away only made matters worse for David. It wasn't until he came clean before God that God was able to clean David's heart. It's the same with us. Covering up our sin only rubs against God and makes us a prisoner to our mistakes. This week, what will you do with your heart? Will you try to cover over your sin and remain a prisoner, or will you confess it and experience God's forgiveness?

WHAT'S WRONG WITH THIS PICTURE?

TAKEN FROM PSALM 73

GETTING READY

Before you begin today's lesson, stop and pray. Take care of anything that might be occupying your mind (i.e., questions for God, asking His forgiveness, etc.), so that your heart is open and teachable before Him. Spend a moment thanking God for His hand on your life—even when circumstances might seem "unfair" on the outside.

THE JOURNEY

Does it ever seem unfair when people who do wrong have it better than those who do what's right?

Asaph sighed as he looked up from his parchment. The words he wrote reflected honest thoughts that came from both experience and observation. . . .

"Truly God is good to Israel, to those who are pure in heart," Asaph stated with confidence. "Yet, as for me, my feet had nearly slipped," he admitted. "When I saw the proud and wicked get their way and have success in life, I struggled. I nearly lost my perspective and my foothold."

Asaph paused to reflect on what he had observed about godless people and how it bothered him. "The wicked have no struggles; they seem healthy and strong—free from the burdens that plague everybody else. They wear pride like a necklace and strut about, clothed in cruelty. They scoff and speak only evil, seeking to crush others. If that isn't enough," Asaph described, "they boast against heaven itself, and people listen to them and turn from God! This . . . this is what the wicked are like! Always carefree and enjoying a life of ease while their riches seem to multiply!"

Although Asaph didn't say so, the words, "it's not fair" lay dangerously close to the tip of his tongue. It was something that had surfaced from the deep struggles of his own heart. "Have I kept my heart pure and lived a godly life for nothing?! The wicked seem to get all they desire, yet I experience trouble all day long!" *What's wrong with this picture?!* Asaph had thought to himself. "I tried to understand why the wicked prosper, but it got the better of me. It wasn't until I came into Your sanctuary, Lord, that I gained a new perspective on the matter. There, I was reminded of the destiny of the wicked," he whispered, "for instantly they will be destroyed and swept away in terror. When Your judgment comes upon them, they will vanish from this life. How foolish I was to be envious of them! My focus was totally wrong, and I reacted like an animal without sense!" Asaph admitted.

Asaph was a Levite musician appointed by David to serve in the worship services (1 Chronicles 16:5). Twelve psalms are credited to his name (Psalm 50, and Psalms 73-83), although some were written by his sons, who inherited his position.

Both Psalm 73 and Psalm 49 are considered "wisdom psalms" and share similar messages, although written by different people! The psalmist in verses 16-17 of Psalm 49 states: "Do not be overawed when a man grows rich, when the splendor of his house increases—for he will take nothing with him when he dies. . . ."

A moment of quietness filled the room as Asaph leaned back in his chair and considered the rest of the words he would write. A sense of awe and worship flooded his heart as he thought about God's faithfulness and goodness. "Even though my spirit was bitter within me as I observed the wicked, You didn't give up on me! You took hold of my right hand and guided me with Your counsel. Whom, Lord, have I in heaven but You? In this whole earth, there is nothing I desire more than You," he exclaimed. "My flesh and my heart may fail," Asaph admitted readily, "but You, God, are the strength of my heart and all that I need forever."

exploring deeper

Quickly turn in your Bible to Psalm 73 and read verses 16-17. Look at the focus of verse 16. Now compare that to the focus of verse 17. Do you see any differences? What were the results of each focus?

DANGER AHEAD

It's easy to lose our focus when we compare our experiences in life with others, or expect rewards and benefits (but don't get them)! Like Asaph, we are prone to question: "Is living a godly life really worth it?!" Such emotions are normal, and you will most likely experience them at some point in your life. Don't let them throw you! It is all too easy to look at this present world and think that's all there is to life. It's not. Don't be fooled. Instead, come before God and ask Him to help you gain His perspective. He will show you what's wrong with your picture, and then give you an even bigger—and better—one to look at! Keep your focus on Him—not on those around you.

IT'S YOUR MOVE...

TAKEN FROM PSALM 101

GETTING READY

Don't read any further until you've stopped to pray and commit this time to the Lord. Praying isn't merely a nice idea or a good habit—it's a necessity! The only way we advance against our enemy is by advancing on our knees—in prayer. Give today into God's hands and let Him help you fight your struggles.

THE JOURNEY

Do you ever find yourself slipping into old habits and doing what you know you shouldn't do?

David knew the path that lay before him. He had seen other rulers travel it—some with success and others with disaster. He knew the road ahead could be treacherous, for it was full of choices, temptations, and raw power. If he wasn't careful, David could end up making the same foolish mistakes Israel's first king—King Saul—had made. That thought made David shudder. As the new king of Israel, David wanted to be all

God wanted him to be, so he might lead the nation of Israel in the ways of the Lord. David knew he had to make a commitment to live a life of integrity.

"O Lord, I will sing of Your loyal love and Your justice," David proclaimed. "I will be careful to live a blameless life and will walk with a blameless heart. Because of this desire and commitment, I won't let my eyes look upon anything vile or offensive that could pollute my mind. Actions that are crooked or evil I will hate, and I'll have nothing to do with them," David vowed. He knew the standards he set now would help to keep him on track in the future when he would face tempting choices or difficult situations. King David didn't want to fall into any traps or cause dishonor to God's name. As a result, he would turn from all appearances of evil and seek to live his life according to a higher standard. David knew the danger that was out there.

"I will have nothing to do with wicked men. Neither will I tolerate those who slander their neighbors or live a life of conceit and pride," he stated. "I'll have absolutely nothing to do with their evil ways. Only those who are blameless will be allowed to serve around my throne. Deceivers and liars will not be allowed to serve me, nor even come into my presence," David finished.

> **It has been said that failing to plan is the same as planning to fail.**

Plan ahead!

P - Pray for your day before your feet hit the floor in the morning.

L - Learn to rely on God's wisdom—not your own. (Read your Bible and memorize key verses that speak to your heart and help you.)

A - Admit your weaknesses and realize where you are most prone to fall.

N - Never kid yourself into thinking you can live the Christian life in your own strength.

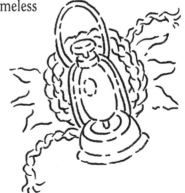

exploring deeper

At first glance, David's words seem pretty harsh and judgmental toward others—but a closer look reveals great wisdom! In your Bible, turn all the way back to Psalm 1 and read it. (Go ahead; it's only six verses long!) The key to understanding why David made the commitment he did is found in this psalm.

Now go back and reread the first verse of Psalm 1. Who is blessed? Next, take a close look at the words: "walk," "stand," and "sit." Do you notice anything interesting about these words?—Do you see the downward spiral of bad influence (walking, then standing, then sitting among the wicked)? These steps come almost unnoticed! It begins in simple ways such as: listening to the wicked, then identifying with them, then becoming like them yourself—without even knowing it!

According to verse 2, what is a way to avoid falling into this trap? Verse 3 describes the results.

THINKING on your FEET

It's so easy for us to fool ourselves into thinking we have everything under control! We make friends without even considering their influence upon us. We compromise, cheat, or lie without thinking of the consequences upon our lives! Soon, we don't realize the company we are keeping. We get caught up in patterns of bad behavior and old habits that are hard to break. Without a plan, we tend to fall right back into what comes easily or naturally for us (see Psalm 1:1). David realized the danger of this and set up "roadblocks" to keep himself from traveling down the wrong path. David had a plan, and he relied on God to help him. Do you? What will your plan be? It's your move....

IT'S A PERSONAL THING

TAKEN FROM PSALM 103

GETTING READY

Before beginning, take a moment to quiet your thoughts and put distractions behind you. Ask the Lord to open your heart and eyes to better understand who He is, that you might see how worthy He is of your worship.

THE JOURNEY

Do you sometimes draw a blank when it comes to worshiping God—unsure what to say or where to start?

"Praise the Lord, O my soul," David wrote, pondering all that God had done for him. "With my whole heart, I will praise His holy name, and not forget all His benefits. For God forgives all my sins and heals all my diseases. He rescues my life from the pit of death and then showers me with His loyal love and tender compassion. God satisfies my deep desires with good things that come from His hand. Under His care, my strength and youth are renewed like the eagle's!" David exclaimed. He sat back

373

momentarily and paused. Words seemed to come almost faster than David could write them all down. *There are so many things to worship and praise God for!* he breathed to himself. Taking up his pen, David continued to write across the parchment.

> The "fear of God" isn't a terrorizing fear like we experience when evil is around; rather, it is based on respect and love. It's a healthy view of God's awesome power.

"God is a God we can know, for He revealed His character to Moses and His wondrous deeds to all of Israel! He is a gracious God—One who is slow to anger and continuously displays His covenant loyalty. God's love is unfailing," David wrote. He briefly thought about his own life and Israel's past history. Even when the nation turned its back upon God and began worshiping false gods and idols, the Lord remained true to His covenant agreement. Even when His people were least deserving, God was there. David knew this was true for his own life as well.

"God hasn't punished our sins as they rightly deserve to be punished," David wrote concerning God's mercy and compassion. "Instead, God's love toward those who fear Him is as great as the distance from earth to the farthest point in heaven. It is God who removes our sins from us and places them far away—as far as the east is from the west. The Lord is like a tender and compassionate father toward those who fear Him. He understands how weak we are, knowing we are but dust. Even though our days on earth are brief—much like withering grass or flowers that bloom and die—God is there and remains constant. His loyal love is with those who know Him—those who keep His covenant and obey Him."

David looked up toward the heavens and sighed. He reflected on all that was there—just as real as the things on earth, yet invisible to his human eyes. "The Lord has made His throne in the heavens and rules everything from there. God's mighty angels listen for His commands and hasten to carry out His plans," David wrote. He knew God was the supreme ruler over the entire universe. Nothing was outside of God's concern or control. David glanced back down at his parchment. He would end his psalm of worship and praise on that note. "Praise the Lord, O my soul," David whispered quietly, then bowed before the Lord in a moment of true worship.

exploring deeper

Open your Bible and turn to this psalm that David wrote (Psalm 103). What does he challenge us to do in verses 1-2? Believe it or not, this is the bottom line of worship!

Skill Time

Worship is simply acknowledging God's worth. It is not a special ceremony reserved for a particular day when we all gather together in a building, but rather something that occurs deep within our hearts. The more we know God, the deeper we will bow on our knee. True worship comes from knowing God in a personal, intimate way, and we come to know Him through reading what He says about Himself in His Word (the Bible).

If you've closed your Bible, get it back out and open it to Psalm 103. Read verses 1-5 and write down on a piece of paper the five things David described and worshiped (praised) God for. (Hint: if you are reading from the NIV, these five things start with the following letters: f, h, r, c, s, r) Carry these around in your pocket today as a reminder. Then (when no one is even aware of it!) refer to your list and spend a moment quietly worshiping God. It can be easily done in the privacy of your own heart.

GOT AN APPETITE?

TAKEN FROM PSALM 119

GETTING READY

Remember to pray and commit your time to the Lord before beginning. Quiet your thoughts and tell God what is on your mind, so He can tell you what is on His. Allow Him to teach your heart and help you get beyond "I know I ought to," to the point of "I can't live without it," when it comes to reading His Word.

THE JOURNEY

In the smorgasbord of life, does the idea of reading your Bible rate the same as the thought of eating dry cardboard?

The psalmist picked up his pen and carefully wrote the first letter of the Hebrew alphabet on his parchment. His heart felt as though it would explode with the feelings he had inside for God's Word, yet he tried to contain himself. He knew the importance of his message and how important it would be for many generations to come. . . .

"Blessed are they whose ways are blameless—people who walk

according to the law of the Lord," the psalmist wrote from experience. "Blessed are those who keep His Word, and seek Him with all their heart. They don't play around with evil, but walk only in God's paths. You have charged us, Lord, to carefully keep Your commands. Oh, that my actions would always reflect your principles! Then I wouldn't be ashamed when I compare my life with Your commands," he wrote. The psalmist paused. He had written eight lines in the first paragraph. Each line carefully started with the first letter of the Hebrew alphabet. *This is good,* he thought to himself. He knew it would be able to be easily memorized and passed along. Taking his pen up again, he began the next eight lines with the second letter of the alphabet, and so he would

The author of Psalm 119 is unknown, although some believe it to be Ezra, who might have written this psalm after the temple was rebuilt. (See Ezra 6:14-15.)

continue. The psalm he was writing was to be special—it was a love letter to God concerning His Law.

"How can a person keep his way pure? By obeying Your Word and following its rules. I have hidden Your word in my heart so that I might not sin against You," the psalmist wrote, acknowledging his own weaknesses and tendencies. "I will delight in Your decrees and not forget Your Word. Oh, open my eyes that I may see wonderful things in Your Law. Teach me, O Lord, and give me understanding. Turn my heart toward Your Word and not toward selfish gain. Turn my eyes away from worthless things, for You are able to use Your Word to guide me and preserve my life. When I suffer, my comfort is found in the promises in Your Word. They are a healing balm to my soul. All Your commands are able to be trusted, and I can stand upon them like a firm foundation. Your Word, O Lord, is eternal—it doesn't change or pass away with the whims of man."

Slowly the psalmist looked up. Already he was halfway through the Hebrew alphabet and going strong. There was still so much more to write. He bent his head down and continued to write. The words flowed from his heart and onto the parchment in beautiful form, showcasing the honor and high regard he had for God's Law.

"To all perfection there is a limit, but Your commands have no limit—they are boundless! Your Word makes me wiser than my enemies, gives me more insight than my teachers, and enables me to have more understanding than my elders! Your words taste sweeter to me than honey, and I yearn to know them more. Even at night I lay upon my bed and think upon Your promises! Your Word, O Lord, is like a lamp to my feet showing me where to go, and a light to my path—helping me to get there. Your Word, O Lord, gives me peace in my heart, so that nothing can cause me to stumble. Through Your Word, You are near to me, Lord—all Your commands are true. Long ago I learned and understood that You have established them to last forever. . . .

exploring deeper

Open your Bible to Psalm 119 and look up verse 32. What does it say? Have you experienced this?

Skill Time

As you can see, God's Word isn't just an ancient book full of rules and regulations, as many are led to believe. It's God's personal letter to each of us. God chooses to use the Scriptures to reveal Himself to us. Through them He can strengthen, communicate, and comfort us. We are able to receive His guidance so our lives will go well. But— all this can only happen as we get into God's Word and hide it in our hearts! So, how is this done?

1. First, you need to read God's Word (Psalm 119 is a great place to start!).
2. Ask yourself, "What does God want me to learn from this?"
   — Is there a sin I need to avoid?
   — An action I need to take?
   — A change I need to make?
3. Find a verse that speaks to your heart and write it down to think about it during the day.
4. Memorize special verses of promise, counsel, or encouragement, and act upon them.
5. Always remember that God never lets His Word return empty. He desires to use it in a special way in your life. Let Him. Now that you've seen how this is done, put it into practice—today!

PEEK-A-BOO!

TAKEN FROM PSALM 139

GETTING READY

If you began at the front of this devotional and have read from cover to cover, congratulations! You now have a great understanding of what the Old Testament is really about, a deeper understanding of who God is, and hopefully, a changed life as a result. Spend a moment thanking God for all He has done and shown you. Thank Him especially that He loves you with a love beyond understanding—no matter how "ugly" you may feel.

THE JOURNEY

Have you ever been afraid to allow people to know the real you, for fear they might reject you?

David lay upon his bed in the quietness of the night, whispering his prayer to the Lord. "O Lord, You have searched me and know everything about me. You know when I sit down or stand up. You know when I come and when I go. You know my every thought—even from a distance! You,

Lord, are familiar with all my ways," David acknowledged. "Such knowledge is too wonderful for me—it is too great for me to know! There is nowhere I can go to run from You; there is nothing I can do to hide who I am. You know and see it all, yet You still accept me."

David thought on that fact for a while. He understood God had created him and knew him intimately—better than anyone else on the face of the earth could know him. He knew his life was not a mistake or an accident, but rather something of purpose and beauty to God. He was part of God's creation.

"I praise You, Lord, because I am fearfully and wonderfully made," David spoke out loud. "It was You who created who I am. You knit me together in my mother's womb. When my body was being formed, it was not hidden from You. Rather, You were overseeing every little detail that went into making me, me. How precious to me are Your thoughts, O Lord. They are so many! If I were to count every time I am on Your mind, it would far outnumber the sand!"

David knew in his heart that no matter what his enemies did to him or what others said—it wouldn't change God's opinion of his worth.

> **Even Paul in the New Testament states that nothing can separate us from God's love—not even death, life, angels, demons, or any created thing. You can read about it in Romans 8:38-39.**

> **Matthew, one of Jesus' disciples, also talked about God's intimate knowledge of us. "Even the very hairs on your head are all numbered" (Matthew 10:30).**

exploring deeper

Quickly turn to Psalm 139 in your own Bible. Read verse 1 and verse 17 aloud. Now, in the place of the word "me," substitute your name and read it out loud once more. Believe it.

DANGER AHEAD

Contrary to popular (false) belief, God doesn't make mistakes, and you are not a worthless piece of trash waiting for someone to find value in you. Someone already has— the One who created you with a purpose and meaning and who knows you inside and out. You can stand on that and hold your head high (but don't let pride get ya!). Whatever you do, don't let others feed you a lie and steal your joy. You are worth knowing.

A SPECIAL MESSAGE
JUST FOR YOU!

The fact that you're reading this page either means you desire to know more about how you can have a personal relationship with God, or you turned here by accident (or even curiosity). Either way, I'm glad you did. Whatever your reasons, this message is especially for you.

GOD SHOWS US IN BOTH THE OLD AND NEW TESTAMENTS THAT:

1. *We are all sinners* (Ecclesiastes 7:20 / Romans 3:23) and can't live up to God's standards of holiness. No matter how hard we try, we will always fall short. This creates a big problem, for it means no human can ever get to heaven by trying to live a good life, or by "keeping all the rules." It also creates another problem, for God is righteous, and He must punish sin.

2. *The wages of sin are death and separation from God* (Isaiah 59:2 / Romans 6:23). Just like death separates us from our loved ones, spiritual death separates us from the love of God. It keeps us from being able to have a right relationship with Him.

3. *The gift of God is eternal life* (Jeremiah 31:31 / Romans 6:23). Because of God's great love and mercy (see John 3:16), He offers a solution to our problem. He sent Jesus the Messiah to die on the cross and pay the penalty of our sins in our place (Isaiah 53:3 / 1 John 5:11-13). It is a gift we did not earn or deserve (Ephesians 2:8-9).

4. *We must receive this gift* (Psalm 130 / John 1:12). Just like a gift is not ours until we accept it, we must choose to accept God's gift of eternal life in Jesus.

In John 14:6 we learn that there is only one way to have our sins forgiven so we can enter into a relationship with God and live with Him in heaven. Jesus is the Way, the Truth, and the Life. No one comes to God except through Him. Jesus is God's gift to us. What God only pointed to in the Old Testament through the sacrifice system, He brought to fulfillment in the New Testament through Jesus! We receive God's gift of eternal life by placing our faith and trust in what He has provided. When we do this, we become children of God and enter into a relationship with God forever.

HOW CAN YOU DO THIS?

Simply pray to God and tell Him what you desire. This requires no special formula or words. God offers you the gift of salvation and is waiting for you to accept it.

Tell God you are sorry for your sins. (Sins are any wrong actions or attitudes—such as anger, pride, selfishness, etc.) Claim Jesus' sacrifice for you as your means of forgiveness. Ask God to forgive you and tell Him you want to enter into a relationship with Him and become His forever. (Psalm 51:1-4 and verses 7 and 10 offer a great model prayer.)

Thank Him for what He has done and promises to do. In 1 John 1:9 we are told that if we confess our sins, God is faithful and just to forgive our sins and cleanse us from unrighteousness. Psalm 32:1-2 states: "Blessed is the person whose sins are forgiven and whose unrighteousness is no longer counted against him!"

If you have done this, you've now begun your life with God. He accepts you as blameless and holy—your guilt is gone! Just like newborn babies need to grow, you need to grow too. You do this by reading your Bible, praying, and seeking to live the kind of life that pleases God.

Congratulations! You've just begun an exciting journey!